HIGH CRIMES AND MISDEMEANORS

The Case Against Bill Clinton

HIGH CRIMES AND MISDEMEANORS

The Case Against Bill Clinton

Ann H. Coulter

Since 1947
REGNERY PUBLISHING, INC.
An Eagle Publishing Company
Washington, D.C.

Library of Congress Cataloging-in-Publication Data

Coulter, Ann H.
    High crimes and misdemeanors : the case against Bill Clinton / Ann H. Coulter.
        p.cm.
    Includes bibliographical references and index.
    ISBN 0-89526-349-1 (alk. paper)
    1. Clinton, Bill, 1946–   —Impeachment. 2. United States—Politics and government—1933–   3. Political corruption—United States—History—20th century. I. Title.
E886.2.C38 1998
973.929'092—dc21   98-29093
                                                                                  CIP

Published in the United States by
Regnery Publishing, Inc.
An Eagle Publishing Company
One Massachusetts Avenue, NW
Washington, DC 20001

Distributed to the trade by
National Book Network
4720-A Boston Way
Lanham, MD 20706

Printed on acid-free paper.
Manufactured in the United States of America

Book design by Marci Hecht

10 9 8 7 6 5 4 3 2 1

Books are available in quantity for promotional or premium use. Write to Director of Special Sales, Regnery Publishing, Inc., One Massachusetts Avenue, NW, Washington, DC 20001, for information on discounts and terms or call (202) 216-0600.

FOR MY PARENTS,

who see virtues in the British system.

CONTENTS

The President, Vice President, and all civil Officers of the Unites States, shall be removed from Office on Impeachment for, and Conviction of, Treason, Bribery, or other high Crimes and Misdemeanors.

—United States Constitution, Article II, section 4

Chapter One

Just Do It

Compared to the long hours and amazingly tedious work of practicing law, political punditry has much to recommend it. In only one respect does practicing law compare favorably with practicing punditry, but it is an important one. In the law, there are standards, rules, and precedents that must be adhered to by everyone—trial judges, opposing counsel, jurors, appellate courts, even, in theory, the Supreme Court. The first principle of law is that like cases are supposed to be treated alike.

Political commentary is completely different. Like cases are treated unalike with such alacrity as to make the head spin. No general principles can ever be adduced. If a pundit opines that there is no constitutional basis for President Bill Clinton's claimed immunity from civil suit, that is assumed to be a political preference, rather than an attempted interpretation of the law… and half the time it is. Pundits left and right[1] switch sides with barely a blush, depending on whose president is being gored.

Nevertheless, there are standards and precedents and rules about the conduct of public men, presidents in particular. It cannot be the case, for example, that President Richard Nixon "shredded the Constitution" for *inquiring* about having the Internal Revenue Service (IRS) audit his political enemies (request declined), but that President Bill Clinton is an innocent victim of—in his wife's words—"a vast right-wing conspiracy" when he *succeeds* in having the IRS audit his political enemies. The evidence for either claim may be disputed—to a point—but the answer to whether politically motivated IRS audits are right or wrong should not depend on who the president is, or who the enemies are.

There are even standards for evaluating the evidence of such misconduct. And these standards, too, must be applied even-handedly if the rule of law is to survive. It cannot be the case, for instance, that, when a Republican president stands accused, he is to be held accountable for the actions of his subordinates, even in the absence of proof that he directly ordered those actions, and that a Democratic president is assumed to be innocent, no matter what the evidence, unless we catch him with a smoking gun in his hand. On videotape.

With each new revelation about President Clinton's apparently corrupt and sometimes illegal behavior, paid and unpaid Friends of Bill (FOBs) take up the public relations gauntlet to announce that previously abhorred conduct is now considered wholly excus-able conduct. "In the end the party would announce that two and two made five, and you would have to believe it.... [T]he logic of their position demanded it.... The heresy of heresies was common sense."[2] Oceania is at war with Eastasia. Two plus two makes five. We're "waiting for the facts to come out" to decide if President Clinton has lied,[3] and Mrs. Clinton is confident the allegations will "evaporate and disappear if they're ever given the light of day."[4]

The only coherent epistemology at the moment is that once Clinton is caught doing it, it's okay. At this rate, the entire country will soon be molesting interns, lying under oath, buying witnesses, flashing subordinates, and rifling through confidential FBI files. The

only thing American citizens must never, ever do is tape a friend—
even to expose government corruption. Free John Gotti! And those
Floridians who secretly taped Newt Gingrich go to prison for life.

Everyone is entitled to his own opinion; everyone is not entitled to his own facts. Precedents, like Watergate, are facts. If a
president's "cutting corners or hoarding dirty little secrets" is
enough to impeach him, as Nixon's attorney general, Elliot
Richardson, said, because "honesty is the best politics,"[5] then a
president's bald-faced lies under oath in a citizen's constitutional
case against him have to be enough. If it is wrong to talk about
pornographic movies to female subordinates, it is wrong to drop
your pants and say "kiss it" to female subordinates. If the woman's
statement plus one corroborating witness was enough evidence
yesterday, it's enough evidence today. Although, ultimately, one
might have a preference for one rule or another, at least we should
all know what the rules are.

There are pretty clear rules and standards for what constitutes
a "high Crime and Misdemeanor," or an impeachable act. Certain
types of conduct have been accepted as valid grounds for
impeachment throughout American history, and under the
British constitutional precedents the Founding Fathers had in
mind when they wrote the impeachment clauses of the
Constitution. The grounds, and even more important, the purposes of impeachment, reach back with remarkable consistency
more than six hundred years.

VICTIM OR THE CRIME

When the framers of the Constitution chose the phrase "high
Crimes and Misdemeanors" to complement treason and bribery
as grounds for impeachment, "they adopted a unique phrase used
for centuries in English parliamentary impeachments, for the
meaning of which one must look to history."[6]

That statement comes from the report assembled by Representative Peter Rodino's House Judiciary Committee, which framed the Articles of Impeachment against Richard Nixon. The so-called Rodino Report, entitled "Constitutional Grounds for Presidential Impeachment," was the work of, among others, Bernard Nussbaum, who would serve as President Clinton's first White House counsel, and Hillary Rodham, who would serve as first lady to President Clinton—the next president for whom impeachable offenses would be an issue.

Here's some history:

- In 1666 Viscount John Mordaunt was charged with impeachment for the high crime and misdemeanor of making uncivil addresses to a woman.

- In 1680 Sir William Scroggs, lord chief justice of the court of the King's Bench, was impeached on account of "his frequent and notorious excesses and debaucheries" bringing "the highest scandal on the public justice of the kingdom."[7]

- In 1701 Edward, Earl of Oxford, a member of the king's council, was impeached for procuring an office for someone "known to be a person of ill fame and reputation."[8]

- In 1881 the Minnesota legislature impeached Judge E. St. J. Cox for "frequenting bawdy houses and consorting with harlots."[9]

Quite noticeably, all but presumably the last of these are not crimes—even misdemeanors—under the criminal law.

Though it will come as a shock to people who acquire their legal knowledge from TV pundits, the phrase "high Crimes and Misdemeanors" has nothing to do with criminal law. The "somewhat startling" proposition that high crimes and misdemeanors need not be crimes at all is, nonetheless, an indisputable fact demonstrated by the "great preponderance of authority."[10]

In fact, there is *no such thing* as a "high Crime and Misdemeanor" in the criminal law. Just as a sea lion is something completely different from a lion, and a mongoose completely different from a goose, the "high Crimes and Misdemeanors" mentioned in the Constitution are completely different from crimes and misdemeanors. Attaching "high" to "crimes and misdemeanors" creates an entirely different animal. And, as Rodham and Nussbaum once explained to the nation, the framers knew that.

Impeachment is not a criminal procedure; the acts that justify impeachment are not necessarily criminal acts; and the purpose of impeachment is not punishment.

Indeed, impeachment is not directed exclusively or even primarily at violations of criminal law: Supreme Court Justice Joseph Story in his great *Commentaries on the Constitution* was especially eloquent on this point. Not only "crimes of a strictly legal character" are impeachable offenses, but also political offenses, growing out of "personal misconduct… so various" that they "must be examined upon very broad and comprehensive principles of public policy and duty."[11]

First used for an impeachment in 1380, the phrase has always referred exclusively to conduct that could lead to an impeachment. Impeachable offenses encompass "a great variety of circumstances… which do not properly belong to the judicial character in the ordinary administration of justice and are far removed from the reach of municipal jurisprudence."[12]

JOHNNY B. GOODE

A *"high misdemeanor" refers* not to a criminal offense just short of a felony, but to misbehavior, bad demeanor. As the Rodino Report explained, "From the comments of the framers and their contemporaries, the remarks of delegates to the state ratifying conventions, and the removal power debate in the First Congress, it is apparent that the scope of impeachment was not viewed narrowly."

Impeachment for misbehavior is not, however, as unlimited as it sounds: the behavior at issue is moral behavior, not Emily Post polite society behavior. According to historical precedent, impeachable misbehavior "means (a) [misconduct] in the execution of office, or (b) *scandalous behavior in his private capacity.*"[13] Or, as Alexander Hamilton put it, the impeachment power is addressed to "the misconduct of public men" or the "violation of some public trust."[14]

In the course of prosecuting one of the greatest impeachment trials in Anglo-American history—the impeachment of Warren Hastings—Edmund Burke said: "Other constitutions are satisfied with making good subjects; [impeachment] is a security for good governors."[15] Burke did not mean that statesmen were supposed to be "good" in the sense of competent, but "good" in the sense of moral: "It is by this tribunal that statesmen [are tried] not upon the niceties of a narrow jurisprudence but upon the enlarged and solid principles of morality."[16] It seems it's the president's principles of morality that are supposed to be "enlarged and solid."

Statesmen who merely transgress "the spirit of the law," Burke said, "can never hope for protection from any of its forms."[17] Other presidents being investigated by independent counsels have understood this and have waived even legitimate legal privileges. President Clinton has invoked every legal stonewall in the book, and even some that aren't in the book.

Although Burke explicitly ruled out trying impeachments "upon the niceties of a narrow [criminal] jurisprudence,"[18] almost any serious crime will evidence a sufficiently diminutive morality as to constitute a "high Crime and Misdemeanor." Still, the standard is morality, not the technicalities of the law. Crimes that are *malum in se*, or wrong in themselves, such as murder or bribery, would certainly fall within the ambit of "high Crimes and Misdemeanors."

Crimes that are *malum prohibitum*, or wrong only because the law makes them so—Occupational Safety and Health Act (OSHA) violations for example—would not.

The moral underpinnings of the impeachment clause can be understood by considering the framers' purpose in crafting a Constitution in the first place. James Madison said the "first aim" of the Constitution was to ensure that men with the "most virtue" would become the nation's rulers. The Constitution's impeachment power was for "keeping them virtuous whilst they continue to hold their public trust."[19]

They were erecting a moral standard because they believed that only virtuous men could maintain a republic. As one constitutional scholar has pointed out, acts unrelated to job performance are proper subjects for impeachment because "a perjurer or a forger simply could not command the public respect indispensable to the administration of justice."[20] Note, though, that even in the case of perjury or forgery—criminal acts—the rationale is not simply that the officer has violated the criminal law, but that such a violation discredits his office, and that failure to punish it would damage the government.

Impeachment was the means by which the Republic would defend itself from officeholders who could no longer command the public's trust. As Hamilton stated: "Men, in public trust, will much oftener act in such a manner as to render them unworthy of being any longer trusted than in such a manner as to make them obnoxious to legal punishment."[21] The framers recognized that the credibility of the government would be undermined and the nation threatened if the president, judges, or other government officers were seen to be personally corrupt or self-aggrandizing, as if they were above the law.

SUBSTANCE AND MEANING

Despite its six hundred years of history, the term "high Crimes and Misdemeanors" has been unfairly described as meaning "whatever a majority of the House of Representatives considers it to be at a given moment in history; conviction results from whatever offense or offenses two-thirds of the other body considers to be sufficiently serious to require removal of the accused from office."[22] This is a statement about procedure rather than substance.

As a procedural matter it is true that, theoretically, the House could impeach and the Senate could convict for an offense that is not a "high Crime and Misdemeanor."

All this means is that no one could stop them, just as no one could stop the Senate from concluding in 1797 that senators are exempt from impeachment. (If they thought they could get away with it, the Senate might conclude that senators are immune from elections, too.) Similarly, the House, Senate, president, and Supreme Court can all pretend that Roscoe Filburn growing wheat on his lot to feed to his livestock "affects commerce" under the Constitution. There is no appeal from an unconstitutional Supreme Court ruling, just as there is no appeal from an impeachment conviction. But the absence of an appeal doesn't mean "high Crimes and Misdemeanors" has no meaning, any more than affecting commerce or any other particular set of words in the Constitution has no meaning.

The general categories of impeachable conduct that developed in the four hundred years of use in Great Britain were these:

- corruption
- betrayal of trust
- abuse of official power
- neglect of duty
- encroachment on Parliament's prerogatives
- misapplication of funds

Examples of impeachable conduct by officeholders included appointing "unfit persons to office" (often relatives and retainers).

These were offices they had the strictly legal right to fill, so at worst this was mere neglect of duty. But appointing "unfit persons" denied the king's subjects the benefits of just and efficient administration. Similarly, Justice Joseph Story included as an impeachable offense "habitual disregard of the public interests, in the discharge of the duties of political office."[23]

English courtiers were impeached for persuading the king to give them excessive gifts. These favors from the crown were not in themselves illegal, but it was held that using their access to the king for personal benefit was an abuse of power.

Obviously, the categories tend to bleed into one another and specific incidents might fall into more than one category. For example, compromising the country's national security interests by leasing ports to the Chinese government or granting waivers for the transfer of sensitive technology could constitute corruption, betrayal of trust, or neglect of duty. Using the FBI and the IRS to harass a civil servant whose pink slip was sought by the president's friend and contributor might qualify as corruption, abuse of power, or neglect of duty (if the president was simply unaware of his subordinate's machinations). Granting perks and government jobs to people whose silence is sought constitutes corruption, abuse of power, and betrayal of trust—perhaps even misapplication of funds.

THE PROMISED LAND

Despite the high-sounding nature of these categories from the old country, oral sex from the interns in the Oval Office will do. Even in England impeachable conduct included personal vices. Men of weak character would place the government in disrepute. As was remarked in one English case, officers of the crown should not act so as to bring "scandal on the public justice of the Kingdom."

But when the impeachment device made its way across the

ocean to America, it was inserted into a Constitution that created a government unlike any other. The different context gave impeachments a different color. Watergate-era cliches about the president "subverting constitutional government" were over- wrought rhetoric then; this is not the standard now. To para- phrase the current "just about sex" line, Watergate was about a two-bit breaking and entering. And unlike with Monica Lewinsky, it wasn't committed by the president, or even by people who worked at his White House, but by people who worked for his campaign committee. Grand-sounding treacheries weren't required by the framers, weren't required for Nixon, and aren't required now. It's enough for the president to be a pervert.

The British categories for high crimes and misdemeanors weren't rejected by the framers so much as they were expanded and reshuffled for use in a different country. The Philadelphia convention in 1787 adopted the impeachment remedy in the process of creating the first government in the history of the world that would have separated powers, checks and balances, and sharply limited powers. And, of course, no king. The reach and purposes of impeachment would be different in a constitu- tional republic. Personal misconduct took on a larger role in impeachments, for example, and policy disputes became irrele- vant to impeachable conduct.

Impeachments in Great Britain had been used as a weapon in the ongoing and turbulent power struggle between Parliament and the king. Describing the standard reason for an impeachment, the Earl of Danby, a leader of the impeachment of Clarendon, said that if he did not succeed in hanging Clarendon for high treason, he, the Earl of Danby himself, would be hanged instead.[24] (And in the "whirligig of politics" the Earl of Danby was in fact later impeached—but only imprisoned.[25]) The king could not be impeached, but Parliament could weaken him by impeaching his ministers.

Consequently, impeachments in Great Britain tended to fall into ponderous, grand-sounding categories such as "abuse of power" and "encroachment on Parliament's prerogatives." Meanwhile, actual impeachments in this country have been for things like "consorting with harlots" and "drunkenness."

The only impeachment convictions ever rendered by the United States Senate were for the high crimes and misdemeanors of: Drunkenness and Senility; Incitement to Revolt and Rebellion Against the Nation; Bribery; Kickbacks and Tax Evasion; Tax Evasion; Conspiracy to Solicit a Bribe; and False Statements to a Grand Jury.[26] While Clinton's defenders act as if an impeachable offense must be some immediate threat to the nation—such as the discovery that the president was conspiring with communist agents to turn over vital missile technology to Red China— impeachment was intended to be used, and always has been used, to remove officers who simply "behave amiss."

Impeachment scholar Raoul Berger remarked of impeachment American-style: "Once initiated to topple giants… impeachment has sunk in this country to the ouster of dreary little judges for squalid misconduct."[27] But the American variations on impeach- able crimes flow directly from the Constitution itself. Power struggles were resolved in advance by the Constitution; others would be resolved with constitutional mechanisms such as presi- dential vetoes, veto overrides, and judicial review.

Another difference between impeachment in Great Britain and impeachment in this country is that Congress does not have the authority to hang or otherwise punish the impeached officers. Some might say that eliminating the possibility of beheading and hanging cabinet officials for "treasons" defined retrospectively by the legislature was a step up.

One additional distinction the Constitution requires is this: policy disputes are not supposed to be resolved by resort to impeachment. Since impeachment was used in Great Britain as a weapon against a king whose veto Parliament could not override, impeachments frequently addressed policy disputes with the king. (These were often resolved with a hanging.) Members of Parliament couldn't stop the king from entering into treaties they didn't like, but they could impeach his ministers who gave the king such "bad advice."[28] This was really a method to "condemn policies which they believed pernicious to the realm."[29]

By contrast, the Constitution gives Congress plenty of tools, short of impeachment, to oppose a president's "pernicious" policies. Moreover, the chief magistrate would not govern by divine right, but by the consent of the people. Elections decide policy; impeachments judge character. Staging impeachments over policy disagreements doesn't make sense in the context of the American Constitution.

That policy disagreements cannot form the basis for an impeachable offense in this country is more than a logical deduction from the structure and purposes of the Constitution. At the Constitutional Convention, Madison explicitly rejected "maladministration" as a ground for impeachment. He said "so vague a term will be equivalent to a tenure during the pleasure of the Senate." (And thus, "high Crimes and Misdemeanors" was adopted instead.)[30]

Other comments from the framers further demonstrate that the purposes of impeachment did not include policy disputes—but did include personal misconduct. Edmund Randolph said, for example: "No man ever thought of impeaching a man for an opinion. It would be impossible to discover whether the error in opinion resulted from a wilful mistake of the heart, or an involuntary fault of the head."[31] Apparently, a "wilful mistake of the heart," when discernable, *would* constitute grounds for impeachment and removal.

When Hamilton described impeachable offenses as "political," he did not mean partisan. The president cannot be impeached for issuing executive orders that are strongly opposed by *New York Times* columnist Anthony Lewis. Rather, high crimes and misdemeanors are "political" in the sense that they "relate chiefly to injuries done immediately to the society itself."[32] Since policy matters are necessarily off the table, in a sense, that leaves only "personal misconduct," or as Edmund Randolph put it, "wilful mistakes of the heart."

Perhaps the more significant American innovation on impeachment was that the chief magistrate could be impeached. Indeed, it was the president the framers had in mind when they drafted the impeachment clauses.

Having just fought a war to get rid of a king, the framers had "the perfidy of the chief magistrate"[33] clearly in their sights when they included broad grounds for impeachment. They discussed the Constitution's impeachment power in terms of removing a president who "misbehaves" or "behave[s] amiss," as two of the delegates put it.[34] Madison wrote that impeachment was meant to remove presidents for "incapacity, negligence, or perfidy."[35] And Hamilton wrote that the entire process of selecting a president was designed to ensure that "some fit person" notable for "ability and virtue" would be chosen for that office. As a back-up mechanism to prevent rogues from holding office, they provided for impeachment.

To have the president's behavior propel the country into a national discussion of whether oral sex counts as adultery would have been a blatant "high Crime and Misdemeanor," if the framers could possibly have imagined any president would sink so low.

THE LAST TIME

But one doesn't have to look back to the Constitutional Convention for the standards. This country last faced the need to remove a president just twenty-five years ago during the presidential scandal known as "Watergate." Half the country actually lived through this most recent precedent for impeaching a president.

On July 27, 1974, the House Judiciary Committee adopted three articles of impeachment against Richard Nixon. The charges against him were neatly summarized in two sentences at the bottom of the indictment:

> *In all of this, Richard M. Nixon has acted in a manner contrary to his trust as President and subversive of constitutional government, to the great prejudice of the cause of law and justice, and to the manifest injury of the people of the United States.*
>
> *Wherefore, Richard M. Nixon, by such conduct, warrants impeachment and trial, and removal from office.*

To say that Nixon was forced to resign for acting in a manner "subversive of constitutional government" is meaningless without knowing what acts comprised that "subversion." In brief, Nixon's subversion consisted of: One presidential lie, one invocation of presidential privilege, and zero criminal offenses. (One month after Nixon resigned, a prosecutor said of some of Nixon's alleged crimes, "None of these matters at the moment rises to the level of our ability to prove even a probable criminal violation by Mr. Nixon."[36])The standard for "constitutional government subversion"—or whatever the impeachable offense is called—should not be a function of poll numbers plus the misery index.

Impeachment, as the country was reminded in 1974, is intended to reinforce the heavy constitutional cables that hold even heads of state to the rule of law. If a president can slip these cables, we no longer have a constitutional republic. We end up with an "Imperial President," as Anthony Lewis and Company ceaselessly intoned during the Nixon presidency, right on up to the election of President Carter (to be reintroduced during the Reagan years).[37]

As Nixon discovered, the president's obligations go far beyond the requirement that he not criminally obstruct justice. Madison

explained, "If the President be connected, in any suspicious manner with any person, and there be grounds to believe he will shelter him, the House of Representatives can impeach him; they can
remove him if found guilty." Using the power of the presidency to
"pardon crimes which were advised by himself" or to "stop
inquiry and prevent detection" of crimes was, according to
Madison, an impeachable offense.[38]

Nixon *talked* about political audits by the IRS, but no political
audits were ever conducted (except of Nixon himself). Nixon
invoked one privilege one time (and this was somewhat legitimate,
since the Supreme Court did in fact recognize a brand new legal
privilege). Nixon permitted his subordinates to delay one investigation once—for two weeks.

The worst that could be said of Nixon's alleged "obstruction of
justice" was that he thought the president had a right to fight a legal
case, just like a private citizen might. But as Nixon's first special
prosecutor, Archibald Cox, said, "[T]here is a radical difference
between what people expect of a president and his aides and what
they will cynically tolerate from time to time in municipal aldermen
or county commissioners." A president cannot act like a municipal
alderman; he certainly should not be able to act like O.J.[39]

If Nixon telling one lie, *not* under oath, constituted the creation of an "Imperial Presidency"[40] demanding the president's
impeachment, what has Clinton created by telling repeated lies,
not only to the public, but under oath?

Lying to the American people is a clear betrayal of trust. There
is no question that this is an impeachable offense, assuming the
"lie" does not fall under the president's duties, such as protecting
the military as commander in chief. That may sound odd, given
how thoroughly politicians are associated in the public eye with
lying. But throughout American history, acknowledged instances
of presidents lying to the nation are both rare and notorious.

In fact, Nixon's lie—that the White House had conducted its own internal investigation of the Watergate break-in and found that no White House personnel had been involved—was actually cited in the first article of impeachment voted by the Rodino Committee. Article I charged Nixon with, among other things, "making or *causing to be made* false or misleading statements for the purpose of deceiving the people of the United States into believing that a thorough and complete investigation had been conducted…" (emphasis added).

The Watergate special prosecutor, Leon Jaworski, said of Nixon's disgrace and resignation: "What sank him was his lying."[41] Even President Nixon's most loyal defenders abandoned his cause when they found that he had indeed lied to the public. Just on one point. "The problem is not Watergate or the cover-up…. It's that he hasn't been telling the truth to the American people…. The tape makes it evident that he hasn't leveled with the country for probably eighteen months. And the President can't lead a country he has deliberately misled for a year and a half."[42] That, incidentally, was how Nixon's speechwriter, Pat Buchanan, explained to Julie Nixon that her father had to go.

Meanwhile, President Clinton has lied repeatedly, openly, and directly to the American people. He does not even seem to care whether there is a plausible sense in which his lies might be justified as half-truths—so long as he can get away with the lie, even temporarily. During the 1992 presidential campaign he brushed off his affair with Gennifer Flowers and his status as a draft-dodger with this doggerel deceit: "a woman I never had sex with and a draft I never dodged." Six years and countless lies later, he had taken to giving the country schoolmarm lectures, knowing his word would not be believed: "Listen to me… I never had sexual relations with that woman [Monica Lewinsky]." Clinton defender Lanny Davis is no Pat Buchanan.

Even the president's few remaining defenders in the criminal defense bar don't bother pretending to believe him anymore. They say his lies about Gennifer, Paula, Kathleen, and Monica don't matter because those are "about sex." No, actually, not all his lies are "about sex"; the lies "about sex" just happen to be the ones he told under oath. It's impossible even to keep track of all the lies he has told. As Democratic Senator Bob Kerrey casually remarked of the president, "Clinton's an unusually good liar. Unusually good. Do you realize that?"[43]

And Senator Kerrey said that before the president started telling his lies under oath in a sworn deposition in front of a federal judge. The evidence that the president perjured himself, and perjured himself repeatedly, during his deposition in the Paula Jones case is overwhelming. So overwhelming, in fact, that Clinton acted like a trapped animal when he was later asked to say simply that it is wrong for presidents of the United States—in the abstract—to commit perjury and obstruct justice.

At a press conference on April 30, 1998, ABC reporter Sam Donaldson posed this question to President Clinton:

> *Now you deny wrongdoing, I understand, but as a standard for presidents what do you think: Does it matter what you do in private moments, as alleged? And particularly does it matter if you have committed perjury or in another sense broken the law?*

Clinton responded:

> *Well, since I have answered the underlying questions, I really believe it's important for me not to say any more about this. I think that I'm, in some ways, the last person who needs to be having a national conversation about this.*[44]

It is astonishing that the president of the United States has so obviously and blatantly broken the law that he feels he should not go on record saying that presidents, as a general matter, should not break the law. Clinton openly announces that he is "the last person who needs to be having a national conversation about" whether it should "matter" if the president is a felon.

U.S. BLUES

Though there are standards and precedents to abide by, impeaching a president is not just a matter of legal technicalities. It is a matter of our duty as citizens. Impeachment may seem like an extreme course, especially when our mutual funds are doing well, but it is a course specifically provided for in the Constitution. The Constitution was drafted by men who had already resorted to more extreme measures than impeachment to remove their colonial governors. They had staged a revolution and drafted a document proclaiming to the world that revolution was their right and duty, when, "in the course of human events, it becomes necessary for one people to dissolve the political bands which have connected them with another."

Americans have become so delirious on the rhetoric of choice that the question of whether to impeach a president, even one who has manifestly committed impeachable offenses, seems like a matter of personal preference, rather than our obligation as citizens of a republic. That isn't how our Founding Fathers put it in the Declaration of Independence. And they were about to alter a government "long established" in a more jarring fashion than a simple little impeachment.

They acknowledged that "[g]overnments long established should not be changed for light and transient causes" and recognized "that mankind are more disposed to suffer, while evils are sufferable, than to right themselves...." But the whole point of the Declaration is that finally there comes a limit to what citizens can tolerate from their government. And then the Declaration does not say merely that citizens have the right to make a change, but that they have a duty: When citizens witness "a long train of abuses and usurpations... it is their right, it is their duty, to throw off such Government...."[45]

This is what it means to be a citizen in a republic—of the self-governing kind and not the banana variety. You can vote for a knave and a clown, but then you have to take some responsibility to correct your mistakes. And those who didn't vote for the clown have a responsibility to rescue the rest of the country from its foolishness. Moreover, there ought to be some responsibility attached to holding office in a government founded on the blood of patriots. (So, why exactly is the Republican Congress doing nothing while waiting for Ken Starr to save the country?)

This is our fundamental political tradition. The governed may be expected to abide a certain amount of evil for the sake of continuity and stability, but there's a limit. When it is easy to imagine Larry Flynt watching television coverage of the president and wondering what the country has come to, the president has got to go.

It has been the president's game to identify his critics as religious right fanatics to play on people's fear of excessive morality in politics. This is odd since the Christian Coalition hasn't made a peep about manifest perversions and apparent crimes, except to endorse the position of Clinton's flacks: like Lanny Davis, it is just waiting "to see the facts."[46] Be that as it may, surely it does not yet require fidelity to a particular religious creed to say the president of the United States should not be having affairs with an intern, lying to the American people, obstructing justice, or perjuring himself in a constitutional case.

Impeachment is not something even a partisan jumps into impulsively. But it's absurd to pretend that only nonpartisan adherents of good government—whoever they are—can call for impeachment. No one ever expected the impeachment of a president to be nonpartisan. It's *supposed* to be partisan. Alexander Hamilton wrote that impeachments would "enlist all [the citizenry's] animosities, partialities, influence, and interest."[47] This was in a tract recommending adoption of the Constitution—along with its impeachment clauses.

In fact, the whole government is supposed to be partisan precisely so that, as James Madison put it, "each may be a check on the other—that the private interest of every individual may be a sentinel over the public rights."[48] If the president's enemies aren't going to be sentinels over him, who is?

The indignant complaint that the people attacking the president are out to "get" him is so illogical it stops you in your tracks. Okay, but then the people defending the president are out to save him, so where does that get us? There are always two sides. The question isn't whether there are two sides—down to the last criminal defense lawyer defending Clinton—but whether there are grounds and reason to impeach the president.

The Declaration of Independence gave only one side of the story, too. It repeatedly blamed the whole thing on King George: "*He* has refused his Assent to Laws, the most wholesome and necessary for the public good.... *He* has obstructed the Administration of Justice, by refusing his Assent to Laws for establishing Judiciary powers." *He* did this. It didn't matter that they were out to get King George and that the Tories had a different opinion.

If this country didn't have the stomach to stand up for its principles, we'd be Canada now. And, anyway, this isn't revolution, so calm down. It is a remedial measure: "Impeachment is the first step in a remedial process—removal from office and possible disqualification from holding future office."[49] (That phrase comes from the report drafted in part by Hillary Rodham.)

In Federalist No. 51, in which Madison commended the

Constitution's reliance on partisan interests, he said: "It may be a reflection on human nature that such precautions should be necessary. But what is government but the greatest of all reflections on human nature?" What kind of reflection on our nature might it be if the country were willing to suffer Clinton to continue as president now that we have learned what kind of man he is?

The consequences of this can hardly be overstated. Democracy runs on trust, without which phrases like the "consent of the governed" are meaningless. It is essentially impossible to have democracy if elected leaders do not tell the truth, everyone knows they do not tell the truth, and no one cares. Presidents who by their deceit spread such cynicism actually do commit "offenses that subvert the system of government." As the Declaration of Independence put it, "Governments are instituted among Men, deriving their just powers from the consent of the governed." Consequently, "whenever any Form of Government becomes destructive of these ends, it is the Right of the People to alter or to abolish it."

Elliot Richardson, the attorney general fired in Nixon's "Saturday Night Massacre," explained the danger of failing to remove a corrupt president:

> [T]here is a serious risk when you investigate corruption. You may do more harm than good if all you do is poke a stick in a muddy pool and stir up the mud without clarifying the water.... [P]oliticians govern their conduct in the light of past experience.[50]

HIGH TIME

If President Clinton can do what he has done and not face impeachment, we will have set an all-new, heretofore unimagined—unimaginable—low-water mark for elected officials. Not just that, but if Congress doesn't have the will to throw him out, Clinton will have established a new standard for the entire country. The new standard will be a total absence of standards. Lying doesn't really matter, as long as it's about sex, because sex doesn't really matter, even if it's gross, exploitive, adulterous, and risky. Go ahead: seize this loophole, to the ruin of your family.

And since manipulating the IRS or FBI from the top is all in the course of business, it must be okay to mislead them and divert them from the other end, too. If you get caught and don't have a good enough legal team to escape, you might have to pay a fine or go to prison. But there's no shame in it. The country doesn't *really* condemn this. We adore a lovable rogue. And we are very, very tolerant. The only thing we won't tolerate is a loser. Nothing matters except winning, and it is fine to lie and cheat and manipulate because honor is just a word, just hot air, and the country doesn't really believe in it.

If Clinton stays, we may as well change our national motto from "In God We Trust" to the old Nike slogan: "Just Do It!"

The last line of the Declaration of Independence is: "And for the support of this Declaration, with a firm reliance on the protection of Divine Providence, we mutually pledge to each other our Lives, our Fortunes, and our sacred Honor." Impeachment isn't a revolution, and no one's lives or fortunes are at risk. It's not even our sacred honor this time. It's just a question of whether the country can patch together a little self-respect.

The Founding Fathers said the price of liberty is eternal vigilance. This book isn't even asking for vigilance. It's just asking people to give a damn. If Americans don't care about this, then they are expecting liberty without paying any price at all.

PART ONE

"Kiss It"

Chapter Two

You Can't Prove I Lied

On July 23, 1973, a sitting United States president was subpoenaed for the first time in 166 years. Citing executive privilege,
President Nixon refused to comply with the subpoenas, instigat-
ing a battle over the tapes in the Watergate scandal that would end
in Nixon's resignation one year later.

That same day, three thousand miles away in San Francisco,
Monica Lewinsky was born.[1] (Six days later, family friend William
Ginsburg would kiss "that girl's inner thighs," as he later told *Time*
magazine.[2])

Almost twenty-five years later, Lewinsky would be on tape saying things about the sitting president that would prompt the president's former top aide, George Stephanopoulos, to remark,
"[T]hese are probably the most serious allegations yet leveled
against the president.... If they're true, they're not only politically
damaging, but it could lead to impeachment proceedings."[3] The
night the story about the Lewinsky tapes broke, Jay Leno said on
the *Tonight Show*, "Let me be the first to welcome President Gore."

Stephanopoulos wasn't the only former Clinton apologist
briefly stunned into honesty. The next day, former White House

Press Secretary Dee Dee Myers said, "If he's not telling the truth, I think the consequences are just astronomical,"[4] and the *Washington Post* editorialized: "This time it's different: The allegations against President Clinton are allegations of extremely serious crimes. If they are true, they cannot be... expected to dissolve in an 'everybody does it' cloud of ambiguity."[5]

Even long somnolent Attorney General Janet Reno woke up and formally requested that Independent Counsel Kenneth Starr's jurisdiction be expanded to investigate whether the president perjured himself, suborned the perjury of others, and obstructed justice. Officials at the Department of Justice "were floored" by the allegations and evidence, according to a source quoted in the *Washington Post.*[6]

For only the second time in the history of the country, the sitting United States president was under criminal investigation. Oh, yes, and Monica lived at the Watergate.

The morning the story broke, January 21, 1998, there was total shock. The independent counsel had tapes with former White House intern Monica Lewinsky unwittingly describing her repeated performance of (as Paula Jones had put it) a "certain type of sex" on the president in the Oval Office. And she was also captured on tape describing the red carpet treatment she had gotten from the president and the president's men to induce her to lie about it under oath—as the president had done already.

But soon a predictable pattern began to take shape. While the country was still in shock, Clinton issued a series of fuzzy, disingenuous denials. He threw in his trademark escape hatches, holding in reserve the possibility of his later saying, *you can't prove I lied.* Clinton has always been so disingenuous.

Then quickly, before the media could finish parsing his nondenial denials, the motives and tactics of the president's opponents became the issue. And then it was yesterday's news—*I've already answered that.* Soon half the American people were telling poll-sters that they were totally copacetic with the idea of the White House as Animal House.

From nine hundred FBI files in the White House to a pattern of IRS audits of Clinton's enemies to selling the Lincoln bedroom, Clinton had already done things Nixon only dreamed about. Now Clinton had leapt over a boundary of propriety Nixon *hadn't even experienced as a constraint.* Behavior that wouldn't have been tol-erated in a presidential aide twenty-five years ago was now accept-able behavior for a president. It is difficult to imagine how Clinton could disgrace the presidency any further.

Clinton flacks have frequently made the preposterous claim that this whole degrading mess was the Supreme Court's fault for allowing the Paula Jones suit to proceed. Implicit in the claim is that American presidents have always engaged in salacious, repre-hensible conduct in the White House and White House interns have always talked about earning their "presidential kneepads." It is as if somehow the Supreme Court had been holding back all this sewage from flooding onto the presidency, and by mere his-torical accident it all caught up with Clinton. In fact, of course, private civil lawsuits against presidents have always been allowed. They certainly have never been disallowed. Other presidents weren't vulnerable because other presidents weren't such pigs.

Clinton's Equal Employment Opportunity Commission (EEOC) demands that companies fire employees who are over-heard calling women "broads."[7] And now he was supposed to have gotten a "certain type of sex" from a twenty-one-year-old unpaid White House intern right there on the presidential seal. In the Clinton view, the president is not to be an exemplar but an excep-tion: the rules that apply to all other Americans just don't apply to President Clinton.

Two weeks after the scandal broke, Wolf Blitzer of CNN said to

President Clinton at a press conference, "Mr. President, Monica Lewinsky's life has been changed forever—her family's life has been changed forever. I wonder how you feel about that and what, if anything, you'd like to say to Monica Lewinsky at this minute?" The president smiled as he mulled the question over and then said, "That's good." He chuckled with the rest of the crowd and continued, "That's good, but at this minute, I'm going to stick with my position in not commenting."[8] His whole presidency has been a complete mockery of the American people. Even now, it was all just a game.

THE UNDERLYING CASE: *JONES* V. *CLINTON*

On May 6, 1994, President William Jefferson Clinton was sued for sexual harassment by one Paula Corbin Jones for an incident that occurred when Clinton was the governor of Arkansas.

Reporters had been crawling all over Little Rock the first year of Clinton's presidency looking for arcana on the new president. (They were all over Atlanta after Jimmy Carter became president, too, but the Georgia State troopers didn't have such colorful stories to tell.) In December 1993 the former governor's sexual exploits were exposed in an article in *The American Spectator*. Jones was outed as an attempted Clinton conquest. But according to an Arkansas state trooper quoted in the article, it wasn't just an attempt—Clinton had scored with Paula. She denied the allegation and requested a public apology from President Clinton. When Clinton denied her allegations with the same sincerity he had denied Gennifer Flowers's allegations, she sued.

Jones alleged that on May 8, 1991, when she was working at a conference for the Arkansas Industrial Development Commission being held at the Excelsior Hotel in Little Rock, Arkansas, a state trooper, Danny Ferguson, approached her, handed her a slip of paper with a hotel room number on it, and said "the governor would like to meet with you."

He reassured Jones and her coworker and friend, Pamela Blackard, by saying, "It's okay, we do this all the time for the governor."⁹ Ferguson then escorted her to a hotel room where the governor was alone. After some small talk in which Clinton informed Jones that her boss was Clinton's "good friend," Clinton began praising Jones's "curves," kissed her, slid his hand up her cullottes, and "lowered his trousers and underwear exposing his erect penis and asked Jones to 'kiss it.'"¹⁰ Jones leapt up to leave the room. Before she could make her exit, Clinton reminded her of his friendship with her boss.

Jones brought suit under a statute that prohibits gender discrimination by government officials¹¹—which the courts have interpreted to include sexual harassment.

Evidence that Clinton had engaged in similar conduct with other women would be valuable for Jones's case. Evidence of "other acts" is crucial in discrimination cases because, as the Supreme Court said, "[t]here will seldom be 'eyewitness' testimony as to the employer's mental processes."¹² As a result, presenting "other women" evidence is now *de rigueur* in sexual harassment cases.

Jones's attorneys would have a lengthy period of time to ferret out all evidence they intended to use at trial. The process is called "discovery," but ought to be called "obscurity," since lawyers spend most of discovery trying to block the other side from acquiring relevant evidence. (Modern lawsuits have very little in common with Perry Mason's TV trials, and not only because witnesses rarely blurt out confessions on the stand, but also because no surprise evidence at all can be sprung on the adversary.)

But Clinton, facing reelection, could not allow "other acts" to come to light. So his lawyers embarked on a three-year campaign of delay with a "trumped-up" presidential immunity claim.¹³ But once discovery finally began in the *Jones* case, Judge Susan Webber Wright ruled—despite Clinton's objections and the considered opinions of most TV lawyers—that Jones's lawyers were entitled to take the depositions of witnesses to Clinton's behavior with other women. Indeed, to exclude evidence of Clinton either making sexual advances toward subordinates or using government resources to pursue sexual conquests would almost certainly be reversible error.[14]

The president's lawyer, Bob Bennett, had conceded far more than that in oral argument before the Supreme Court. Bennett told the court that any other women Clinton "has come into contact with" could probably be deposed by Jones's attorneys:

MR. BENNETT: *[Jones's attorney], as he claims, [is] going to be deposing all of the troopers; and* any time the president of the United States has come into contact with a member of the opposite sex, he intends to inquire of that; this is a conspiracy complaint; they talk about pattern of conduct....

JUSTICE SOUTER: *Mr. Bennett, do you think all those events are relevant to this case?*

MR. BENNETT: [S]ome trial courts might say they are *[emphasis added]*.[15]

Consequently, Jones's lawyers followed up on leads to any woman who might be able to provide evidence in the Paula Jones case of such "prior acts" by defendant Clinton. This kept them busy. In addition to information about other women they elicited from the Arkansas State Troopers, the Jones team received some anonymous phone calls tipping them off to yet other women who may have been approached by Clinton since he lost the taxpayer-funded escort service he had had in the troopers. It was an anonymous phone call in January 1997, for example, that led them to a former White House volunteer, Kathleen Willey. The caller told Jones's attorney, "I had a similar thing happen to me...."

Then, around October 1997, Jones's new attorneys and their financial backer, the Rutherford Institute, received phone calls alerting them to a former White House intern named Monica Lewinsky,[16] who had been blabbing to former White House employee Linda Tripp—who had the conversations on tape. As luck would have it, Lewinsky's claimed sexual relations with the president consisted exclusively of the "type of sex" Jones said Clinton urged on her.

Clinton's evidently successful redeployment of the "kiss it" line with Lewinsky on the government's time would help Jones's lawyers establish Clinton's *modus operandi*. But that was not Lewinsky's only use to Jones. The president had also succeeded with Lewinsky in another matter: he had silenced her. This would go a long way toward explaining to a jury why several women who had already been deposed in the *Jones* case were admitting to solitary meetings with Governor Clinton in the wee hours of the morning, but only for… policy discussions. In December, Jones's lawyers issued subpoenas to both Monica Lewinsky and Linda Tripp.

Jones's attorneys hadn't deposed either Lewinsky or Tripp on the eve of Clinton's deposition. That night, however, one of Jones's lawyers informally interviewed Tripp to fill in details of the anonymous phone calls.

Tripp had agreed to an informal meeting with Jones's attorneys in hopes of avoiding a formal deposition. She had only recently discovered that her home state of Maryland was one of the few states that prohibit people from taping their own phone conversations without telling the other person on the line; she had not told Lewinsky. A formal deposition in the *Jones* case would thus have required her to state under oath that she had broken the law, unless she was prepared to lie about this or plead the Fifth. But she was one of the rare witnesses in this case who seemed to take things like sworn statements seriously. Since Jones's suit was a civil rather than criminal case, her lawyers did not have legal authority, as a criminal prosecutor would, to grant Tripp immunity in exchange for her testimony about the tapes.

THE TAPES

Linda Tripp had quite a few tapes—about twenty in all.

Tripp had developed a relationship with Lewinsky, a fellow Clinton White House expatriate, when they both ended up with jobs in the Pentagon press office. This was not a coincidence: The Pentagon press office had become a dumping ground for troublesome women in the Clinton White House, courtesy of a Clinton appointee, Assistant Defense Secretary Kenneth H. Bacon. Bacon would perform many favors for the man who appointed him.

Linda Tripp was a problem for the White House on account of her position as executive assistant in the White House Counsel's Office, the locus of numerous Clinton scandals. As we will see, from the Travel Office putsch to the botched investigation of Vince Foster's office, which led to the forced resignation of Tripp's boss, Bernard Nussbaum, the Counsel's Office generated crisis after crisis. Tripp had sat outside the offices of Bernard Nussbaum and Vince Foster.

Tripp's bird's-eye view of the office, combined with her penchant for wry observations—such as her e-mail missive referring to Nussbaum and two others as "the three stooges"—had put Tripp in the hot seat on more than one occasion. It was Tripp to whom Kathleen Willey had run immediately after emerging from a meeting with President Clinton in November 1993, claiming she had been groped by the commander in chief. And someone at the White House knew it, as evidenced by the "talking points" Lewinsky would later pass to Tripp.

While Tripp had become a problem by earning spots before congressional investigative committees, Lewinsky had become trouble by earning her "presidential kneepads," as Lewinsky herself put it. The two vexatious women were sent to the Pentagon press office, where they met and became friends. What happened after that seems almost inevitable in retrospect.

In numerous conversations, Lewinsky recounted to Tripp intimate and lascivious details of her two-year term as "Special Assistant to the President for B— J—," as Lewinsky had proposed for her title. Lewinsky's salacious confidences regarding her lengthy affair with the president would be red meat for Jones's lawyers.

After Paula Jones's lawyers subpoenaed Lewinsky and Tripp, Lewinsky began telling her friend of Clinton's attempts to ensure that she lie under oath about the affair. Clinton, she said, had offered the assistance of FOB and Washington power lawyer Vernon Jordan. Jordan was to help Lewinsky prepare an affidavit for the *Jones* case as well as set up job opportunities in New York as a payoff for her affidavit denying that she had had a sexual affair with the president.

Lewinsky was playing hardball. She turned down a job offer from United Nations Ambassador Bill Richardson, even after Richardson met her in her apartment building for the interview. She was refusing to give an affidavit denying the affair until Jordan came through with a private-sector job in New York. He eventually did: Lewinsky received a $40,000-a-year job offer from Revlon, where Jordan sits on the board.

Tripp had been tape-recording it all for about six months, capturing descriptions of oral sex with the president in a small study off the Oval Office, and capturing as well Lewinsky's attempt to suborn Tripp's perjury. Toward the end of twenty-some hours of tape, Lewinsky expresses her horror at the prospect of Tripp truthfully describing their previous conversations in her deposition in the *Jones* case. The "Big Creep," as Lewinsky calls Clinton, would find out that she has been blabbing in technicolor, that she has been talking like a—well, like a twenty-four-year-old intern.

Lewinsky pleads with Tripp to lie to Jones's lawyers about what Lewinsky has been blathering to Tripp in earlier segments of the tapes: That she had been performing sexual acts on Clinton since she was twenty-one years old. Lewinsky says, "I'll give you one-half interest in my condo in Australia"—if Tripp would corroborate Lewinsky's proposed lies with her own lies. More interesting is Lewinsky's query to Tripp, "What if I can assure you had job security?"[17]

Even if Lewinsky was fantasizing an oral-sex–only "affair" with the president and lying to Tripp about it for hours on end, month after month, Lewinsky is on tape suborning perjury. It doesn't matter if the oral sex stories were false, the product of an overactive and highly unusual twenty-four-year-old's imagination. Lewinsky asked Tripp to lie about those conversations—to say that conversations that happened didn't happen. The substantive truth of those discourses is irrelevant to Lewinsky's attempt to get Tripp to lie about them. Indeed, Lewinsky never tried to persuade Tripp that her claims of sex with the president had been invented: Monica as fantasy-weaver was the White House's post-scandal spin. Lewinsky is on the tapes asking Tripp to lie under oath about what Lewinsky had told her. That's suborning perjury.

Tripp may have become the century's greatest villain for making the tapes. But imagine what she would be if she hadn't, but still told the truth under oath. That, in any event, was what worried her. Tripp had already made news as the last person to see Vince Foster alive. Most fatefully, she had made news as a near-witness to Kathleen Willey's Oval Office groping. Tripp had given the White House spin on the incident, but was criticized by the president's lawyer for adulterating the spin with the truth.

In fact, this was Tripp's motivation to make the Lewinsky tapes. After the story of Kathleen Willey broke on August 11, 1997, Tripp was quoted in *Newsweek* saying that she had seen Willey come out of Clinton's office disheveled, but "happy and flustered"—pre-

cisely the spin the White House had been trying to put on Paula
Jones's encounter with Clinton in the Excelsior Hotel. Bob
Bennett still called Tripp a liar in the same *Newsweek* article: he
didn't want to allow Tripp's claim that Willey was disheveled to go
uncontradicted. Angered by Bennett's attack, Tripp began taping
her telephone conversations with Lewinsky. If she was ever
required to testify about these conversations, no one was going to
be able to call her a liar.

Clinton's people would learn two lessons the hard way: Don't
call Paula Jones trailer-park trash, and don't call Linda Tripp a liar.

STARR STRUCK

But there was a chink in Tripp's armor. As a resident of Maryland,
she lived in one of a minority of jurisdictions that forbids taping
telephone conversations without both parties' consent, a fact she
says she had not known when she made the tapes. The offense is
minor and rarely prosecuted, but might well have been prosecuted
in this case as political payback. She wanted to make one good,
juicy, legal tape, to protect herself free and clear.

On Friday, January 9, 1998, her then-lawyers agreed to wire her
personally so she could tape Lewinsky somewhere outside of
Maryland the following Monday. Over the weekend, however,
they listened to her tapes. When Monday arrived, they told her
they wanted to take the tapes to Bob Bennett, so he would know
that he had better settle the *Jones* case in a hurry.

There was no way Tripp was handing the tapes over to Bennett.
He was the precise reason she was making the tapes in the first
place. Tripp fired her lawyers and went to Independent Counsel
Kenneth Starr on Monday, January 12. Tripp had a prior relationship with Starr through the Vince Foster and Travelgate investigations. Starr, who was already investigating Vernon Jordan for
arranging lucrative payments to Arkansas FOB Webster Hubbell

(*see* Chapter 16),[18] had to act fast: the story was already starting to leak. Starr's office decided to wire Tripp for lunch with Lewinsky the next day.

Monica Lewinsky had plans to meet Linda Tripp for lunch on Tuesday, January 13, 1998 at the Ritz Carlton bar in Pentagon City, Virginia, just across the river from Washington, D.C. Coincidentally, that was the day after Tripp had walked out on her first set of lawyers and taken her story to Ken Starr. When Lewinsky showed up at the Ritz, Tripp was wired. As Lewinsky and Tripp talked, FBI agents and Starr's deputies listened in. Both women had been subpoenaed in the *Jones* case about a month before. Lewinsky had already given the court an affidavit denying a sexual relationship with Clinton, which Bennett was about to use during the president's deposition.

Still in the dark the next day, Lewinsky, while driving Tripp home from the Pentagon, handed Tripp three typewritten pages titled "Points to make in an Affidavit." The talking points told Tripp how she should recall events in an affidavit to be submitted in the *Jones* case.

On Wednesday, January 14, 1998, Tripp formally retained a new lawyer, Jim Moody.

On Thursday, Starr presented his evidence to Attorney General Janet Reno, requesting an expansion of his investigation of Hubbell and Jordan to include the president's and Jordan's role in similarly fixing Lewinsky's testimony. According to a report in the *Washington Post*, "Justice officials were shocked by the allegations," and "there was no question about approving Starr's request."[19] Reno quickly forwarded Starr's request to a three-judge appeals court panel.

The next day, Friday, January 16, Starr's deputies approached Lewinsky as she sat down to lunch with Tripp, again at the Ritz Carlton. They took her upstairs along with Tripp for a chat. Did Starr's deputies browbeat little Monica? On the contrary.

Typically prosecutors who had captured a witness on tape prattling about her perjurious statements under oath and attempting to suborn another person's perjury would be told, *You've got fifteen minutes to make the most important decision of your life.* If Lewinsky was told anything like that, Starr's deputies or Starr himself immediately backed off.

Lewinsky informed the prosecutors that she wanted to talk to her mother before making a decision, rather than talking to a lawyer. Given who her lawyer turned out to be, this would have been a good call if her mother hadn't been who she was. (With her daughter in the hands of the most determined prosecutor in the country, she decided to take the scenic route, taking the train from New York rather than flying.) Did Starr's deputies take *this* opportunity to browbeat Monica? No, they agreed to wait all day for Lewinsky's mother to take the train, while taking Monica for lunch in the Pentagon City Mall, followed by a shopping foray at Crate & Barrel. This is not how people caught discussing their felonies on tape are typically treated. Earning her "presidential kneepads" had brought some perks.

Also on Friday, January 16, 1998, Starr's investigation was expanded by order of the Special Division of the D.C. Circuit to investigate "to the maximum extent authorized by the Independent Counsel Reauthorization Act of 1994 whether Monica Lewinsky or others suborned perjury, obstructed justice, intimidated witnesses, or otherwise violated federal law other than a Class B or Class C misdemeanor or infraction in dealing with witnesses, potential witnesses, attorneys, or others concerning the civil case *Jones* v. *Clinton*."

President Clinton could certainly be one of the "others" covered by the order and perjury is a violation of "federal law other than a Class B or C misdemeanor or infraction." But the order did not specifically mention "the Big He," as Monica calls President

Clinton on the tapes. Nor by Friday, January 16, had "the Big He" given any testimony yet in the *Jones* case: the order was entered the day *before* Clinton perjured himself at his deposition.

On Saturday morning it probably took only a few minutes after the oath was administered at 10:30 AM before "the Big He" launched one of his whoppers. The perjury investigation could probably have been in full swing by 10:35 AM. But it would not be for another four months that the public would definitively learn that Starr was expressly "investigating allegations of misconduct against the President."[20]

On Saturday, as President Clinton was being deposed by Jones's lawyers, a friend of the Lewinsky family, Los Angeles lawyer William Ginsburg, flew to Washington to represent the former White House intern.

Chapter Three

Prevaricator in Chief: The President's Deposition

The next day, Saturday, January 17, Jones's lawyers took President Clinton's deposition, an out-of-court legal procedure in which lawyers question witnesses under oath. This was the first time a sitting president had ever been deposed in his own case.[1] Armed with Tripp's recollection of Monica's midnight confessions,[2] Jones lawyer James Fisher asked the president detailed questions about his relationship with Lewinsky.

The president's lawyer, Bob Bennett, attempted to block the questioning about Lewinsky altogether by brandishing her post-Revlon affidavit and saying, as he put it, "that there is absolutely no sex of any kind in any manner, shape, or form, with President Clinton," and requesting that she not be required to give testimony in the *Jones* case. Judge Wright, however, allowed Fisher to proceed with questions to the president, following up this line of inquiry.[3]

And what a line it was.

As Fisher asked increasingly detailed questions about "Jane Doe #6," Lewinsky's public designation, Clinton surely realized the jig was up:

Q: Have you ever met with Monica Lewinsky in the White House between the hours of midnight and six AM?

A: I certainly don't think so.

Q: Have you ever met—

Whoops! The prevaricator in chief needed to expand on "I certainly don't think so":

A: Now, let me just say, when she was working there, during, there may have been a time when we were all—we were up working late. There are lots of, on any given night, when the Congress is in session, there are always several people around until late in the night, but I don't have any memory of that. I just can't say that there could have been a time when that occurred, I just—but I don't remember it.

He had a master's precision of knowing just when to lie outright, and when to dissemble.

Not only did Jones's lawyers know about Lewinsky, they knew about the Workers And Visitors Entrance System (WAVES) logs maintained by the Secret Service that document the precise time and general purpose of all visits by outsiders to the White House. Lewinsky had visited Clinton at the White House more than three dozen times since leaving her White House employ, including on December 28, 1997—about ten days after she had been officially subpoenaed in the *Jones* case.

The only cover for these meetings was that Lewinsky would list Betty Currie, the president's secretary, as the person she was visiting. Apparently, this had not thrown Jones's lawyers off the scent.

Q: [H]as it ever happened that a White House record was created that reflected that Betty Currie was meeting with Monica Lewinsky when in fact you were meeting with Monica Lewinsky?

A: Not to my knowledge.[4]

The next day, Clinton personally called Currie to the White House for an emergency coaching session on what her recollections about Lewinsky's visits should be.

The White House would later refuse to turn over the WAVES logs to an eager press, though it had done so the year before during congressional probes of Clinton fund-raising practices.[5] Eventually, Jones's attorneys would subpoena the WAVES logs.

Despite the White House's dogged attempts to portray the Monica scandal as "only about sex," the looming question for both Jones's lawyers and Clinton himself during the deposition was clearly whether the president had obstructed justice in the *Jones* case by trying to prevent Jones's lawyers from finding out about Lewinsky—such as during that December 28 meeting in the White House.

Indeed, one of the strangest aspects of the president's deposition was that Judge Wright and Bob Bennett were required to ask Clinton to speak up whenever the questions veered toward the possibility that he had suborned Lewinsky's perjury. The most booming glad-hander ever to occupy the Oval Office had suddenly lost his voice. And he started talking like George Bush. As the questions went from whether the president had discussed Lewinsky's testimony with her to whether the president had arranged for the U.N. ambassador to get her a job, Clinton's answers became confused and inaudible. In an especially nice touch, the president stalled for time by repeatedly commenting, "I want to be as accurate as I can."

Q: Did you ever talk with Monica Lewinsky about the possibility that she might be asked to testify in this case?

A: Bruce Lindsey, I think Bruce Lindsey told me that she was, I think maybe that's the first person told me she was. *I want to be as accurate as I can.*

MR. BENNETT: *Keep your voice up, Mr. President.*

THE WITNESS: Okay.

A: But he may not have, I don't have a specific memory, but I talked with him about the case on more than one occasion, so he might have said that.

*   *   *

Q: I believe I was starting to ask you a question a moment ago and we got sidetracked. Have you ever talked to Monica Lewinsky about the possibility that she might be asked to testify in this lawsuit?

A: I'm not sure, and I'll tell you why I'm not sure. It seems to me the, the, the,—*I want to be as accurate as I can here.* Seems to me the last time she was there to see Betty before Christmas we were joking about how you-all with the help of the Rutherford Institute, were going to call every woman I've ever talked to and I said, you know—

MR. BENNETT: *We can't hear you, Mr. President.*

Clinton instinctively reverted to attacking Jones's lawyers as members of a vast right-wing conspiracy out to get him—"we were joking about how you-all with the help of the Rutherford Institute, were going to call every woman I've ever talked to…." In fact, Jones's lawyers were interested only in calling in every woman Clinton had ever attempted to grope, proposition, or seduce. That group just happened to be strongly correlated with every woman the president had ever talked to.

Q: Is it your understanding that she was offered a job at the U.N.?

A: I know that she interviewed for one. I don't know if she was offered one or not.

Q: Have you ever talked to Bill Richardson about Monica Lewinsky?

A: No.

Q: What is his title?

A: He's the Ambassador to the U.N.

JUDGE WRIGHT: *I'm sorry, I didn't hear that.*

WITNESS: He's the Ambassador to the U.N.

Q: Have you ever asked anyone to talk to Bill Richardson about Monica Lewinsky?

A: I believe that, I believe that Monica, what I know about that is I believe Monica asked Betty Currie to ask someone to talk to him, and she talked to him and went to an interview with him. That's what I believe happened.

Q: And the source of that information is who?

A: *Betty.* I think that's what *Betty—I think Betty did that.* I think Monica talked to *Betty* about moving to New York, and I, my recollection is that that was the chain of events.

Before the end of his garbled responses on efforts to suborn perjury, the president had finally settled on the fall guy: Betty Currie. "Betty did that" quickly became the leitmotif of Clinton's deposition.

One of the most amusing exchanges in the entire deposition—in the entire case, really—is when Clinton is asked about the gifts he and Lewinsky exchanged. The Jones lawyers clearly knew a lot more than he thought *anyone* knew. Feeling the probe go deeper and deeper, the president played the liar's game of trying to elicit all known facts from his interlocutor before formulating his own "recollection"—

Q: Well, have you ever given any gifts to Monica Lewinsky?

A: I don't recall. *Do you know what they were?*

Q: A hat pin?

A: I don't, I don't remember. But I certainly, I could have.

Q: A book about Walt Whitman?

A: I give—let me just say, I give people a lot of gifts, and when people are around *I give a lot of things I have at the White House away*, so I could have given her a gift, but I don't remember a specific gift.

The story is, upon learning of the *Leaves of Grass* love token her husband had given to Lewinsky, Mrs. Clinton was finally shocked. She is said to have been aboard an Amtrak train when she first got wind of this part of her better half's perfidy, and gasped, "He gave me the same book after our second date!"[6] (It must be said that the book was the perfect courtship gift for Clinton, combining prurience with personal disclaimers. There are lines like "You settled your head athwart my hips and gently turn'd over upon me," but also, "Do I contradict? Very well then I contradict myself.")

And what are all those "things I have at the White House" he's been giving away? Official portraits? Does he have a lot of dresses and hat pins lying around the White House?

Q: Do you remember giving her an item that had been purchased from The Black Dog store at Martha's vineyard?

A: I do remember that, because when I went on vacation Betty said that, asked me if I was going to bring some stuff back from The Black Dog, and she said Monica loved, like that stuff and would like to have a a piece of it and I did a lot of Christmas shopping from the Black Dog, and I bought a lot of things for a lot of people, and I gave Betty a couple of the pieces and she gave I think something to Monica and something to some of the other girls who worked in the office. I remember that because Betty mentioned it to me.[7]

Again, "Betty did that."

Q: Has Monica Lewinsky ever given you any gifts?

A: Once or twice. I think she's given me a book or two.

Q: Did she give you a silver cigar box?

A: No.

Q: Did she give you a tie?

A: Yes, she has given me a tie before. I believe that's right. Now, as I said, let me remind you, normally when I get these ties, I get ties, you know, together, and then they're given to me later, but I believe that she has given me a tie.[8]

*   *   *

Q: Did you have an extramarital sexual affair with Monica Lewinsky?

A: No.

Q: If she told someone that she had a sexual affair with you beginning in November of 1995, would that be a lie?

A: It's certainly not the truth. It would not be the truth.

Q: I think I used the term "sexual affair." And so the record is completely clear, have you ever had sexual relations with Monica Lewinsky, as that term is defined in Deposition Exhibit 1, as modified by the Court?

A: I have never had sexual relations with Monica Lewinsky. I've never had an affair with her.

In response to widespread reports that Clinton believed oral sex did not constitute adultery,[9] Jones's attorney's had posited a definition of "sexual relations" in Deposition Exhibit 1 broad enough to circumvent the typical Clintonian escape hatch. It was not so broad, however, as to encompass a slap on the buttocks, as

James Carville has claimed, unless Carville believes a slap on the buttocks would be capable of "arous[ing] or gratify[ing]" sexual desires. The definition was—

> (1) contact with the genitalia, anus, groin, breast, inner thigh, or buttocks of any person *with an intent to arouse or gratify the sexual desire of any person*;
> (2) contact between any part of the person's body or an object and the genitals or anus of another person; or
> (3) contact between the genitals or anus of the person and any part of another person's body.[10]

No room for weasel words there. Clinton denied under oath that he had engaged in the sexual acts described by Lewinsky in florid detail, on hours of tape—tapes which were at that very moment in the possession of the independent counsel.

When Clinton got back to the White House he canceled dinner plans and called Betty Currie at home to ask her to come to the office the next day, though it was a Sunday and there was no crisis imposing special duties on anyone else. He reportedly ran her through a series of questions and answers about her understanding of his dealings with Lewinsky: "We were never alone, right?" When White House Press Secretary Mike McCurry was later asked to explain this odd behavior, he said the president called Currie in for extra, overtime duty that Sunday because he needed to refresh *his* recollection. McCurry did not explain why the president needed to refresh his recollection for questions he had already answered under oath on videotape and therefore, as far as he knew then, would never again have to answer.

Prior to the deposition, Clinton had apparently already refreshed his recollection enough to recall things he had forgotten throughout the 1992 campaign. One of the most peculiar exchanges during the deposition was this:

Q: Did you ever have sexual relations with Gennifer Flowers?

A: …The answer to your question… is yes.

Q: On how many occasions?

A: Once.

Q: In what year?

A: 1977.

During the campaign, Clinton had said that Flowers was a "friendly acquaintance,"[11] and that "the affair did not happen."[12] On *60 Minutes* he affirmed that he was, as the questioner put it, "categorically denying that [he] ever had an affair with Gennifer Flowers," earnestly insisting, "I have absolutely leveled with the American people."[13] Whoops. Flowers had not only testified under oath about the affair, but had also published a book describing sex with Clinton in immoderate detail.

The odd thing was that Clinton bothered to deviate at all from the "deny, deny, deny" strategy he had outlined for Gennifer Flowers years ago on *her* tapes. Flowers had made tapes of some of her conversations with then-Governor Clinton that pretty clearly corroborated her claimed affair with him. Presumably, Clinton lawyer Bob Bennett was aware of the Flowers tapes and had sternly advised his client about the penalties for perjury. Clinton had, after all, conceded the authenticity of Flowers's tapes by apologizing to then-Governor Mario Cuomo of New York for remarks he had made on the tapes—while denying their authenticity as to anything suggesting he had had an affair with Flowers. Clinton can be heard on the tapes remarking that Cuomo "acts like a Mafioso," and calling him a "mean son of a bitch." After Flowers released the tapes, Clinton moved quickly to shore up the Italian vote, saying, "If the remarks on the tape left anyone with the impression that I was disrespectful to either Governor Cuomo or Italian-

Americans, then I deeply regret it." (Cuomo initially refused the "if/then" apology.)

Still: "Once"?

Chapter Four

The Monica Story Breaks: Clinton's Legacy Is Formed

Late on Saturday night, January 17, the day of Clinton's deposition, Matt Drudge broke the story of the Lewinsky-Tripp tapes in his "Drudge Report" on the Internet in a "World Exclusive." Three nights later, the *Washington Post* released the story on its web site, running it as the front-page story of its Wednesday edition. (And *Newsweek*'s web page included a lengthy section on why their senior editors in New York had spiked Michael Isikoff's story that Saturday, which would have been the original "World Exclusive" on the Lewinsky matter.)

As each additional fact came out, day after day, and hour after hour, the possibility that there would be an innocent explanation became increasingly remote. All the pieces would fit together only if the true explanation was the one Lewinsky gave on the tapes, rather than the version in her affidavit. Apart from the immortal "kiss it," the remainder of Clinton's legacy was formed that week.

On Wednesday, January 21, MacAndrews & Forbes, which owns Revlon, released a statement admitting that Lewinsky had been offered a public-relations job with Revlon on the recommendation of Revlon board member Vernon Jordan. In light of the circumstances, the statement said, they were rescinding the offer. Revlon had extended the offer a few days after receiving a call from Jordan requesting that Lewinsky be made a job offer. Jordan made the call on January 8, the day after Lewinsky had signed the affidavit. Job offer in hand, Lewinsky submitted her signed affidavit to the *Jones* court on January 16.[1]

Also the next day, the president, looking very guilty, said "there is no improper relationship." When asked if there ever was an improper relationship, he replied he would cooperate fully with the investigation. Somehow, that didn't end the matter.

Again and again he denied that he had used Lewinsky for oral sex, saying, "These allegations are false." But leaks from Clinton's deposition had recently established that Clinton had finally come clean about the Flowers affair, which he had also once described as "false." Clinton's individualized understandings of words appeared to include interpreting the word "false" to sometimes mean "true."

On January 26, the day before his State of the Union address, the president went before the cameras from the Roosevelt Room of the White House, with the little woman at his side. He said: "I want to say one thing to the American people. I want you to listen to me. I'm going to say this again. I did not have sexual relations with that woman—Miss Lewinsky."

That still, somehow, didn't end things.

The very first news reports on the Lewinsky tapes noted that an important piece of evidence of Lewinsky's credibility on the tapes would be the WAVES logs kept by the Secret Service. Lewinsky had told Tripp of sex sessions with Clinton since she had left the White House in April 1996. If she was telling the truth, the logs would have to show the former low-level staffer being cleared to enter the White House since April 1996. The White House would have every reason to divulge the logs to the press voluntarily if they were Lewinsky-free. The White House did not release the logs.

Interestingly, according to sources at the White House cited in the *Washington Post*, the logs were not released this time around because with the Lewinsky matter "the danger is legal and thus far more serious."[2] So while White House flacks fanned out across the nation's airwaves to insist the investigation was only "about sex," not obstruction of justice, perjury, suborning perjury, or witness tampering, the White House kept the visitor logs under wraps—because of the legal issues at stake in the Lewinsky matter.

Jones's lawyers had, however, subpoenaed the Secret Service logs. At first, the administration refused to produce them, citing: *executive privilege*, the Nixon dodge. The logs were eventually produced. The records showed that Lewinsky had visited the White House thirty-seven times since she began working at the Pentagon. It was later learned that some of Lewinsky's visits to her pal Betty Currie took place while Currie was on vacation.

Clinton's former press secretary, Dee Dee Myers, said she hadn't visited the White House that many times since leaving. "There's no way to convince the American people that thirty-seven visits to the White House by a former intern is routine. That's extraordinary... and raises a lot of questions."[3]

Soon Clinton's answers to questions during his deposition came out. Not only had he lied about Gennifer Flowers, but he had also admitted he might have given young Monica a brooch, a dress, a hat pin, a book of poetry, and other assorted items. Giving a single dress to each of the hundreds of female White House interns alone would have been a dazzling financial feat, even for a president who was not simultaneously amassing enormous legal bills.

RECIPE FOR PERJURY

On one small point, Clinton's deposition testimony contradicted Lewinsky's sworn affidavit. She had sworn in paragraph 8 of her declaration: "The occasions that I saw the President after I left employment at the White House in April, 1996, were official receptions, formal functions or events related to the U.S. Department of Defense, where I was working at the time. There were other people present on those occasions."[4]

By contrast, Clinton remembered right off the bat seeing Lewinsky outside his office in late December 1997. No official reception, formal function, or other event, just Monica right outside his office. And this he remembered without having the luxury of time to refresh his recollection and confer with lawyers before answering, as had Lewinsky. The leader of the free world recalled a chance meeting with a former White House intern that had evidently not made much of an impression on the intern. It must have slipped her mind.

He did interpose a cover for their meeting: his secretary, Betty Currie. In fact, it was Currie whom Lewinsky had come to see. "She came by to see Betty sometime before Christmas. And she was there talking to her, and I stuck my head out, said hello to her."[5] First Currie had asked Clinton to bring some gifts to Lewinsky from The Black Dog, and then she starts inviting Lewinsky to drop by the White House to visit. That Betty palling around with Monica was going to cause the president no end of trouble.

In an immunity-less proffer negotiated by her lawyer, William Ginsburg, Lewinsky told a different story altogether: it was at that late December meeting,[6] she says, that Clinton told her to say her visits to the White House were to see Currie, and not to see him. Betty Currie has testified that Lewinsky and the president were sometimes alone in his office, though she apparently does not know if they had a sexual relationship.

SUPER LAWYER VERNON JORDAN

Then there was the matter of Vernon Jordan. In the tape-recorded conversations, Lewinsky says super lawyer Jordan informed her that perjury in civil cases is rarely prosecuted. In her proffer to the independent counsel, Lewinsky said she told Jordan she had had sex with Clinton and that she planned to lie to the court, without cavil from Jordan.[7] After testifying before the grand jury, Jordan said, "I did not in any way tell her, encourage her, to lie."

Jordan did, however, get her a job and get her a lawyer—who would help her draft her perjurious affidavit denying she had ever had sexual relations with the president. Jordan's strenuous efforts on behalf of a twenty-four-year-old former intern would be odd enough if she had been *his* intern. Lewinsky's only connection to Jordan was through Clinton.

According to Lewinsky's proffer to the independent counsel in early March, Clinton advised her that she could avoid giving a deposition in the *Jones* case if she were in New York.[8] Jordan told the grand jury that he personally gave the president regular progress reports on his efforts to get Lewinsky a job. He partially confirmed Clinton's statement that Betty Currie was the one who referred Lewinsky to him. Yet he also explained that he assumed the referral was made at the president's request.[9]

Jordan insisted, "[M]y efforts to find her a job were not a quid pro quo for the affidavit that she signed."[10] On NBC's *Today* show Hillary Clinton explained Vernon Jordan's herculean efforts to land a job for the Valley Girl intern by noting "how outgoing and friendly Vernon Jordan is" and saying that "he has helped literally hundreds of people—and it doesn't matter who they are."[11]

THE TALKING POINTS

Most mysterious were the talking points. On Wednesday, January 14, 1998, two days before Starr's deputies confronted Lewinsky at the Ritz Carlton Hotel—and the day after they had wired Tripp to tape a conversation with Lewinsky—Lewinsky handed Tripp a typed, three-page, single-spaced document titled

"Points to Make in an Affidavit." In addition to advising Tripp to be a "team player," the document told her exactly how—providing Tripp specific points to make that would benefit Clinton in the sexual harassment suit.

The proposed "recollections" were not exclusively, nor even primarily, about Lewinsky. They were about Kathleen Willey—whom Tripp was on record as having seen emerging from the Oval Office "disheveled" on the day Willey says she was groped by the president. Tripp was instructed to declare:

> *You now do not believe that what [Willey] claimed happened really happened. You now find it completely plausible that she herself smeared her lipstick, untucked blouse, etc. You never saw her go into the Oval Office, or come out of the Oval Office. You have never observed the President behaving inappropriately with anybody.*

As to Lewinsky herself, the talking points advised Tripp to denounce Lewinsky as "this huge liar," and to claim, "I found out she left the WH because she was stalking the P[resident] or something like that." Finally the talking points requested that Tripp submit her affidavit to "Bennett's people" for review before turning it over to Jones's lawyers. Once again, Lewinsky, if not "the Big He," is caught dead to rights suborning perjury—even if she is "this huge liar."

Like Craig Livingstone—the former bar bouncer turned White House director of personnel security who was caught with nine hundred FBI files in the White House—the only explanation for the talking points is that they materialized out of thin air.

If Lewinsky did type the talking points—and phrases like "this huge liar" suggest that possibility—there is little doubt that she was coached by someone, presumably a lawyer. The points read like a valley girl's transcription of a lawyer's advice. Most implausibly, the talking points concern a certain "Jane Doe" in the *Jones* case who would not be at the top of Lewinsky's concerns. Willey was of great concern to Clinton; Lewinsky was mainly concerned with getting a job in New York and preventing "the Big Creep" from finding out that she been talking about their "affair." The request to let "Bennett's people" review the final declaration doesn't make any sense coming from Lewinsky. By all accounts, Monica was primarily interested in Monica.

The leading candidates for talking points coach are Vernon Jordan, Clinton aide Bruce Lindsey, and of course the only person who would personally benefit from Tripp's suborned perjury—Clinton himself.[12] Lewinsky reportedly loathed Lindsey, and Jordan reportedly is not an idiot. Of the three, Clinton is the only one known to have left messages on Lewinsky's home answering machine.

Though it seems incredible that the president of the United States would be coaching a twenty-four-year-old former intern on how to tamper with a witness, it is also incredible that the president of the United States would be getting oral sex from a twenty-something intern, sending her love tokens, and leaving messages on her answering machine.

Moreover, according to news accounts of Lewinsky's proffer, Clinton was the one who told her how to commit another felony. Clinton is said to have advised the intern that she could trip up the Jones lawyers' subpoena for any gifts he had given her if she relinquished possession of the gifts. Following his advice, Lewinsky packed up the gifts and sent them to Betty Currie. Then Betty Currie took them straight to Ken Starr.

Lewinsky was left holding the bag again: even if Clinton never laid a finger on Lewinsky and really was just consulting her about monetary policy, she is the only person who clearly concealed these gifts from the court in the *Jones* case. Concealing subpoenaed evidence from a court is obstruction of justice, a felony.

As Lewinsky plaintively notes on the tapes, the only reason she is in this mess is because Clinton wouldn't settle the Paula Jones case. Lewinsky at least has no doubt about who is telling the truth. She tells Tripp that Clinton will never settle with Jones because "he's in denial." Jane Doe #6 explains to Tripp why she is willing to commit perjury for Clinton: "I will deny it so he will not get screwed in the case." Presciently, she continues: "[B]ut I'm going to get screwed personally."[13]

PRIAPUS'S PERJURY

Either the president was getting oral sex from Lewinsky while being sued for sexual harassment by Paula Jones, perjured himself about this relevant evidence sought by Jones's attorneys, suborned Lewinsky's perjury, and persuaded Lewinsky to tamper with another witness in the case, or Lewinsky is "this huge liar."

In order to believe the "this huge liar" scenario, one would also have to believe, among many, many other implausible things:

- Lewinsky developed a fantasy affair with the president that she was capable of droning on about to several people in vivid detail over a period of at least one year.

- Lewinsky's fantasy would include a derisive and belittling portrait of the president's private parts.

- The fantasy of a twenty-one-year-old girl would have her repeatedly performing oral sex on a fifty-year-old man (with physical limitations noted above) and with no further sexual satisfaction for her.

- The fantasy of a twenty-one-year-old girl would also not include any significant romantic accoutrements.

- Lewinsky would try several tacks to persuade Tripp to deny knowing of the affair, including offering to pay Tripp's medical expenses for a foot operation and offering her a one-half interest in Lewinsky's condo in Australia. But it would never, ever occur to Lewinsky to just come clean and admit to Tripp that the whole story was a fantasy to begin with.

- By dint of her sheer force of will, Lewinsky managed to secure a job interview conducted at her apartment complex with Clinton friend and Ambassador to the United Nations Bill Richardson. She would have the job offered, decline it, and then lyingly tell Tripp that the interview and job offer were implicit paybacks for her perjurious affidavit in the *Jones* case.

- Also on her own, Lewinsky would procure the assistance of Clinton friend and power lawyer Vernon Jordan and then, again, lyingly tell Tripp that the legal assistance and job offer from Revlon were an implicit payback for her perjurious affidavit in the *Jones* case. Inexplicably corroborating Lewinsky's payback fantasy, Jordan would later admit that he kept the president informed of his efforts on Lewinsky's behalf.

- Entirely on her own initiative, Lewinsky sought advice from a lawyer on how she could tamper with Tripp's recollection of an incident having nothing to do with Lewinsky—to wit, Tripp's encounter with Kathleen Willey. Following the lawyer's counsel, Lewinsky typed up a memo titled "Points to Make in an Affidavit," instructing Tripp how to discount Willey's smeared lipstick and untucked blouse.

- Also on her own initiative, Lewinsky advised Tripp in the talking points memo that Tripp show her affidavit to Clinton's lawyer in the *Jones* case before submitting it to Jones's lawyers.

- Lewinsky had a completely innocent reason to pay three dozen visits to the White House after leaving her job

there, including dates when Lewinsky's close friend—
hard-working, discrete Betty Currie—was on vacation.

■ It is normal for a middle-aged, married man to be leaving messages on a twenty-something's home answering
machine and exchanging gifts with her. (The president
confirmed this under oath in his *Jones* deposition,
specifically admitting that Lewinsky had given him a tie,
and "a book or two," and that he had given her gifts from
The Black Dog, and "could" have given her a Walt
Whitman book and a hat pin.)

These are just some of the things one is required to believe in
order to believe the president didn't perjure himself, didn't suborn Lewinsky's perjury, and didn't persuade Lewinsky to tamper
with another witness in the case.

No one is "waiting for the facts to come in," any more than O.J.
is looking for the real killer.

Chapter Five

Kathleen Meets Paula

Lewinsky was not the only Jane Doe who would be "screwed personally" on account of Clinton's offer to screw her presidentially. Soon even soccer mom Kathleen Willey came in for it from the White House. Willey was a fervent Clinton loyalist, just like all the women who would later tell pollsters they thought Willey was a liar. As she told *60 Minutes* interviewer Ed Bradley, she would have carried Clinton's grope "to the grave" with her if she had not been outed to Paula Jones's lawyers and ultimately compelled by a court to answer questions under oath in the *Jones* case.

Paula Jones's first set of lawyers had issued a request for Willey's deposition on July 29, 1997. A few months earlier, Jones lawyer Joseph Cammarata had received an anonymous telephone call from a woman claiming to have relevant evidence in Paula Jones's suit against President Clinton. The woman told Cammarata, "I had a similar thing happen to me in 1993."[1]

Though the anonymous caller may not have actually been Kathleen Willey[2]—and she has explicitly denied being the caller— the tipster talked at great length about "herself" and her experience with the sexual predator-in-chief but would not give her name. She said the "similar thing" occurred a few years back when she met with President Clinton to make a request for a White House job with more responsibility.

The gist of her story was that the president took her into a private office adjacent to the Oval Office where he began to "comfort" her regarding her troubles. He hugged her, and then moved from feeling her pain to feeling certain of her body parts, as well. The rest of her story largely tracked the contours of Jones's allegations in her complaint regarding Clinton's sexual advances in the Excelsior Hotel: Willey pulled away and left the room.

The Jones team went to work to learn the identity of the anonymous caller. From the tip that her husband had committed suicide (and consequently was listed on many of the right-wing Clinton-associate death lists) Jones's lawyers determined that it was Kathleen Willey, whose husband committed suicide on November 29, 1993.

On August 1, 1997, *Newsweek* reporter Michael Isikoff broke the story. This was the article that contained a quote from Clinton lawyer Bob Bennett about Linda Tripp that would induce her to begin taping her conversations with Lewinsky. Once those tapes were to come out, Tripp would be denounced on a pro-Clinton "fact sheet" for such outrages as being "Thought by Neighbors to Be a Republican." But back when she was being asked about Willey, she was a good Clinton loyalist.[3]

Tripp gave Isikoff the White House spin:

> *Linda Tripp, then an executive assistant in the White House counsel's office, recalls bumping into Willey in the West Wing after Willey had allegedly left the Oval Office. Willey was "disheveled. Her face was red and her lipstick was off. She was flustered, happy and joyful," Tripp told NEWSWEEK. Willey said she had to talk to Tripp right away. According to Tripp, Willey said the president had taken*

*her from the Oval Office to his private office, a small adjoining hide-
away, and kissed and fondled her. She was not in any way "appalled,"
Tripp told NEWSWEEK.*

*Tripp, who says she and Willey were once friendly but are no
longer, agreed to speak to NEWSWEEK "to make it clear that this
was not a case of sexual harassment."*

Just a sentence or two later Bennett insulted Tripp, saying she was
"not to be believed." Soon Tripp was cuing up the tape machine.

In the rest of the article, Isikoff reported on Willey's encounter
with the president on November 29, 1993, as told by her friend
Julie Steele.[4] In her first quoted version of the facts—and there
would be several—Steele said Willey had told her about being
groped by the president the night it happened, and said Willey
was "distraught." Willey was not quoted by Isikoff.

Before the article went to print, Steele called back to say she had
lied. In fact, she now said, Willey only told her about the presidential
fondling a few weeks after it had occurred and, frankly, didn't seem
so damned upset about it. In that second in a series of stories she
would eventually give, Steele said she had lied at Willey's request.[5]

For his part, Clinton's first version of *his* story, as given by his
lawyer, Bennett, was that he had "no specific recollection of meeting [Willey] in the Oval Office."

Meanwhile, Willey was fighting Jones's lawyers like a wildcat.
Willey held her job as a member of the United Service
Organization's Board of Governors as a Clinton appointee. Not
surprisingly, Willey was not eager to leap into the Paula Jones fra-
cas by taking a public stand against her benefactor, President
Clinton. She said she was "outraged" at Jones's attempt to pull her
into the case.[6]

First, she retained a lawyer to block the deposition. Her lawyer,
Daniel A. Gecker, promptly moved to quash the subpoena—a

motion he could not possibly have won—and issued a statement from Willey saying she "continues to have a very good relationship with the President," and "does not have any information that would be relevant to the *Paula Jones* case."[7]

At first, these dilatory tactics worked. Jones's lawyers agreed to delay the deposition on their own accord.

That gave the president's friends time to work on Willey. The Clinton White House began its response to the Willey revelation by denying that she had ever worked in the White House. Once that response became inoperable, the White House took the position that it would neither admit nor deny whether Willey had ever worked in the White House. This actually happened.

Next the White House attempted to discredit Willey, by explaining, through Clinton lawyer Bennett, that she may have been confused by the president's attempt to *comfort* her after her husband's suicide. But it was "preposterous" to suggest that Clinton had "made a sexual advance."[8] Unfortunately, her husband's body was not discovered until the day after President Clinton felt her pain.

Bennett objected to Willey's deposition on the grounds that she "has absolutely no knowledge or information of any relevance regarding Paula Jones or her allegations." Defying the legion of TV lawyers sagely nodding their assent to Bennett's claim, and just about everyone else to report on it,[9] the court ordered Willey to give her deposition to Jones's attorneys.

THE WILLEY DEPOSITION

She didn't go down without a fight though. Throughout the deposition, taken on January 10, 1998, getting her to answer simple questions was like getting the president to answer questions about Lewinsky. Willey was practically spitting her monosyllabic answers at Jones's attorneys. Every time she was asked to say what happened next, Willey answered with the highly abbreviated, but nonperjurious, "I left." She had clearly been extremely well prepared by her lawyer. Unless Jones lawyer Donovan Campbell phrased his questions in precisely the right way, she denied it. Lesser lawyers would have walked away from the Willey deposition empty-handed.

Page after page of the Willey deposition reads like this:

Q: At any time during this meeting with Mr. Clinton did he physically do anything other than sit behind his desk....

A: No.

Q: Did you, during this meeting with Mr. Clinton, did you ever physically do anything other than sit in front of his desk?

A: No.

Q: How did the meeting with Mr. Clinton conclude?

A: I left.

Q: Is there anything that you said before you left that you haven't told us here today?

A: I don't think so.

Q: Is there anything that Mr. Clinton said to you during that meeting that you have not told us here today?

A: No.

Q: At any time during that meeting did Mr. Clinton approach you physically?

A: In the Oval Office?

Q: At any time in your meeting with him that day. In any meeting that day.

A: Yes.

Q: Please explain that situation.

A: Do you want to know—*what do you want to know?*

Even when Campbell had finally maneuvered Willey to the precise location of the presidential grope—"at the door in the private hallway leading back into the Oval Office"—Willey was not exactly forthcoming:

Q: And then what happened?

A: Then he hugged me again and said that they would try to help me.

Q: And was that at the door in the private hallway leading back into the Oval Office?

A: Yes.

Q: And please describe the exact physical nature of the hug.

A: It was a hug.

Q: Is that all? Just an embrace?

A: It was a hug.

Q: Can you describe it any more fully than that?

A: Just a big hug.

Q: Did you hug him back?

A: I think so. I mean, I think so. I mean, I don't really recall if I did or not.

Q: After that hug, what happened after that?

A: Well, it continued.

Q: Okay, please describe exactly how it continued.

A: The hug just continued longer than I expected.

Q: Can you give us an estimation as to how long the hug continued?

A: No.

When Campbell asked point-blank about any kissing, Willey at first admitted only to "an attempt":

Q: Please describe that as fully as you can.

A: He attempted to kiss me.

Q: Mr. Clinton did?

A: Yes.

Q: On the lips?

A: Yes.

Q: Anyplace else? On the neck?

A: No.

Q: And what was your response to that attempt?

A: Surprise.

Q: Did you allow him to kiss you?

A: I don't think so.

Q: Was he successful in kissing you?

A: I can't remember.

Willey's obstinacy finally drew a rebuke from the court. When Willey claimed not to "recall" whether Clinton had touched any part of her body apart from the hug, the judge interjected:

> *I think what Mr. Campbell wants to know is if there was any physical contact between you and the president which had a sexual connotation, and I think you can answer that.*

Still Willey obfuscated. Later the court again instructed Willey to answer the questions, saying, "We've got to move along."

Finally the "Simon Says" game paid off:

Q: Did Mr. Clinton ever place his hands on any part of your buttocks?

A: I don't remember....

Q: You can't categorically say he did not; is that correct?

A: Correct.

Q: Did Mr. Clinton ever seek to take either of your hands and place it on his body anyplace?

A: Yes.

Q: Please describe that....

A: He put his hands—he put my hands on his genitals.

Q: Which hand?

A: I don't recall.

Q: And approximately how long did that last?

A: I don't recall.

Q: What was your reaction?

A: It was very unexpected.

Q: Were you surprised?

A: Yes.

Q: Did you resist?

A: Yes.

Q: How?

A: I just resisted.

Q: Did you try to push him away?

A: Yes.

Q: Were you successful?

A: Yes.

Q: Immediately successful?

A: I don't recall the time frame.

Q: Did you attempt to withdraw your hand from his genital area?

A: Yes.

Q: Promptly?

A: Yes.

Q: Were you successful?

A: As best I recall.

*   *   *

Q: Could you tell whether he was aroused?

A: Yes.

Q: And was he?

A: Yes.

Q: After you withdrew your hand from his genital area, what's the next physical thing that happened during that encounter?

A: I left.

*   *   *

Q: Did you have to gain release from his embrace in order to leave the room?

A: Yes.

*   *   *

Q: Did Mr. Clinton attempt to touch your breasts?

A: I think so.

Q: And what's the basis for your thinking so?

A: I have a recollection of that.

Q: Was he successful?

A: Yes.

*   *   *

Q: Can you tell us whether the touching of your breasts occurred before or after Mr. Clinton took your hand and put it on his genitals?

A: I don't recall.

*   *   *

Q: Did you ask him to stop?

A: I don't think I verbally did.

Q: Do you think you did nonverbally?

A: Yes.

Q: By what?

A: By resisting.

Q: At any time during—from the beginning of this hugging incident that you're just now describing up through to the point in time that you broke away and left the room, did he say anything to you?

A: Yes.

Q: Please tell us what he said.

*   *   *

A: I recall him saying that he had wanted to do that for a long time.

Q: Was he referring to the physical contact?

A: I don't know.

"I DID TO HER WHAT I HAVE DONE TO SCORES AND SCORES OF... WOMEN..."

About a week later, during his deposition in the *Jones* case on Saturday, January 17, 1998, Clinton said under oath that he "emphatically den[ied]" Willey's account. But he contradicted his lawyer's earlier statement that he had "no specific recollection of meeting [Willey] in the Oval Office."

Q: Mr. President, did Kathleen Willey ever give you permission to touch her breasts?

A: No, I never asked, and I never did.

Q: Did she ever give you permission to kiss her on the lips?

A: No.

Q: Did you ever attempt to kiss her on the lips?

A: No.

Q: Did you ever attempt to touch her breasts?

A: No.

Q: Did Kathleen Willey ever give you permission to take her hand and place it on your genitals?

A: No, she didn't.

Q: Did you at any time have any form of sexual relations with Kathleen Willey?

A: No, I didn't.

In the midst of answering questions about his allegedly groping of a White House volunteer, Clinton was able to recall his moralistic opposition to the consumption of alcoholic beverages:

Q: What did you have to drink?

A: I don't remember.

Q: Was it alcoholic?

A: Oh, no, no, I don't serve alcohol there in the office of the White House.

Q: Not ever?

A: Never.

No, it might interfere with his sexual potency.

Q: All right. Having read a summary of her testimony, are you aware that she has testified that you kissed her in the hallway between the Oval Office and the private kitchen?

A: I am aware of that.

Q: And you're aware that she testified that you took her hand and put it on your penis?

A: I'm aware of that.

Q: All right, and you deny that testimony?

A: I emphatically deny it. It did not happen.

The president's explanation for this *fifth* woman to accuse him of making sexual advances (Gennifer Flowers, Sally Perdue, Paula Jones, Dolly Kyle Browning)—falsely, he had said of all five, though moments later he would retract his Flowers denial—was that Willey was crazy. The other ones were gold-digging tramps, Willey was a looney bird and should properly be headed to the sanitarium. He repeatedly mentioned her husband's suicide, fudging the timeline to bolster his claim that he was merely "trying to help her calm down and trying to reassure her." In fact, Mr. Willey's body wasn't found until the day *after* Mrs. Willey's little tête-à-tête with the president. No matter, she was crazy and he was being comforter-in-chief: "Her husband killed himself, she's been through a terrible time…. She's been through a terrible, terrible time in her life." What a gallant.

Q: Do you know why she would tell a story like that if it weren't true?

A: No, sir, I don't. I don't know. She'd been through a lot, and apparently the, the financial difficulties were even greater than she thought they were at the time she talked to me. Her husband killed himself, she's been through a terrible time. I have—I can't say. All I can tell you is, in the first place, when she came to see me she was clearly upset. I did to her what I have done to scores and scores of men and women who have worked for me or been my friends over the years. I embraced her, I put my arms around her, I may have even kissed her on the forehead. There was nothing sexual about it. I was trying to help her calm down and trying to reassure her. She was in difficult conditions. But I have no idea why she said what she did, or whether she now believes that actually happened. She's been through a terrible, terrible time in her life, and I have nothing else to say. I don't want to speculate about it.

Q: Has she ever asked you to pay her money in return for her not disclosing this story?

A: Not to my knowledge.

Q: Do you recall at any time in that meeting with Kathleen Willey saying to her, "I wanted to do that for a long time"?

A: No, sir. Let me remind you, Kathleen Willey asked for this meeting with me. I didn't ask for the meeting with her. I didn't say anything like that.

That question about whether Willey wanted money in exchange for her silence hinted at one of the more explosive allegations to come: in another month the independent counsel would be investigating Willey's claims that the president's men had attempted to buy her silence. It also demonstrates that even before the White House released what it thought would be exculpatory letters from Willey to the White House, Jones's lawyers had guessed that Willey had reacted to the sexual harassment with a subtle form of blackmail—exactly what the letters revealed.

After November 29, 1993, the day Willey says she was groped by the president, she became a favorite for Clinton patronage jobs. She was not shy about asking for them either. Just a little more than a year after Willey's encounter with Clinton, the former stewardess—who had no college degree or other accomplishment, and who had been an unpaid volunteer at the White House—wrote to the president of the United States to ask him for an ambassadorship.

Such jobs are often patronage positions. But Willey and her husband had not been major contributors—the couple had given only $4,000 in 1992.[10] One wonders: Why was Clinton being Willey's patron?

Chapter Six

The *60 Minutes* Interview

Once it became clear that Willey's ultimately truthful deposition in the *Jones* case was going to be made public when Jones's lawyers filed their reply papers to Clinton's motion for summary judgment,[1] Willey agreed to appear on CBS's *60 Minutes* to tell her story to interviewer Ed Bradley. Presumably, Willey figured the best defense was a good offense. It would not be difficult to predict that Clinton's attack dogs would soon be deployed against Willey.[2]

This time Willey described her encounter with the president unreservedly. Since Paula Jones's account of Clinton's assault had come out only in the crabbed legalisms of a formal complaint, Willey's *60 Minutes* interview provided the first clear picture of Clinton's *modus operandi.*

Having had time to improve upon his opening gambit of "kiss it," Clinton led off with, "Why don't you come into my study?" As had eventually been dragged out of Willey during her deposition, she said the grope session began with a hug that "lasted a little longer than I thought necessary."

She continued:

WILLEY: And then he—then he—and then he kissed me on—on my mouth, and—and pulled me closer to him. And—I remember thinking—I just remember thinking, "What in the world is he doing?" I—I just thought, "What is he doing?" And, I—I pushed back away from him, and—he—he—he—he—he's a big man. And he—he had his arms—they were tight around me, and he—he—he touched me.

BRADLEY: Touched you how?

WILLEY: Well, he—he—he touched my breast with his hand, and, I—I—I—I was—I—I was just startled.

BRADLEY: This wasn't an accidental grazing touch?

WILLEY: No. And—then he—whispered—he—he—said in—in my ear, he said "I've wanted to do this ever since I laid eyes on you." And—I remember—I remember saying to him, "Aren't you afraid that somebody's going to walk in here?" The—and, he said—he said, "No. No, I'm—no, I'm not." And—and then—and—and then he took my hand, and he—and he put it on him. And, that's when I pushed away from him and—and decided it was time to get out of there.

BRADLEY: When you say he took your hand—

WILLEY: Right.

BRADLEY: and put it on him—

WILLEY: Uh-hum.

BRADLEY: Where on him?

WILLEY: On—on his genitals.

BRADLEY: Was he aroused?

WILLEY (sighing): Uh-hum.

BRADLEY: He was.

WILLEY: Uh-hum.

BRADLEY: What were you thinking?

WILLEY: I thought, "Well, maybe I ought to just give him a good slap across the face." And then I thought, "Well, I don't think you can slap the President of the United States like that." And— and I just decided it was just time to get out of there.

As a soccer mom who had fallen for the White House spin that Paula Jones was a trailer-trash gold-digger, Willey was *shocked*. "I just could not believe that had happened in that office. I could not believe the recklessness of that act." The sleaziness of what Clinton did to Willey does surpass the Jones assault in one way. As Willey noted, the president was a friend of her husband's, too: "[H]e knew my husband also. I mean, he was my husband, and he was in trouble. And I was there, asking a friend who also happened to be the president of the United States, for help." Of course, Ed Willey, Jr., would never learn of Clinton's perfidy; he was committing suicide about the time the president was groping his wife.

Bob Bennett made a command performance on *60 Minutes* following Willey. (Earlier in the week, Bennett had refused to appear on the program.) Bennett's appearance was memorable principally for his incapacity to take his eyes off his shoes. The president's reaction, he said, "in my presence was one of shock, bewilderment, outrage, that anything, any impropriety could be suggested."

Once again, the president had been wronged by another lying woman. Willey, Bennett said, was simply not telling the truth. She was just like Paula Jones, Gennifer Flowers (his emphatic denial now inoperable), Monica Lewinsky (on tape), and other women not yet described here: Sally Perdue, Dolly Kyle Browning, and Elizabeth Ward Gracen (whose own emphatic denial was about to become inoperable) as well as all their corroborating witnesses— Pamela Blackard, Debbie Ballantine, Lydia Cathey (Paula Jones's sister), three state troopers, Lauren Kirk (Flowers's roommate—denial now inoperable), and Linda Tripp. Clinton just has lousy luck.

Gracen, incidentally, had publicly denied a sexual liaison with Clinton in 1992 at the request of Clinton's then-campaign manager, Mickey Kantor.[3] She recanted her denial in the midst of the Monica scandal in order to *support* the president. Gracen finally admitted she had had sex with the then-governor in 1983, when she was twenty-two. Gracen said she was coming clean in order to make it absolutely clear that Clinton had not used force on her. That's gallantry in the era of Clinton. One can't help imagining the conversation over breakfast in the White House residence that morning—Hillary: *Oh look Bill! That sweet Elizabeth Ward has told the press you didn't use force when you had sex with her while I was home taking care of little Chelsea in 1983. Isn't that nice of her?*

Even with Gracen's helpful remarks, Kathleen Willey's charges were devastating to Clinton. As former Clinton aide George Stephanopoulos said, the charges were "tough" for Clinton because Willey was a "credible person," and the incident took place "right next to the Oval Office."[4]

Chapter Seven

Blasting the Bimbos

Like a bear gnawing his leg off to escape from a trap, Clinton instinctively reverts to attack mode against any woman who admits, willingly or unwillingly, to a sexual encounter with him. Fortunately for his agents in the attack squad, Clinton rarely chose women like Hillary or Susan Thomases for his sexual conquests, so he didn't have to worry about alienating his feminist loyalists when the conquests later had to be smeared as trailer-park trash. This must have been a great help when it came time to destroy the president's women.

Clinton can be heard on the Flowers tapes saying, "I just think that if everybody's on record denying it you've got no problem.... If everybody kinda hangs tough, they're just not going to do anything. They can't." Any woman ungrateful for the opportunity to have accommodated Clinton's sexual needs would have to hang by herself.

Soon after Monica made headlines in January, Clinton aide Paul Begala indicated the White House would be reviving the Clinton scandal management technique of total stonewalling combined with attacks on his accusers. He commented, "It got us through the snows of New Hampshire, it'll get us through this."[1]

About a week later, former Clinton aide George Stephanopoulos posited a "different, long-term strategy," saying people around Clinton were "already starting to whisper" about deploying an "Ellen Rometsch strategy" to deal with the Lewinsky scandal.[2] Stephanopoulos was referring to FBI Director J. Edgar Hoover's reported use of damaging information contained in the FBI files of various congressmen to scare them off an investigation into President John F. Kennedy's liaison with Ellen Rometsch, an East German spy. Apparently, the former presidential aide was suggesting, the White House would find dirt on Clinton's detractors to shut them up.

Stephanopoulos's claim was alarming. A few years earlier, in 1995, the Clinton White House had been caught with about nine hundred FBI files containing sensitive background information on former White House employees. It was known that the White House had not hesitated to plumb the files for dirt on at least one White House enemy, Billy Dale. Some former White House employees whose files may have been illegally obtained by the Clinton White House had gone on to jobs with Congress and with the press. Stephanopoulos said, "I think some around him [Clinton] are willing to take everybody down with him."[3]

According to former Clinton adviser Dick Morris, the White House "secret police" in all likelihood put the screws to Assistant Defense Secretary Kenneth H. Bacon to force the release of embarrassing information about Linda Tripp, a clear violation of the Privacy Act. The employee who actually leaked the private background data on Tripp has stated under oath that he did so on orders from Bacon, a Clinton appointee who had done favors for the White House in the past.

Clinton's defenders claim they are waiting for the process to play itself out, waiting for more evidence. But meanwhile, Clinton interferes with the process by using his office to throw muck at his accusers. Americans are allowed to say unpleasant things about their leaders. Americans are allowed to go to court to redress grievances. If he has no comment, he has no comment. But the president shouldn't be poisoning the well against people with grievances against him.

Trashing the women seemed almost acceptable in an era in which everything, including the law, is political spin. But Paula Jones wasn't Bob Dole. None of these women was a political candidate running against the president; all were witnesses against him.

BIMBO ERUPTIONS DURING THE 1992 CAMPAIGN

The media smear strategy was old hat for the Clinton team. Back in 1992 investigative reporter Michael Isikoff elicited this priceless phrase from top Clinton campaign aide Betsey Wright: "If the campaign needs a hatchet woman, I am more than willing to be it."[4] As it happened, the soccer mom's favorite candidate did need a hatchet woman, a couple of hatchet men, a whole hatchet team, in fact, to quell—also in Wright's famous words—"bimbo eruptions."

Wright told Isikoff that almost $28,000 in payments to a law firm listed in the Clinton campaign's Federal Election Commission report for the month of May actually paid for a private investigator, Jack Palladino. The campaign soon abandoned the law firm as a front for payments to the private eye and simply listed his fees as "legal expenses." Isikoff reported that Wright admitted to him: "I don't think I've used him [Palladino] on anything except bimbo eruptions." In retrospect, Palladino's "legal fees" were a real bargain compared with the ones Clinton has been paying Bob Bennett.

Palladino scoured the women's backgrounds in hopes of getting family members or old friends to malign the girls or, barring that, uncovering Republican affiliations to support the first lady's theory that a "vast right-wing conspiracy" was out to get the president.

NO MORE FLOWERS

Though he once had sweet nothings to whisper in her ear, after Gennifer Flowers told the world of her affair with Bill Clinton, he reportedly denounced her to his troopers in terms unbecoming the president who claims credit for the Violence Against Women Act. He called her a "f—ing slut," and demanded to know "What does that whore think she's doing to me?"[5]

That isn't how he always talked to her. On the tapes of their telephone conversations she produced to prove the affair, she was "baby." Back when he needed her silence, he also made sure Flowers was set up with a nice government job with the state of Arkansas. On the tapes, after Clinton assures her that their affair would be unprovable "if they don't have pictures," Flowers worries, "the only thing that concerns me... is the state job." No problem for Slick Willy. He advises her, "Yeah, I never thought about that, but as long as you say you've just been looking for one, you'd check on it. If they ever ask you if you've talked to me about it, you can say no." Good thing he's now admitted to the Flowers affair. The tapes alone were completely mystifying to American journalists.

Things changed for Flowers when she decided to tell the truth. Suddenly she wasn't "baby," but a bimbo and gold-digger: When asked on *60 Minutes* about Flowers's allegation, Clinton said, "That allegation is false." The next day he called her a liar and questioned her motives, saying, "She didn't tell the truth. She hired a lawyer a year ago, a year and a half ago, to say that anybody that said that was a liar and would be sued. And she admitted that she changed her story for money."[6] He explained the "baby" tapes by admitting that their relationship was "friendly."

Then the Clinton campaign P.I., Palladino, went to work on discrediting Flowers, in the end producing, according to Betsey Wright, "an affidavit or two" that would allegedly link Flowers to a right-wing conspiracy.

Flowers's former roommate, Lauren Kirk, corroborated Flowers's story in an interview with the *New York Post*'s Cindy Adams during the 1992 campaign ("There can be no doubt that she and Bill Clinton had sex with one another"). Thereafter, Kirk lost her job.

PERDUE CHICK

Sally Perdue, a former Miss Arkansas, is another woman who claims to have had an affair with Clinton. After rumors circulated just before the 1992 Democratic National Convention that the fifty-three-year-old Perdue was about to go public with the affair, Palladino sprung into action.[7]

He called around to Perdue's family members, friends, and acquaintances until finally locating one single estranged relative who was willing to malign Perdue. Palladino made sure the disgruntled relative was known and available to the press. Thereafter, Perdue was largely ignored by the press—when not mentioned in passing as a bimbo gold-digger—save one appearance in July 1992 on the *Sally Jessy Raphael Show.*

Perdue soon began receiving a series of threatening visits, phone calls, and letters. Perdue claims to have been visited by a man on August 19, 1992, who informed her that "keeping [her] mouth shut would be worthwhile." Perdue said she was told: "If I was a good little girl, and didn't kill the messenger, I'd be set for life: a federal job.... I'd never have to worry again. But if I didn't take the offer, then they knew that I went jogging by myself and he couldn't guarantee what would happen to my pretty little legs." She didn't take the job and was soon fired from her job in the admissions office of Lindenwood College (Missouri).[8]

KEEPING UP WITH JONES

Paula Jones has of course endured every trick of the Clinton "bimbo eruption" task force. Remember, it wasn't Ken Starr who brought the lawsuit that threatened to destroy Clinton's presidency.

Of course, no one in Clinton's camp dared say the president

would never, *never* do such a thing as Jones alleged. What they *did* say was that Jones was trailer-park trash and had a few skeletons of her own. Clinton lawyer Bennett has managed to produce two women loyal to Clinton, but barely acquainted with Jones, who claim Jones was thrilled—full of "bubbly enthusiasm"—after her encounter with Clinton. Poor little Paula was so reviled with the claim that she was doing it for money—unlike Bob Bennett, presumably—that she promised to donate any recovery to charity.

After Jones's wholly predictable, but almost wholly unpredicted, 9-0 victory in the Supreme Court on Clinton's frivolous "presidential immunity" claim, Bennett openly announced that his legal strategy of choice was to smear Jones. Comparing Jones to a dog on a Sunday morning talk show,[9] Bennett declared that he would wage a war of personal destruction against Jones for presuming to exercise her constitutional rights. "We've thoroughly investigated this case. If Paula Jones insists on having her day in court and her trial, and she really wants to put her reputation at issue as we hear, we are prepared to do it."

One doesn't have to accept the feminist argument that a woman's sexual history is never, ever relevant[10] to a sex case to see that there was no legal justification for Bennett's threat to delve into Jones's sexual history.

Even if Jones were everything James Carville says she is, Clinton's defense was that he can't even remember meeting her—not that she consented. When Jones's new lawyers dropped her defamation claim against Danny Ferguson, there was no possible legal basis for him to depose any of Jones's disgruntled former suitors.[11] Trashing Paula as a legal strategy had to be abandoned. Bennett would have to rely on Clinton's handmaidens in the media to wage the smear campaign against Paula's reputation.

WEE LITTLE WILLEY—INDUCING LARYNGITIS

Soon people around Clinton were behaving in a way that could easily be mistaken for attempts to buy Willey's silence. As with Lewinsky and Gennifer Flowers, Willey was first approached with carrots. Willey told *60 Minutes* interviewer Ed Bradley[12] that she had been talked up "extensively" by Nathan Landow, the former chairman of the Maryland Democratic Party and a major Democratic contributor. She said she could not elaborate because Landow's dealings with her were being investigated by the grand jury.

According to leaks to *Newsweek* about Willey's appearance before the grand jury, Willey testified that Landow told her, "Don't say anything." Taking a page from Clinton's talking points on the Gennifer Flowers tapes, Landow told her that as long as she said "nothing happened," they couldn't prove anything.[13]

At first, Landow dismissed Willey as a "distant acquaintance." But then it turned out he had chartered a private jet to fly Willey to his beachfront estate in Maryland in October 1997, at a cost of more than $1,000. Willey also testified that she had been offered an all-expenses-paid trip to New York for a Christmas shopping spree. Landow said the only reason "distant acquaintance" Willey had come to his estate by chartered plane was to visit his daughter, Harolyn. Landow also said the suggestion that he tried to influence Willey's testimony was "totally false."[14] Between Harolyn Landow and Betty Currie, women seemed to be constantly causing Clinton no end of trouble.

When it looked like Willey might be planning to tell the truth, the White House wasted no time in applying the screws to their very own soccer mom. On *60 Minutes*, Willey said Bob Bennett met with her before her deposition in the *Jones* case. After telling her that the president "just thought the world of [her]," Bennett said, "now this was not sexual harassment, was it?" When she failed to provide the proper assent, Bennett said "Well it wasn't unwelcome, was it?" Willey says she told Bennett "it" was unwelcome. (In another week Bennett would sit through Clinton's deposition listening to the president say there *was* no "it"—welcome or otherwise.) She told Bennett that she intended to testify truthfully in Jones's civil case against the president. Then, in what Willey said she believed was meant as a threat to persuade her to lie, Bennett advised her to get a criminal lawyer.

The day after Willey's *60 Minutes* interview, the White House tried to dig Clinton out of the hole but only managed to dig him in deeper. The White House produced ten private letters Willey had sent the president between May 1993 and November 1996. Willey's incident with the president had taken place on November 29, 1993. The White House intended the letters to be exculpatory because they included sentiments such as "Take heart in knowing that your number one fan thinks of you every day"(November 1994). Why would she write so warmly to a man who had sexually assaulted her?

That would have been an excellent point to make—had Willey been suing Clinton for sexual harassment. But she wasn't. Willey could have done cartwheels out of the Oval Office and high-fived everyone in the hallway after being groped by the president of the United States, and it would not have diminished her value to Paula Jones as a witness. The only legally relevant question about Willey's allegations to the Jones lawsuit was whether it happened, not Willey's personal reaction to it.

Willey was giving testimony—had been forced by the court to give testimony—in someone else's lawsuit for sexual harassment. So the credibility issues that are normally raised when a woman sues for sexual harassment alleging an offensive act were irrelevant. This wasn't a "He said/She said" issue; it was a "He said/They forced me to tell the truth under oath" issue.

Willey's forced admission that Clinton had groped her and placed her hand on his genitals when she came to ask him for a paying job was probative evidence tending to support Jones's claim that he had done "the same thing" to her.

Because she was a witness and not a party to a sexual harassment lawsuit, the letters tend to support Willey's story because they suggest that Willey believed the president owed her something. Before Willey's November 29, 1993, encounter with Clinton, her letters are standard, besotted soccer mom letters to the liberal savior. Only *after* the alleged presidential groping do her letters to the president contain job requests. Extravagant job requests.

The White House said it had provided all the letters from Willey it could find. In a typical pre-grope letter she gushed, for example, "I watched you at the press correspondents' dinner on Saturday evening you were hilarious at least you haven't lost your sense of humor! Thanks again for all your help don't let the bastards get you down!"[15]

At the time of the presidential grope, Willey was a volunteer at the White House, and her most urgent need was money. She was liable along with her husband Ed Willey on a note repaying $274,000 he had stolen from his clients. She had come to Clinton to ask for a paying job because of her family's financial difficulties.

It soon turned out, however, that money would not be a major concern. Willey's husband had committed suicide the same day she asked the president for a paying job. Ed Willey's insurance company settled her claims on the policy for about a million dollars. That would have been more than enough to repay Mr. Willey's clients. But the defrauded clients would never receive the money they were owed from the insurance company's payout. Willey's lawyer shielded the bulk of the insurance settlement from her creditors by transferring it to Willey's children, who had not cosigned the note promising repayment. Willey was not going to be out on the street.[16]

Since most of her future earnings would go toward paying her creditors, her job requests to the president after the groping incident tended to focus on glamourous jobs that would give her credibility, such as international junkets and ambassadorships, rather than high-paying jobs. Though Clinton did not comply with Willey's absurdly presumptuous request for an ambassadorship, he did appoint her to positions on international delegations and prestigious government organizations that would normally go to scholars, lobbyists, lawyers, and major campaign contributors.

About two weeks after the distressed Willey met with Clinton to ask for a paying job—only to be groped instead—Willey met again with Clinton. Soon thereafter she was offered a part-time job in the White House Counsel's Office as a "staff assistant." She started the job some months later, in April 1994, and was fired six months after that for "lacking the necessary skills"—she couldn't type.[17]

Being fired from a secretarial job in October 1994 apparently struck Willey as an excellent stepping stone to an ambassadorship in the Clinton administration. She promptly dashed off a letter to the president requesting one. On October 18, 1994, Willey wrote to Clinton:

> *Thank you so much for taking the time to meet with me. Since I've seen you, I have had the opportunity to talk with [various aides in the Clinton administration.] I have invested almost three years with your campaign and administration and am not very willing to depart yet. I would like to be considered for an ambassadorship or a position in an embassy overseas....*
>
> *I don't need to remind you of my willingness to help you in any way that I can.*

Several months later, Willey had toned down her ambitious career plans, informing the president: "I would very much like to be considered for" a position on the International Union for the Conservation of Nature.[18]

Clinton wrote a note to his staff on the back of this letter: "Is this what Shelia Lawrence did? Can we do this for her?"[19] Shelia Lawrence was the fourth wife and widow of Clinton donor/ambassador Larry Lawrence, who later would have to be disinterred from Arlington Cemetery for lying about his nonexistent war record. She would later bring a lawsuit against Arianna Huffington for claiming Shelia was one of Clinton's mistresses.

Though Willey never landed an ambassadorship, in 1995 the former airline stewardess without a college degree was sent by the president on two international junkets with the State Department. Willey was the only participant in the two conferences "with no apparent expertise in the issues under discussion"—biodiversity and social development.[20] Then, on September 20, 1996, President Clinton appointed her as a member of the United Service Organization's Board of Governors.

Soon such international junkets became the enterprising soccer mom's taxpayer-funded Club Med. One of her letters to the commander in chief about one such boondoggle sounds like a letter from widows' summer camp:

> *I learned so much and made many new friends.... I also spent one day in a rain forest, followed by a day diving the coral reef on the island of Sulawese, experiences which I will never ever forget.... While I am very much in need of employment, I think that the Clinton-Gore campaign needs me too.*
>
> *I am free to travel and work on your behalf for the next year.... Fondly, Kathleen.*[21]

Willey is either a woman of incredible cheek, or she had something on the president. In any event, the letters sure weren't the exculpatory evidence the White House thought they would be.

A few days after releasing Willey's oddly presumptious letters to the president, the White House turned up its opposing witness. Any woman who accuses Clinton of sexual impropriety can expect some distant relative or erstwhile friend to start telling the most hideous stories about her. Just as not all accusers are necessarily to be believed, not every accuser of an accuser is to be believed. The negative character witnesses produced by the Clinton team often have credibility problems of their own. Former Willey friend Julie Steele was no exception.

Steele attacked Willey's credibility by claiming that Willey had asked Steele to lie for her on several occasions; Steele claimed she had lied for her friend. Supposedly, Willey first asked Steele to lie to *Newsweek*'s Michael Isikoff by exaggerating Willey's distress about the presidential grope.[22] Then Willey asked Steele to tell a boyfriend of Willey's that Willey was pregnant with his twins, as some complicated form of retaliation no one can understand. By her own account, Steele unhesitatingly told both lies.

Assuming the imaginary pregnancy story was true, it certainly seems peculiar and disreputable. (You wouldn't think Clinton's defenders would have the cheek to be commenting on anyone else's disrepute.) But even if true, neither the bizarre pregnancy story nor even the claim that she asked Steele to embroider her distress are particularly relevant to the truth of Willey's claim that Clinton groped her. Steele's material information to Jones's lawsuit was that Willey told her about the grope soon after it occurred.

That much, Steele stands by. For obvious reasons, such contemporaneous accounts are important evidence in harassment cases. But even if Willey never said anything to Steele about the incident, there is another even more contemporaneous witness: Linda Tripp. Tripp saw Willey emerge from Clinton's office in a state of disarray immediately after Willey's November 29, 1993, encounter with the president and moments later stepped outside with Willey for a cigarette, where she got the full account.

Then it was gleefully reported that Willey had floated her story as a book proposal, requesting $300,000 as an advance. The proposal, however, was declined. Being a woman who has been groped by Clinton was evidently not a big story. Most absurdly, Steele herself thought that being the *friend* of a woman who had been groped by Clinton might be: She tried to sell her story to *Star* magazine, some months before concluding that Willey was not so credible, after all.

Like Willey's effusive personal letters to the president, the fact that Willey may have tried to peddle her story might have worked to impugn her credibility in some contexts, but not in this one. Willey had not come forward voluntarily. Left to her own conscience, Willey was perfectly happy to allow the White House to smear Paula Jones as a lying, white-trash slut, even though Willey had to consider it likely, on the basis of her own experience, that Jones was telling the truth.

The court in the *Jones* case had compelled Willey's testimony because her own encounter with Clinton was relevant evidence in Paula Jones's legitimate constitutional claim against the president. Still, Willey had done everything in her power to avoid giving Jones's lawyers her deposition. Her stonewalling answers in the deposition could not make her reluctance to come forward more clear. Moreover, as for the credibility of Willey and Clinton lawyer Bob Bennett on *60 Minutes*, only one of them was getting paid to say what he said. Bennett isn't working *pro bono*.

The White House made known the crazy phone calls Willey made to her husband's creditors late at night in the days after his death. She had been married to a thief.

But by the time Willey stepped forward, denouncing the various Jane Does as lying, lunatic gold-diggers was beginning to lose its sting. The Clinton campaign had once launched the same attacks on Gennifer Flowers—who, as he had now admitted, had been telling the truth all along.

GOOD TRIPP

Contrary to attacks on Tripp's motives (for instance, the pro-Clinton "fact sheet" that said Tripp was "Thought by Neighbors to Be a Republican"), Tripp was not a Bush Republican spying on the Clinton White House. Contrary to White House–propelled leaks of Linda Tripp's background file, she was not a thief. Contrary to the implicit point of both attacks, it would be irrelevant to the question of whether Clinton obstructed justice if she were a conservative Republican or a reformed teenaged thief.

Tripp was a career civil servant, which is why she stayed on to work in the Clinton administration until August 1994, when she was assigned to the Pentagon Press Office. As her former lawyer, Jim Moody, said, "She is not enemy of this [Clinton's] administration. She is a proponent of the truth."[23]

The next Clinton administration attack on Proponent-of-the-Truth Linda Tripp took the preposterous form of accusing her of a "contradiction of the truth," as Secretary of Defense William Cohen put it.[24] Suddenly the Clinton administration was acutely interested in the truth.

A career employee at the Pentagon, Clifford Bernath, leaked information from Tripp's personnel file to Jane Mayer of *The New Yorker*, telling Mayer that Tripp had denied ever having been arrested for a crime on her security clearance form.[25] The release of this datum seemed to establish that Tripp had lied on her security clearance form: Mayer had already located a thirty-year-old arrest for "grand larceny," when Tripp was seventeen years old.

Leaking this information to a reporter was a bald violation of the Privacy Act. The Clinton administration may have become interested in the truth, but it remained cool toward the law.

For a while, countless newspaper headlines blared that Tripp had "lied" in her security questionnaire about a grand larceny charge. Tripp stood accused in the media of having committed two felonies—the original "grand larceny" charge as well as the felony offense of making false statements to the government in her 1987 security form. Secretary Cohen assured anxious truth-lovers that Tripp's malefaction would "be the subject of some inquiry." Lying in the Clinton administration, Cohen said, was "a very serious matter."[26]

The Clintonian code of ethics was getting confusing. If it was okay to lie under oath about adultery, why wasn't it okay to lie in a security clearance form about an alleged theft that occurred thirty years ago? Youthful delinquency was not the sort of thing that was typically held against upstanding citizens thirty years later. In some circles, adultery, to say nothing of perjury in a civil rights case, still was.

In any event, the accusation turned out to be false in material details: the larceny charge had been thrown out, and the judge had told Tripp to forget about it. Legally, it had never happened. Within a week the Pentagon had cleared Tripp of any wrongdoing.

According to the uncontradicted explanation given by Tripp's lawyer, the entire incident resulted from a "prank" played on Tripp by her friends—which should also be in quotes. While generally misbehaving at a hotel with a group of her teenage peers, someone in Tripp's crowd had lifted some jewelry and money and planted it in Tripp's purse, a fact duly noted by the judge, who threw out the larceny charge and reduced Tripp's charge to "loitering." The friends admitted to the felony larceny charge. The judge assured Tripp it would not go on her permanent record, and told her to forget about it,[27] which manifestly, she had.

In the end, there was no "grand larceny" charge and there was, consequently, no lie on her security form, as the Pentagon concluded. There was, however, a pretty clear violation of the Privacy Act by the Clinton administration's releasing information from Tripp's personnel file.

How had such outlandish charges been unleashed? There were a number of suspicious details.

Linda Tripp was not just any government employee. She was the woman who had revealed the biggest political scandal at least since Watergate—and perhaps for people who know what "Watergate" actually was—in the history of the Republic. The tapes she kept demonstrated not only that the president had lied to the public, but also that he had lied under oath in a lawsuit accusing him of violating a citizen's constitutional rights. Billy Dale may have been inconvenient, but Tripp was radioactive. It was hard to explain this as anything but a targeted political hit.

Moreover, the trumped-up larceny story came out at a propitious moment for President Clinton, coinciding with two severe PR setbacks for the defendant in *Jones* v. *Clinton*. As luck would have it, the Tripp smear broke the same weekend Kathleen Willey told her story of her encounter with the president on *60 Minutes*. Two days earlier, on Friday, Paula Jones's lawyers had released the depositions of Clinton's various distaff accusers, including Willey, Dolly Kyle Browning, and other "Jane Does," as they were called in their depositions. (Further confusing the Clintonian code of ethics, Clinton lawyer Bennett denounced the "Jane Doe" depositions as "a pack of lies"[28]—even though the sworn statements to which he referred were *only about sex*.)

More insidious, though, discovering who in the Clinton administration had broken the law by releasing information from Tripp's file soon became a shell game. No one has been fired. No one has been held accountable.

Initially, Clifford Bernath, the Pentagon flunky who had released the information to Mayer, insisted to the press that he alone was responsible for the leak. But, in a deposition on April 30, 1998, he admitted under oath, "I didn't do it on my own." Rather, he said his boss, Ken Bacon, had specifically directed him to release the information from Tripp's 1987 security clearance form. In his contemporaneous notes, Bernath wrote that Bacon had "made clear it's priority."[29]

Bacon, too, at first told the press that Bernath's testimony was "not accurate." But then, when called upon to give statements under oath, he recanted the "not accurate" part. In his own deposition on May 15, Bacon admitted that he had directed Bernath to provide the sensitive information to *The New Yorker*'s Mayer.

Bacon had been called upon by the Clinton administration to help out with nettlesome Clinton women before. He was the Clinton appointee who allowed for the Pentagon press office to be used as a dumping ground for women in the White House— which had brought Tripp and Lewinsky together.

EARNING HER PRESIDENTIAL KNEEPADS

As a matter of course, when the Lewinsky story broke, it was quickly made known that she used to wear low-cut blouses. The day after his deposition, Clinton was in the White House coaching his personal secretary, Betty Currie, to recall that he had resisted Lewinsky's sexual advances toward him.[30] Man of God Billy Graham quickly excused the lovable rogue: "The ladies just go wild over him." Graham and Elizabeth Ward Gracen could form a tag-team defending the president's promiscuity.

If Lewinsky hates Linda Tripp for allegedly betraying her, wait until she sees what "the Big He" has in store for her if she ever starts talking. Then she will really start earning her presidential kneepads.

Chapter Eight

Persecuting the Prosecutor

Denouncing Clinton's women as gold-digging whores—one once convicted of "loitering"—was not the only renewed attack. On the Flowers tapes Clinton says, "It would be extremely valuable, just to have, like I told you before... an on-file affidavit explaining, you know, you were approached by a Republican and asked to do that [allege a sexual relationship]."

The Republican attack machine excuse was reinvigorated to the point of comedy on NBC's *Today* show when the first lady spoke of the "vast right-wing conspiracy that has been conspiring against my husband."[1]

STARR'S REINCARNATION AS A HARDLINER

Descriptions of Starr—by those who know him, not those who fear him—invariably make him sound like Jimmy Stewart in *It's a Wonderful Life*. Until he was secretly inducted into the vast right-wing conspiracy (presumably the same day as Monica Lewinsky, the *Washington Post*, and the *New York Times*), conservatives never fully trusted him. He had that Supreme Court aspirant's gleam in his eye. He tried to walk away from this investigation in

95

1997, it was assumed, to preserve his viability as a High Court nominee. One of Starr's prosecutors resigned in disgust when Starr issued a report—unsigned—concluding that Vince Foster's death was a suicide, with very little new investigation.

Lawyers from the Bush Justice Department laugh at Starr's media reincarnation as a hard-liner. "His brief in *Cruzan*, for example," one lawyer remarked, speaking of the Supreme Court's right-to die case, "refused to denounce substantive due process root and branch. It was the work of a Powell-ite, or of someone who had seen what happened to the great man [Robert Bork]." As a federal judge, he once wrote an opinion in favor of the *Washington Post* in a libel action (*Tavoulareas* v. *Piro*) that some lawyers viewed as an Establishment suck-up. So much for the vast right-wing conspiracy's small tent.

Even his conservative critics, though, say his ethics are unimpeachable. Many of Starr's colleagues have remarked upon what a shock it must have been for him to descend into Clinton's Potterville and discover that not every man's word is his bond.

Clinton flacks Paul Begala and James Carville's efforts notwithstanding, the legal community seemed not to have even noticed that the Clinton attack squad had trained its sights on poor honest Ken. The president could have resigned, and federal prosecutors would still have been too busy talking about William Ginsburg's aberrant behavior to notice. "Starr has got to be going nuts, dealing with such an idiot. He's never dealt with someone like this." The reason for lawyers' obsession with Ginsburg was this: Starr didn't need Monica any more; about twenty-four hours into the investigation, Monica needed Starr. A credible threat of prison awaited Lewinsky whether she chose Door #1, Door #2, or Door #3.

It is a mark of Starr's old-school rectitude that his reaction to Ginsburg's bizarre tactics was austerely described in the *Washington Post* simply as "los[ing] patience with the young woman and her lawyers."[2] It is a mark of Starr's dangerousness to the administration that the White House started screaming about leaks from Starr's office. (If the "leaks" distraction ever fades, perhaps James Carville will reinstitute his December 1996 threat that Starr was "one more mistake away from not having any kneecaps.")

CLAIMS OF "LEAKS"

The "leaks" story, like the vast right-wing conspiracy story before it, was complete lunacy. For openers, the leaks kept throwing a monkey wrench into Starr's investigation. Just as Starr was trying to wire Monica, presumably to send her on another limo ride with "the other one," as she refers to Vernon Jordan on the tapes, the story broke. At that point, Starr's prosecutors walked away from Lewinsky, saying, "We've blown the opportunity to wire her. She's radioactive because of the Drudge Report." (This is according to Ginsburg's self-leaked information in *Time* magazine.[3])

The nuclear bomb in terms of leaks was the one about Betty Currie, loyal Democrat and personal secretary to President Clinton. According to the *New York Times*, Currie told Starr she was called into the office by Clinton the day after his deposition in the *Jones* case, whereupon Clinton coached her to say she had never seen him alone with Lewinsky. Worse, Clinton instructed Currie to retrieve the gifts he had given Lewinsky—consistent with Lewinsky's taped remarks that Clinton had told her if she didn't have the gifts, she wouldn't have to turn them over to Jones's lawyers. Currie retrieved the gifts all right. Then she apparently took them straight to Starr.

The moment the *New York Times* (newly inducted vast right-wing conspirator) printed this front-page story on Currie's testimony, she lost all her value to Starr as a source. (She must have also lost the warm sense of camaraderie around the office. Currie still sits outside the president's office.) Perhaps most devastating,

Starr lost the invaluable element of surprise in producing the gifts during Lewinsky's, and perhaps Clinton's, grand jury testimony.

Despite claims in the media that Starr's office was leaking this information, there was precisely zero evidence to support the allegations. Stuart Taylor of the *National Journal* (formerly a legal reporter for that right-wing conspirator, the *New York Times*) stated on national television that "any number of [the leaks], I've heard from the lips of witnesses and lawyers who aren't connected to Judge Starr's office, more or less verbatim, the way they were published in other publications."

Michael Isikoff of *Newsweek* (formerly of that right-wing conspirator, the *Washington Post*) is probably responsible for reporting more of the Lewinsky story than any other single reporter. Isikoff said of the leaks issue on NBC, "We don't discuss where [leaks] come from. I will say in this particular case of the—of the new White House aide, we do source it to sources close to the president's defense. So that may help you on that one small matter."

When Clinton personal attorney David Kendall filed a court motion under seal to protest the alleged "leaks," his court papers were immediately leaked to the press. As a consequence, the Currie bombshell took second place to Kendall's allegations of Starr's leaks on the evening news. Clinton administration officials have admitted that they routinely contact lawyers for witnesses before the grand jury (who, like Clinton, are not subject to any grand jury secrecy rules) to ask about their testimony. Clinton's lawyers, not Starr's, have both motive and opportunity to leak.

There is simply no conceptual framework under which leaking important information like this would constitute good legal strategy for Starr. And Ken Starr was no William Ginsburg.

OUTING STARR'S DEPUTIES

As with the smeared Jane Does, the White House did not limit its attacks on Starr's office to legitimate, if groundless, criticism.

Soon Starr's deputies would find their sex lives under attack. The White House was trying to smear members of Starr's staff with embarrassing personal stories—including trying to out a closeted homosexual. This wasn't a matter of a "two-way street," as Bennett had said when he threatened to go after Paula Jones's sexual history. Neither Jones nor any members of the independent counsel's office were being sued for sexually assaulting a subordinate on the job, nor were they being investigated for perjuring themselves about their personal sex lives in order to obstruct justice. This was pure political blood sport.

According to Doug Ireland, reporting in *The Nation*, "Three members of the media confirmed to me that [White House media counsel] Sidney Blumenthal… had indeed been spreading" rumors about the homosexuality of a Starr staffer. Reporters refusing to out the independent counsel staffer were threatened with their own outings.[4]

Michael Kelly wrote in early March that in "the past month, Starr's Washington office has logged what Starr's chief deputy, Jackie M. Bennett, Jr., says are close to a hundred calls from reporters inquiring about false and damaging accusations against the independent counsel's prosecutors…. Other recent calls to Starr's office from journalists reportedly have concerned such pertinent matters as whether a member of the investigation was a closeted homosexual and whether another person was involved in a sexual relationship with a reporter."[5]

The White House first denied and then admitted that the president's personal lawyers had retained Washington private investigator Terry Lenzner to dig up dirt on Starr and his staff. Bennett claimed this did not constitute investigating "personal lives" on the preposterous grounds that the investigator would not be using any illegal methods of gathering evidence: "There is public information available," Bennett said, "which, of course, it is our duty as counsel to research and gather." Divorce records, police reports, and statements from disgruntled acquaintances are "public," but why is it Bennett's "duty... to research and gather"? Suppose Starr and his deputies *were* drug-addicted sexual perverts. What does that have to do with whether Clinton committed perjury, suborned perjury, or obstructed justice?

Blumenthal said the allegation that he was trying to out members of Starr's staff and reporters were "totally false."[6] He attributed the story to a "smear" campaign, according to the *Washington Blade*, "though he was not willing to speculate who might be waging such a campaign." So now, *The Nation* and the *Washington Blade* have been inducted into the vast right-wing conspiracy, too.

Chapter Nine

Starr Turn: The White House's Secret Weapon

Whenever Clinton goes, just remember, it might have happened four months earlier had it not been for Monica Lewinsky's attorney, William Ginsburg. Shortly after Ginsburg was replaced with two lawyers, it was reported that the president was "preoccupied and depressed."[1] No big surprise there. Ginsburg had presumably contracted Judge Ito disease and lost his mind with all the publicity. Apart from Lewinsky ridiculing the president's manhood, Ginsburg provided the major comic relief of "Tailgate."

In a brief, shining moment of lucidity, when the story broke in January, Ginsburg said: "If the president of the United States did this—and I'm not saying he did—with this young lady, I think he's a misogynist." He was soon perseverating retractions. On further reflection he apparently concluded that if the president of the United States was being serviced by an unpaid intern in the Oval Office, he's a fine man. (At least Lewinsky's "libido" wasn't "imprisoned" while she was servicing the president, as Ginsburg later said it was.[2])

Everything Ginsburg did seemed calculated to harm his client. As Harvard law professor Alan Dershowitz said, Lewinsky was going to need a replacement lawyer "who is prepared to charge Ginsburg with ineffective assistance of counsel."[3]

Months earlier, Ginsburg's peculiar strategy had already set off quiet but incessant murmurings among criminal lawyers. "It's mind-boggling what a poor attorney [Ginsburg] is, and equally mind-boggling is the public's lack of realization [of that fact]." "Ginsburg has a very bizarre view of how these things usually work. He appears to have learned criminal law from a 1950s crime movie." "[Starr] offered her immunity [on the first day] if she wore a wire—what lawyer in his right mind would turn that down?!" "[Ginsburg] has done such an awful job, blabbering like he's some brilliant technician. But all the talking heads are fawning over him because they want to interview him." "He looks a lot like my Uncle Irv. I think that's the only thing that explains it. This is probably what my Uncle Irv would do."

These were just some of the comments from criminal lawyers on the strange behavior of William Ginsburg. Naturally, therefore, the media was focused like a laser beam on the legal behavior of... Independent Counsel Ken Starr. To set the record straight, Starr had Lewinsky over a barrel. Lewinsky had only one defense, which her own lawyer almost completely sabotaged.

It was a common misconception that fickle little Monica held the whole ball of wax with her decision about whether to make a clean breast of it, and that if she pleaded the fifth, everyone would pack up and go home. If Starr wanted her testimony, he would get it. Starr could have compelled her testimony before the grand jury (and in any trial other than her own). He could have simply unilaterally imposed limited federal immunity on her testimony, forcing her to waive her Fifth Amendment rights.

All the Fifth Amendment requires is that a person not be compelled by the government to give self-incriminating statements and then be criminally prosecuted for those very statements. Any immunity granted pursuant to a compelled waiver of the Fifth Amendment simply returns things to the status quo ante. Any evidence the government knew about or later learns about—independent of Lewinsky's grand jury testimony—could be used against her in a criminal prosecution.

If Lewinsky was compelled to testify and she did not tell the whole, complete truth in her compelled testimony, she could have faced additional prosecutions for perjury or false statements in that testimony. Starr can also compel her testimony in any subsequent prosecution against, say, Vernon Jordan or President Clinton. Moreover, since Starr is the independent counsel he has all the powers of the attorney general. If he alone decided he needed her testimony, he would get it, or she would go to jail—just as another Clinton "close friend," Whitewater partner Susan McDougal, did when she refused to testify.

If Lewinsky had had an attorney who knew something about criminal law, he would have immediately demanded that she throw herself on Starr's mercy and sing her little heart out to the grand jury for days on end. Even if she had done all that, she would still have had to keep her fingers crossed. As with compelled testimony, all she would have immunity from is Starr's use of her own testimony before the grand jury in any subsequent prosecution against her. He could still have prosecuted her for perjury, suborning perjury, witness tampering, and obstruction of justice, with all the evidence he had, apart from her own statements to the grand jury.

The "full immunity" Ginsburg kept demanding on television talk shows doesn't technically exist under federal law. It exists in 1950s crime movies. The only advantage Lewinsky would have gained by cooperating was that Starr might have agreed to sign an informal letter agreement stating that he personally would not prosecute her for certain crimes. Typically, such letter agreements do not forswear prosecution for all of a witness's crimes, just the most serious ones. It is a myth that people who commit crimes can walk away scot free if they turn state's evidence. Generally, the most they can hope for is leniency in a plea bargain.

That was the closest Ginsburg was ever going to get to "full immunity," and he wasn't likely to get it after spending eighteen hours a day on TV denouncing Starr. Starr didn't need Lewinsky or her loopy publicity-seeking attorney. So why wasn't Lewinsky's lawyer finding out what Starr's favorite chocolates and flowers were, rather than criticizing Starr on national television?

Until the *Beverly Hills 90210* girl figured out that her lawyer was yet another older man in her life willing to sell her down the river, Lewinsky was in trouble. On the basis of just the evidence *Newsweek* had, to say nothing of what Starr had—the dress, the brooch, the hair pin, the twenty-plus hours of tape, the talking points, the testimony of Linda Tripp, Ashley Raines (a White House staffer who heard Lewinsky describe her relationship with the president), Secret Service agents, and her mother—Lewinsky's own statements before a grand jury were not going to make or break any criminal case against her—or the Big Creep.

Remember: Lewinsky was alleged to be on tape, first, babbling to Linda Tripp about Lewinsky's affair with the president and, second, pleading with Tripp not to tell Jones's lawyers about those earlier conversations. That is suborning perjury. Lewinsky was the one who handed off the "Points to Make in an Affidavit" document to Linda Tripp. That is witness tampering. Lewinsky, according to press leaks, had taken gifts given to her by the president to Betty Currie—so that they were not in her possession when Jones's lawyers requested them. That is concealing evidence. Three felonies, even if she were fantasizing an oral-sex–only affair with the president.

No wonder the president was "depressed" when she got rid of Ginsburg.

Chapter Ten

A Cancer on the Country

John Dean warned President Nixon of a "cancer" growing on his presidency on account of some bad apples who had worked their way to positions of influence in the Nixon administration. This time around it's a little difficult to conceive of the cloud following Clinton from Little Rock to Washington as a staffing problem. Trouble follows Clinton whether he is in the Excelsior Hotel or the Oval Office, whether his associates are James and Susan McDougal (his Whitewater partners) or Vernon Jordan and Betty Currie, or whether his subordinates are Arkansas State Troopers or former bar bouncer Craig Livingstone. It's hard to explain this as a coincidence.

Clinton's defense is essentially that he is not impeachable because his conduct is so disreputable that the framers could not have conceived of it. This is the important part of the incessant claim that the president is not subject to impeachment or indictment and that "no one cares" because his offenses are only "about sex."

The framers never expected a man like Clinton to become president. Rather, they anticipated, with "great probability," that any man elevated to the presidency would have certain characteristics; he would be "a man of abilities, at least respectable." The office of the president—and to some extent the Senate—would require men of "character" notable for their "wisdom" and "integrity."[1] But they also assumed that the office would elevate the man; it would "naturally beget a livelier sense of duty and a more exact regard to reputation." This was, in fact, one of Hamilton's arguments for a single president in opposition to a populace fearful of getting another king. Vesting all the executive power in a single man, Hamilton argued, would cause him to "feel himself under stronger obligations."[2]

The "stronger obligations" and "lively sense of duty" the framers counted upon were obligations and duties to the entire country. In this regard, the president was quite unlike members of Congress, who would carry their local "prepossessions" or biases with them, as James Madison said in Federalist No. 46.[3] When the president has an impaired sense of duty and obligation to the nation, and absolutely no "regard to [his] reputation," the infirmity would naturally be expected to infect the entire country.

Instead of reflecting Americans' virtues and aspirations, President Clinton reflects the country's dark side. He has debased not only the White House, not only the administration, but the entire country, not only by what he has done but also by how he has defended himself. Nixon was impeached in part for lying to the American people himself and for engaging his White House intimates in a pageant of obfuscation. Clinton has done worse than lie: he has told lies that no one can believe, and forced those around him to lie as well. And then he and his cronies have denied not only the facts but even basic standards of decency.

Nixon eventually resigned in shame; Clinton's legacy is that he has no shame, no sense of duty or obligation to the country, and no concern for his own reputation. O.J. is the model for Clinton's second term. He has no alibi, no story whatsoever, and he has left a trail of DNA across a string of Jane Does. He just says he didn't do it and refuses to explain anything further.

In this recurring nightmare of a presidency, we have to have a national debate about whether he "did it," even though all sentient people know he did. Otherwise there would be debates only about whether to impeach or assassinate. Or the relative merits of the terms "scumbag" and "pervert." No one believes he's not guilty, except the usual 30 percent of people who remain willfully ignorant on every subject.

Clinton's shameless refusal to leave office voluntarily has led directly to monstrous "factions" of hypnotized zombies spouting the absurd. Like a cancer, his own lack of integrity has infected the nation. By refusing to go gracefully—as gracefully as is possible under the circumstances—he has dragged the whole country into a public debate about the indefensible. "Parties more or less friendly... to the accused" are forced into taking absurd positions. People who used to say controversial, but not preposterous, things are now having to twist themselves into pretzels to defend him. The line of defense shifts away from protests that the president is innocent to charges that the accusers have bad motives. (Even if their accusations happen to be true.) The cost of not impeaching him is to see Clintonesque arguments become standard political dialectic.

More is at stake than how we define fitness for office: it's how we define politics. Or, finally, how we define truth. There has always been a certain amount of disingenuousness in politics, but now that's all there is. Ruthless political gamesmanship has overtaken the law and finally overtaken the truth. Politicians are allowed to reshape our understanding of facts and truth, because it's all just political spin.

Clinton draws on every sick theme of our culture to win politically. He has such mastery of popular psychoses, he could be Jerry Springer. Under Clinton the country has grown accustomed to believing that there is no truth. Deconstruction has escaped from the twilight zone of the Ivy League and taken hold of our political life. Truth is political. Law is political. The law is a hook that you use, but, really, it's all about your feelings. Motives are the only things that exist, the only things that can be discussed. Paula Jones has a bad motive, Ken Starr has a bad motive, so the truth is secondary. Half the country is perfectly comfortable with the idea that since Starr is out to "get" Clinton, it doesn't matter that Clinton's guilty.

This obsession with "motives" is repeated by Clinton's flacks— *Starr is out to get the president; it's just about sex; he's spent $40 million.* Instead of plausibility, the issue is loyalty. Even if Clinton takes a demonstrably counterfactual position, his partisans rally to him because he said it. They have become Clintonized to say there are no facts, no evidence, the president is telling the truth. *The president said it is not true. We must believe what the leader says.* It has become a game to see who can say Clinton is innocent with the most sincerity. Eleanor Clift and Lanny Davis march forth like robots, saying anything their leader tells them to say because they are loyal. They may as well tell us South Korea invaded North Korea. It makes you want to slap them to break the hypnotic trance.

The contradictory claims of the two Clinton camps illustrate the reduction of truth to spin. The first lady and Eleanor Clift scream that the charges are false, thrown by scummy people. Geraldo Rivera and Bill Maher say they don't doubt the allegations, but it doesn't matter because it's all about sex. If truth were still the standard, the contradiction would be unsustainable. But both make good spin. Meanwhile Starr's great—and only—crime, apparently, is that he can't spin. Starr's critics' mantra, endlessly repeated, is that he has no feeling for public relations; he's very clumsy. Just as the truth doesn't count against Clinton, it doesn't count for Starr. When the framers said a republic cannot be sustained without virtue, this is more or less what they had in mind.

In early February *Human Events* called Gloria Steinem's office for a comment on the Lewinsky allegations. A spokesman for Steinem explained that "laryngitis prevents her from responding at this time."[4] Later she recovered her voice. It was a mistake.

On the op-ed page of the *New York Times* about a month later, once the laryngitis had lifted, Steinem announced the new Clinton-era standard of sexual harassment: The boss gets one free grope. Referring to Kathleen Willey's allegations during the *60 Minutes* interview, Steinem wrote:

> *The truth is that even if the allegations are true, the President is not guilty of sexual harassment. He is accused of having made a gross, dumb and reckless pass at a supporter during a low point in her life. She pushed him away, she said, and it never happened again. In other words, President Clinton took "no" for an answer.*[5]

So the dividing line between chivalry and a legal cause of action is the use of force—until Clinton actually rapes a woman. If you stop at *some* point after grabbing your female subordinate's breast and placing her hand on your crotch, it is not sexual harassment.

Most fabulous was Steinem's admission that laws against sexual harassment were never intended to stop sexual harassers. Rather, sexual harassment law is a tool to be used against ideological enemies of the feminist movement. Steinem called complaints about feminists refusing to criticize the president for turning the White House into his personal brothel "another case of the double standard." Again, paraphrasing doesn't do her justice:

> *[I]f the President had behaved with comparable insensitivity toward environmentalists, and at the same time remained their most crucial champion and bulwark against an anti-environmental Congress, would they be expected to desert him? I don't think so.*[6]

Perhaps not. But if the president's "insensitivity toward environmentalists" consisted of breaking a law others were required to follow, say, dumping pollutants in a lake, people would expect the law to be enforced against the president, even if he was "good on environmental issues." If instead, environmentalists reacted by saying, *That's not a pollutant, That's not a lake*, they might expect to see a drop in their credibility on environmental issues. Laws that are enforced only against people with certain points of view aren't laws, they're ideological weapons.

Law as thought control was already the official position of the Clinton administration in the case of sexual harassment. Clinton's EEOC has been at the forefront of pushing "sexual harassment" cases that consist of nothing more than "offensive" speech in the workplace. Nazis can march in Skokie, but don't call your secretary "honey." No wonder the feminists are devoted to him. They don't care about breast-grabbing; they want to know what you think.

At least now we know.

THE PRESIDENT LYING

One of the most terrible things Clinton has done to the country is to make it respectable to lie. He was already pushing the envelope on lying. He claimed during his first campaign that he didn't inhale, and that he had no idea how he had ended up with a low draft number, and that he had "absolutely leveled with the American people" about Gennifer Flowers. Monica Lewinsky was just the *reductio ad absurdum* of all this. It had never been so obvious that Clinton was lying—baldly and repeatedly—to the American people.

When the story first broke President Clinton assured the public he would provide as many of "the facts" as he could, "sooner rather than later," in keeping with his "obligation to cooperate with the investigation." Then it was a total stonewall. Words mean nothing. "[T]he very existence of external reality was tacitly denied by their philosophy."[7]

It may be illogical, but it is natural for people to think that if the president of the United States can lie, how can it be such a big deal if they lie, too? Fancy lawyers go on national TV to announce various exceptions to the quaint little anachronism of truth-telling. We have it on the authority of Susan Estrich, among others, that lying about sex is okay.[7]

This is absurd.

If we're going to have sex crimes, it cannot be that people are allowed to lie about sex. Rape, child molestation, sodomy, indecent exposure, prostitution—these are all sex crimes. People may have disagreements with the substantive law—for example, by opposing the application of sexual harassment laws to politicians who are "good" on abortion—but whatever the substantive law is, it is not okay to lie in judicial proceedings. The laws cannot be abstracted from the judicial proceedings necessary to enforce the law. If lying about sex doesn't count, then there cannot be sex crimes.

Is lying about sex okay if a woman levels a false allegation of rape or sexual harassment? Or only when a man falsely denies a charge of rape or sexual harassment? Paula Jones, Kathleen Willey, Gennifer Flowers, Dolly Kyle Browning, and the troopers have all given statements under oath "about sex." Would it be okay for them to have lied? Lying is never okay.

It may sound trite, but truth is all that separates us from the cave. People cannot communicate if they cannot assume that most of what they hear is true. Truth is prerequisite for a society to survive, for capitalism to flourish, and for a system of law to dispense justice, rather than raw power.

This is evidenced by a casual review of the nations that prosper as well as those that muddle along. One of the countries least famous for its respect for the truth is France—the country whose morals we are being asked to emulate in the era of Clinton. Phony sophisticates suggest that only the lowbrow would fail to embrace the idea of Monica standing by the president's coffin next to Hillary, just as former French President Francois Mitterrand's wife stood next to her husband's mistress. Consider Nobel Laureate Milton Friedman's prognosis for countries such as France that share Clinton's view of the truth:

Q: You've mentioned what you see as the institutional prerequisites for capitalism. Do you think there might be cultural prerequisites, too?

FRIEDMAN: Oh, yes. For example, truthfulness. The success of Lebanon as a commercial entrepot was to a significant degree because the merchants' word could be trusted. It cut down transaction costs.

It's a curious fact that capitalism developed and has really only come to fruition in the English-speaking world. It hasn't really made the same progress even in Europe—certainly not in France, for instance. I don't know why this is so, but the fact has to be admitted.[8]

PERJURY "ABOUT SEX"

The importance of truth-telling is of a much higher order in a judicial proceeding. There can be no system of justice if people feel no particular obligation to tell the truth under oath. Society recognizes that by imposing serious penalties for lying under oath. Perjury is completely unacceptable, even if you are in small claims court because your dog ate the neighbor's flowers. It is certainly unacceptable when the president of the United States is answering questions under oath because he has been accused of violating someone's constitutional rights.

If, as apparently everyone in America believes[9]—except Hillary Clinton, Eleanor Clift, and Vic Kamber—the president lied to the American people about his relationship with "that woman—Miss Lewinsky," he has also perjured himself in a legal proceeding. During his deposition in the *Jones* case, with a federal judge presiding, President Clinton stated, under oath, "I have never had sexual relations with Monica Lewinsky. I've never had an affair with her." And "sexual relations" was expressly defined to encompass the "certain type of sex" Clinton is believed to have engaged in with Lewinsky.

Members of the bar ought to be apoplectic that the president of the United States appears to have committed perjury. At least one member of the judiciary is duly alarmed by how casually the press has treated perjury by members of the Clinton administration. Federal Judge Royce Lamberth sentenced Ronald Blackley, the chief of staff to former Agriculture Secretary Mike Espy, to twenty-seven months in prison for making false statements under oath. In sentencing Blackley, Judge Lamberth said, apparently referring to William Ginsburg:

> *A lawyer, who must have been on another planet—actually he was just from Hollywood—recently claimed that no one is ever prosecuted for false statements under oath in a civil proceeding.... This Court has a duty to send a message to other high-level government officials, that there is a severe penalty to be paid for providing false information under oath.*

Judge Lamberth said his sentence should demonstrate "the seriousness with which this issue should be viewed by all" because "democracy depends upon trust between the people and government officials."

You can lie to Gloria Steinem, but don't lie to Judge Lamberth.

OBSTRUCTION OF JUSTICE "ABOUT SEX"

President Nixon wouldn't turn over documents, claiming one legal privilege, one time. He won, and consequently a new privilege was created. Clinton has invented wild legal doctrines to cover up his

relationship with a White House intern—among other Jane
Does—and we have to "wait for the facts to come in."

So far, Clinton has blocked the search for the truth with these
"trumped-up argument[s]," as former Clinton adviser Dick
Morris put it:

- The president can't be sued civilly for conduct that took
  place before he took office;
- The president's aides do not have to give testimony to a
  grand jury about purely private conduct;
- White House lawyers cannot be called to testify about
  the president's personal conduct;
- Secret Service officers cannot be asked to testify to anything about the president, or the president's consorts.

He is president, so, his legal arguments go, he does not have to
give evidence or respond to legal complaints. And to think Nixon
had inaugurated the "Imperial Presidency."

Admittedly Nixon did not invoke his one privilege in an investigation "about sex" he personally engaged in or pressed upon
unwilling females. He raised it in an investigation about a third-
rate burglary he didn't commit.

The only presidential privilege Clinton had not claimed was
the one floating around the Internet:

> Going to hell would interfere with the president's ability to carry
> out the duties of his office, and God's judgment would violate the sep-
> aration of powers. Sins are therefore excused in the case of a sitting
> president, at least if the economy is good.

The president's invocation of presidential immunity, executive
privilege, attorney–client privilege, and "protective service privi-

lege" to obstruct information from coming out about his relationship with Monica Lewinsky is about as plausible.

To state the obvious, White House discussions—at the highest possible level—about Monica Lewinsky cannot possibly be protected by a privilege for presidential communications about military and diplomatic secrets. They are, as his defenders say, "personal matters." Personal matters are not beyond the reach of impeachable offenses; they are beyond the reach of any legal privilege immunizing executive communications from production to a grand jury.

Nixon may have been paranoid about national security leaks and the "opposition government" in the midst of the Vietnam War. And covering up the existence of the "Plumbers"—the private group Nixon authorized in order to plug national security leaks— may well have constituted obstruction of justice. But he wasn't some horny hick in the White House asserting contrived privileges to cover his getting oral sex from the interns.

Warren Harding must be turning flips of delight in his grave to know that at least he isn't Clinton. No one has ever been caught like Clinton, in this tawdry combination of sexual perversion, witness tampering, and perjury. The most frothing-at-the-mouth Nixon haters never thought Nixon had himself committed perjury—even over a small matter like national security leaks during wartime. There was a dignity about Nixon unimaginable with Clinton. This is the most complete ignominy in American history.

PART TWO

Abuse of Power

Chapter Eleven

Job Creation, Clinton Style: The Travel Office Massacre

Poor, inconvenient Billy Dale. He had the misfortune of holding a White House job—director of the Travel Office—coveted by of one of the Clintons' Hollywood friends, Harry Thomason. To get rid of Dale, the idealistic first couple deployed the full force of the federal government against him. The FBI, the Justice Department, the IRS—even an independent contractor who happened to be working in the White House one weekend—were all called in to look for dirt on Dale.

The White House must have assumed that anyone could be found guilty of a crime if only investigated. Unfortunately for the Clintons, that assumption proved false. Investigations into the Clintons, after all, usually uncovered wrongdoing. On closer inspection, almost every wild accusation against the Clintons would turn out to be true—from the first lady's work on Castle Grande—a fraudulent land deal in Arkansas—to the sale of a burial plot at Arlington Cemetery. But Dale was clean as a whistle. Civil Society: 1; the Clintons: 0.

Clinton did have the authority to fire Dale, who served at the president's pleasure. It just happened that seven presidents before

Clinton had not seen fit to fire Dale, and it also just happened that a generous campaign contributor wanted Dale's job. Firing a veteran public servant to make room for a big Hollywood producer is the sort of rank cronyism and hypocrisy that one might have vainly hoped the Clintons had left behind when they came to the White House to usher in "the most ethical administration in the history of the Republic."

The framers believed that one of the virtues of having just one president rather than a body of presidents was that a single man would be less inclined to engage in such cheap cronyism. As Hamilton explained in Federalist No. 76, the president "will have fewer personal attachments to gratify than a body of men who may each be supposed to have an equal number; and will be so much the less liable to be misled by the sentiments of friendship and of affection. There is nothing so apt to agitate the passions of mankind as personal considerations, whether they relate to ourselves or to others...."[1]

Still, Clinton could have just come clean and explained that, while he appreciated Dale's vote (and Dale *had* voted for Clinton), what he really needed was money, so Dale had to be fired to accommodate a campaign contributor. While Clinton might not have been "putting people first," as his campaign booklet had promised, that's not an impeachable offense.

But that's not what Clinton did. Rather, his administration ginned up every oppressive mechanism the federal government had to offer in order to wage a full-fledged assault on an inconvenient man, Billy Dale. The Clinton administration used government agencies to investigate, audit, and prosecute Dale, in a desperate, *post hoc* attempt to portray cronyism as some sort of good government maneuver. That is the very definition of abuse of power. It doesn't get any clearer than this. If what the Clinton administration did to Dale is not impeachable, the Clintons have pulled ahead and, in the end, routed Civil Society.

THE FOBS

Harry Thomason, the Hollywood television executive famous for producing such shows as *Evening Shade* and *Designing Women*, was a major Clinton fund-raiser.[2] He is an old friend of Bill and Hillary Clinton, having first met the future president when Thomason was an Arkansas high school football coach in the 1970s. (One of the most priceless descriptions of the Thomasons' kindness to the Clintons was this: "It was the Thomasons who served as their ambassadors to Hollywood in 1991 when the Clintons were thought of as hicks."[3])

Thomason had helped "produce" various campaign events, culminating in his orchestrating the January 20, 1993, presidential inauguration. Following the inauguration, Thomason was given a White House pass and a White House office. Ironically, Thomason's job was to create events to burnish the president's image. He was to report to the president.[4]

Thomason was part-owner of an air-charter consultant firm, TRM, Inc., that had teamed up with the Clinton campaign's travel agency, World Wide Travel, to help arrange press travel during the campaign. Little Rock–based World Wide Travel was a hotbed of FOBs—including the very "generous" Riady family (about whom we will learn more later), longtime Clinton supporter Jackson T. Stephens, and the Rose Law Firm, where Mrs. Clinton was a partner.[5] World Wide Travel officials themselves had, of course, contributed to Clinton's campaign.[6]

While roaming about the White House, Thomason spread rumors about the Travel Office. He was the first one to plant in the heads of Mrs. Clinton and President Clinton the idea of removing the long-serving White House employees.[7] Thomason told Hillary Clinton that the Travel Office staffers were disloyal and should be replaced.

FUTURE EX-CODIRECTOR OF THE
WHITE HOUSE TRAVEL OFFICE

Another FOB with an interest in World Wide Travel usurping the functions of the White House Travel Office was Clinton's third cousin, twenty-five-year-old Catherine Cornelius. Her contributions to Clinton were murkier. During the campaign she had worked with World Wide Travel, coordinating travel arrangements for the press. Cornelius assumed that travel arrangements, among other things, would continue in the White House as they had in Little Rock.

Before Clinton had even taken office, Cornelius had written up a plan for World Wide's takeover of the White House Travel Office—with herself at the helm.

Clinton put Cousin Cornelius on the White House staff as a secretary to David Watkins, assistant to the president for management and administration. During her mere two months in Watkins's office, Cornelius kept up her campaign to oust the Travel Office staff. Just three days after Clinton's inauguration, Cornelius sent out a memo describing herself and another White House aide, Clarissa Cerda, as the future codirectors of the White House Travel Office. On February 15, 1993, Cornelius and Cerda coauthored an eight-page memo describing their planned reorganization of the Travel Office and, again, calling themselves "codirectors." They denounced the Travel Office staff as "complacent" and "overly pro-press."[8]

In April, Cornelius was reassigned to the coveted White House Travel Office. However, she was not yet codirector—only a spy on a reconnaissance mission for Watkins.[9] More than a month later, the day the Travel Office staff was fired, Watkins noted in a memo to Mrs. Clinton that Cornelius "had been observing the Travel Office for 45 days" and that she believed the office was engaging in "criminal activity." Coincidentally, right about the time Cornelius began "observing" the Travel Office, papers started disappearing.[10]

Among the vanishing papers was an expense log that would ultimately be crucial to Billy Dale's defense. The log never turned up.[11]

It must be said that, though the Travel Office staff was neither disloyal nor corrupt, some of the accounting methods Dale employed were sloppy and unorthodox, which created an opening for unsubstantiated charges of criminality. But the breadth of the accusations Thomason and Cornelius leveled at the office suggests that even they did not really believe the criminality charges.

One of Cornelius's indictments of the Travel Office was that the employees used "sexist" language,[12] which created a hostile environment—something that could not be tolerated in Bill Clinton's White House. Thomason claimed they were disloyal—a view, he told Watkins, that was shared by the first lady.[13]

THE PRESIDENT AND FIRST LADY'S FORGOTTEN ROLES

While Cornelius was snooping around the Travel Office, Hollywood producer Thomason was taking his case directly to the president and first lady. Not long after the inauguration, Thomason met directly with President Clinton to outline his plan for the White House to award a half-million–dollar consulting contract to TRM.[14] The president forwarded Thomason's memo, promoting the venture to top White House aides. This was not an idle gesture: Clinton also attached a label marked "action" on the memo and added a personal handwritten notation—"These guys are sharp. Should discuss with [Leon] Panetta [head of the Office of Management and Budget] and [Philip] Lader [deputy White House chief of staff]."[15]

According to Watkins's notes from April 16, 1993, Thomason told him that Travel Office employees were probably receiving 5 percent kickbacks from airline bookings.

On May 12, 1993, Thomason again met with the president in

the morning and Hillary later in the day. Thomason then went to Watkins and told him that he had spoken with the first lady about the Travel Office situation and that she was "ready to fire them all that day."[16]

On May 13, 1993, Thomason had a meeting with the first lady at the White House. The next day, she directed Watkins to fire the Travel Office staff. According to Watkins's notes, Mrs. Clinton explained, "We need those people out—we need our people in—we need the slots." She told Watkins that "Harry" had a plan for the Travel Office.

A few days later, Mrs. Clinton was pressing the planned takeover on Thomas F. "Mack" McLarty, then–White House chief of staff. According to McLarty's notes of the May 16 dinner meeting, after briefing the first lady on the Travel Office employees, he felt "pressure" from her to take quick action: "May 16: HRC Pressure."

The next day—May 17, 1993—McLarty talked to Watkins about Mrs. Clinton's concerns. Watkins later wrote that he felt he had to fire the Travel Office employees or there "would be hell to pay." A May 17 memo on the firing was faxed to President Clinton in California and "cc'd" to "Hillary Rodham Clinton." That day, aboard Air Force One, presidential aide Bruce Lindsey briefed Clinton on the impending firings.[17]

Indeed, this is just some of the mountains of evidence—in the form of sworn statements, White House admissions, and contemporaneous notes—that put President and Mrs. Clinton's fingerprints all over the decision to replace the Travel Office staff with "our people," as Hillary delicately put it.

Mrs. Clinton has consistently denied playing any role in the Travel Office firings, despite reams of documents and testimony turned up by congressional investigators that contradict this assertion. In a deposition given to the House Government Reform and Oversight Committee on March 21, 1996, Hillary Clinton said, "I had no decision-making role with regard to the removal of Travel Office employees."

The president, too, claimed to be out of the loop on the Travel Office firings. On May 25, 1993, President Clinton said, "I had nothing to do with any decision, except to save the taxpayers and the press money. That's all I know."[18]

"PUTTING PEOPLE FIRST"—THE PUTSCH

Watkins fired the seven Travel Office employees on May 19, 1993. Cornelius and World Wide Travel moved in immediately. Watkins gave Dale and his staff ninety minutes to pack up and move out. He informed them their White House passes would be no good after 5 PM that day. As Dale tearily packed his belongings from more than three decades of White House service, Catherine Cornelius moved in, asking Dale questions about the operation she had just acquired. The Travel Office employees were driven just off White House grounds in the back of a van and deposited on the Ellipse.[19]

In a "soul-cleansing" memo written some months later, but that would not be produced for another three years, Watkins explained that the Travel Office firings were Mrs. Clinton's doing: Vince Foster and Harry Thomason, Watkins wrote, "regularly informed me of [the first lady's] attention to the Travel Office situation—as well as her insistence that the situation be resolved immediately by replacing the Travel Office staff.... We both knew that there would be hell to pay if... we failed to take swift and decisive action in conformity with the first lady's wishes."[20]

The White House cover-up has remained the same. In all, five separate federal agencies would attempt to get to the bottom of the Travel Office firings. Representatives from all five agencies later testified that they had encountered steady roadblocks in their investigation, with the White House withholding documents, facts, or witnesses. Michael Shaheen of the Department of Justice labeled the White House's lack of "cooperation and candor" as "unprecedented."[21] And as William Clinger's House Government Reform and Oversight Committee noted in its report on the Travel Office firings, "Never before has a President and his staff done so much to cover up improper actions and hinder the public's right to learn the truth."[22]

THE SCRIPT REQUIRED CRIMINALS

Amazingly, Hillary and White House image-polisher Thomason had originally envisioned the Travel Office firings as a great public relations coup: the populist first couple putting an end to government corruption, removing deadwood at the White House, and saving the taxpayers money.

But this public-relations ploy backfired. The press quickly figured out what was really going on, and was not thrilled with the bald-faced political patronage that cost seven career employees their jobs. The dismissive remark of Thomason's wife, Hollywood producer Linda Bloodworth-Thomason, that taking over the White House Travel Office was "the equivalent of taking over a lemonade stand," didn't help matters.[23]

Still, so far, nothing much new here. The jobs of long-serving White House employees were for sale in the Clinton White House, just like, as we will see, the Lincoln bedroom and foreign policy.

It was the White House's relentless attempt to return to the original script, to portray the dumped Travel Office employees as crooks, that constituted an abuse of power unparalleled— undreamed of—by any previous administration.

The problem was, to pull off the image-enhancing version of the firings, the White House needed the Travel Office employees actually to be corrupt and thieving. So no matter how weak the evidence was, White House aides continued to accuse the employees of corruption and kickbacks in the press, finally bringing in the FBI and the IRS to locate some criminality. That was what the image was supposed to be, not White House cronyism. Dale's failure to be a crook wasn't going to get in their way.

SMEAR

The day of the purge—May 19, 1993—the president set the tone. Explaining his role in the firings (none) Clinton elaborated: "All I know about it was I was told the people in charge of administering the White House found serious problems there and thought there was no alternative."[24]

The same day, White House Press Secretary Dee Dee Myers held a press briefing to inform reporters that an independent audit of the Travel Office had uncovered evidence of "gross mismanagement" and "very shoddy accounting practices." Harry Thomason and Director of Media Affairs (and Cornelius boyfriend) Jeff Eller followed up in "off-the-record" briefings, telling reporters that the FBI was looking into "kickbacks" at the Travel Office.

(Eller had already tried to help his girlfriend's career plans by asking FBI agents for damaging information on the Travel Office employees.[25] When it came out in the press that the leaker's inamorata was none other than Cornelius, Eller expressed his empathy for the fired employees by bitterly complaining: "It's unfortunate that my personal life is getting dragged into this."[26])

Even months after Dale's November 1995 acquittal on embezzlement charges, the first lady was still trying to portray him as a crook. She explained to ABC's *20/20* that her interest in the Travel Office firings was limited to "the financial mismanagement" in the office.[27]

All seven Travel Office employees were fired and then defamed by the announcement of an FBI investigation, even though only two Travel Office employees, Dale and his assistant, had anything to do with the office finances.[28]

ABUSE OF FBI FILES

Around the time of the firings, someone in the White House asked Director of Personnel Security Craig Livingstone for Billy Dale's file—despite the fact that later testimony indicated that no one at the White House even knew who Craig Livingstone was or what he was doing there. "I do remember that the files were discussed," said Livingstone's former executive assistant, Mari Anderson, under oath.[29] Anderson elaborated in her sworn statement, "I know Craig [Livingstone] discussed them [on the telephone], but with who, I don't remember.... Craig was talking on the phone, and he asked [me or office assistant Lisa Wetzel] to go and pull these files, and I gave them to Craig."

Apparently, Livingstone was unable to accommodate the request fully: He did not have Dale's "raw" FBI file, with all the unsubstantiated rumors FBI agents had been able to unearth. This is odd since the White House cover story on why Livingstone was mistakenly in possession of about nine hundred FBI files— including many on former cabinet members and other high-level staffers in the Reagan and Bush administrations—was that Livingstone had been conducting a review of all current White House staff. Dale's file would fit into that description the way James Baker's file, for example, wouldn't. In any event, now that Dale was on the White House enemies list, Livingstone moved to correct the oversight.

In December 1993—seven months after Dale had been fired and Livingstone himself had revoked Dale's security clearance— Livingstone's office requested Dale's raw background file from the FBI. (Craig Livingstone had been the person in charge of "securing" the Travel Office after Dale and his coworkers were fired.) The request form said, "The person named above is being considered for: ACCESS (S)" to the White House. Dale had been banned from the White House in May 1993. Still, his FBI file arrived at

Livingstone's office on January 6, 1994, and stayed there until December 1, 1994.

Livingstone and his office were not a few loose cannons; the assumption that sensitive FBI files could be plumbed for opposition research was apparently widespread at the Clinton White House. FBI Agent Dennis Sculimbrene said under oath that three White House political appointees had already asked him for derogatory material on all seven White House Travel Office employees even before the May 19 massacre. The three were Associate White House Counsel William Kennedy, Watkins's deputy Patsy Thomasson, and Cornelius's boyfriend Jeff Eller.[30]

FBI INVESTIGATION

William Kennedy did not stop at attempts to ferret out damaging information from the Travel Office employees' FBI files. On May 12, right about the time when Thomason was again pleading his case directly to President and Mrs. Clinton, Kennedy contacted FBI headquarters directly to demand an investigation of the seven employees on the basis of Cornelius's unsubstantiated allegations.

James Bourke, the FBI supervisor who took Kennedy's call, politely suggested to Kennedy that, to initiate an FBI investigation, he would need to come up with more specific claims of wrongdoing than, for example, the fact that a female employee had been shunned by the staff,[31] or that the same female employee believed that staffers were living beyond their means. And Bourke did not even know that the same female employee had designs on running the office herself or that two days earlier Hollywood producer Thomason had sent a memo to the White House complaining, again, that UltrAir—the charter airline Billy Dale used—had shut out his own company from providing White House travel.[32]

Moreover, Kennedy could not even tell the FBI agent whether

the alleged "kickbacks" involved the federal government's money at all. Kennedy said he'd get back to Bourke.

The next day, May 13, Kennedy was more specific. This was the day Hillary was demanding that Watkins fire "those people" to open up slots for "our people." He said the demand for an FBI investigation of the Travel Office came from "the highest levels" of the White House, and if the FBI refused to begin investigating the Travel Office within the next fifteen minutes he would turn to a more responsive federal agency: the IRS.[33]

Only after Kennedy had demanded an FBI investigation into the Travel Office within "fifteen minutes," and after he had made a non-idle threat to call in the IRS, did anyone at the White House attempt to ascertain whether there was any basis for an investigation. The White House still had no evidence of corruption in the Travel Office, apart from the claims of financially interested parties Cornelius and Thomason.

The White House turned to an accounting firm that happened to be in the White House anyway, helping Al Gore with his "reinventing government" ploy. White House Deputy Counsel Vincent Foster, Jr., asked KPMG Peat Marwick to glance through the Travel Office books the following weekend to see if anything was amiss. Even this eleventh-hour review was not an official audit; a single auditor simply performed an informal review of the Travel Office's books. He discovered what anyone who had worked with Dale would have known: Dale's records on about $7 million worth of yearly travel by the press were not in tip-top shape. About $18,000 of the press's money was unaccounted for, and various other payments were undocumented.

Dale was not given a chance to respond to the charges.

On the basis of this slipshod, *post hoc* rationalization for an FBI investigation that had already been authorized at the "highest levels" of the White House, the White House forced the FBI to investigate.

This allowed the White House to justify the firings later as the result of a criminal probe, which resulted from the Peat Marwick review. In fact, however, the events went in precisely the opposite direction: the decision to fire the Travel Office staff was followed by the White House's demand for a criminal probe by the FBI, which was followed by an informal review of the Travel Office books by Peat Marwick.

Three days after the firings, the White House released a statement from the FBI stating that Peat Marwick had produced "sufficient information for the FBI to determine that additional criminal investigation is warranted." Publicizing an FBI investigation this way contravened FBI standing policy of never confirming or denying pending investigations. This much the White House later admitted, saying it was a mistake.[34]

But it was too late for the Travel Office staff: they were already tarred with the publicity of a criminal investigation. As Mrs. Clinton would say of charges against her beleaguered husband, a lie makes it halfway 'round the world before the truth can get its boots on.

Dale was ultimately brought up on embezzlement charges for depositing $68,000 of the media's money in his personal account. He denied, and the government was unable to prove, that he had ever used the floating account for his personal use. The prosecution probed the Dale family's finances in minute detail, but on November 16, 1995—two and a half years after his firing—Billy Dale was acquitted of all criminal charges.

THE TAX MAN COMETH

When Kennedy threatened to call in the IRS if the FBI didn't gin up an investigation, he wasn't kidding.

Precisely eight days after Kennedy issued this threat, IRS officers showed up unannounced at the offices of UltrAir and began an unorthodox audit. If there had been any "kickbacks," as Thomason had alleged, UltrAir would have been the airline paying them. The auditors asked to see UltrAir's books concerning flights arranged through the White House Travel Office.

The UltrAir audit turned out to be highly unusual in many respects. Typically, an IRS audit is performed with respect to a company's tax returns. UltrAir was formed in 1992; it had not yet had occasion to file a single tax return.[35]

Two years later the IRS concluded that there were no problems with UltrAir.

The IRS did not stop at auditing UltrAir. Both the former head of UltrAir, Charles Caudle, and Billy Dale himself were personally audited. The IRS must have been sorry Caudle turned up on the White House enemies list: it turned out the IRS owed Caudle nearly $5,000.[36]

In June Kennedy told two other members of the White House Counsel's Office that he had spoken to the commissioner of the IRS, Margaret Milner Richardson, about Billy Dale and reported that she was "on top of it" and that IRS agents were "aware."[37] Commissioner Richardson had been a friend of Mrs. Clinton's since their days at Yale Law School; she had also been a Clinton campaign contributor and an aide on the Clinton transition team.

Eventually, Billy Dale was personally audited by the IRS. In case this needs to be stated: White House lawyers are not supposed to have advance warning of even random IRS audits.

Coincidentally, Dale was first warned that he was going to be audited personally when being questioned by the IRS about the Travel Office accounts. He described this in testimony before the House Government Reform and Oversight Committee:

> Well, I can tell you that, I don't remember the date but somewhere along October–November of 1993, I got a summons from the IRS to appear in my attorney's office and bring all documents pertaining to the Travel Office. I went and it was our understanding that they were going to question me about the excise tax and how the White House

Travel Office had handled it. And as the meeting was drawing to a close, they had asked me a lot of personal questions, what kind of an automobile did I drive and things like that, and they looked at me and they said, "Don't be surprised if you hear from Baltimore and they want to audit you."

Representative Carolyn B. Maloney (D-NY) followed up Dale's disturbing account by accusing politicians of "playing politics instead of shaping policy"—but she was attacking *the Republicans*. She went on to praise herself—"at the risk of sounding constructive"—by proposing that the committee address an imaginary problem: how to "depoliticize" the Travel Office.

The difficulty with this was the office had never been "politicized." Dale had begun working at the White House in the Kennedy administration—playing Santa Claus on the telephone for little Caroline—and moved into White House travel operations during the Johnson administration. He had served seven presidents—three Democrats and four Republicans. The office had not become "politicized" until the Clinton White House purged the entire office because it needed "the slots," accused Dale of embezzling funds, ginned up an FBI investigation and prosecution against him, arranged for a compliant IRS to audit this public servant, and then turned to reliable flacks like Representative Maloney to defend the White House from legitimate inquiry.

ALL THE PRESIDENT'S FAULT

In some respects, what was done to the White House Travel Office employees is the worst of the Clinton scandals. There is no more pernicious abuse of power than using the police powers of the federal government for personal or political gain. The most damning charges against Nixon had been that he had attempted to use the office of the president to influence the FBI and the IRS.

He got an FBI investigation delayed for two weeks, and he was completely ignored by the IRS.

The very first indictment of Nixon in the second article of impeachment charged that he had attempted "to obtain from the Internal Revenue Service, in violation of the constitutional rights of citizens, confidential information contained in income tax returns" and had attempted "to cause" IRS audits or other income tax investigations. And, incidentally, this was for "endeavor[ing]" to politicize the IRS "personally and through his subordinates." Poor Tricky Dick could never actually get the IRS to audit one of his enemies. He couldn't even get them to back off from auditing him while he was president.

Still: he asked. Technically, Nixon stormed around his office bellowing about it, and a low-level functionary took him at his word and asked, but even that was once an alarming fact in this country. In the wake of Watergate, rules were quickly adopted prohibiting the White House from having any contact with the IRS, precisely to avoid the merest potentiality of political abuse of this powerful government agency.[38]

Nixon was also charged with "impairing the due and proper administration of justice" for attempting to have the FBI "conduct or continue" investigations. The accusation was that he had tried to gin up FBI investigations and to use information obtained by the FBI "for purposes unrelated to national security, the enforcement of laws, or any other lawful function." In fact, Nixon wanted one man investigated, and he wanted FBI information on that one man: Daniel Ellsberg, a former Pentagon official who was leaking national security secrets to the *New York Times*. If that was "unrelated to national security," what are the implications for an FBI investigation of a public servant whose job Clinton's friends wanted?

In any event, like the IRS, J. Edgar Hoover also ignored him, which is why Nixon brought in the Plumbers to plug national security leaks, some of whom were later caught at the Watergate Hotel....

Indeed, the famous "smoking gun" tape was the direct result of the fact that the FBI would not accede to the Nixon administration's demands—as is discussed on the tape. Consequently, Nixon listens to Chief of Staff Bob Haldeman's proposal that he and John Ehrlichman, the chief domestic policy adviser, ask the CIA to tell the FBI to keep stay away from the money trail leading from the Watergate burglars. Nixon accedes to the proposal but then, two weeks later, personally instructs the FBI director himself to "just continue your aggressive and thorough investigation." A two-week delay of an investigation that would reveal the president hiring the equivalent of Terry Lenzner (Clinton's private investigator), not to dig up dirt on his critics, but to plug national security leaks—that was once considered an impeachable offense in this country.

Twenty-five years later the Clinton administration uses the IRS and the FBI—and this time these agencies are responsive—to persecute an innocuous public servant whose job Clinton's people wanted. Nixon acted from defensiveness; Clinton acts from cupidity. At least Nixon tried to bend these agencies to his will to stop leaks of national security information; at least he tried to manipulate the agencies to protect his people rather than to attack his enemies; at least he was rebuffed; and at least President Kennedy had his sexual trysts with grown women who were getting paid.

One realizes how low President Clinton has brought the country when you start thinking *Bring back the Plumbers! Bring back the paid prostitutes!*

On the other hand, there is no "smoking gun" tape of Clinton acceding to his aides' proposals to obtain Billy Dale's FBI file, or to have the FBI investigate Billy Dale, or to have the IRS Commissioner (and FOB) Peggy Richardson audit Billy Dale and UltrAir (as well as eight out of ten other Clinton critics, *see* Chapter 13). As Bob Woodward remarked, there are "a lot of suspicious circumstances," but there is no Deep Throat.[39]

But the smoking gun tape was only important, because the Nixon administration *never got anyone audited and never got the FBI to investigate anyone.* The indictment of the Nixon administration was Nixon and "his men" had contemplated doing things the Clinton administration has actually done. The smoking gun tape revealed that Nixon had permitted his subordinates to try to interfere with an FBI investigation and to try to instigate political IRS audits—in both cases unsuccessfully.

It is true that Clinton's four misbehaving subordinates received letters of reprimand for their roles in the Travel Office firings— after those roles were revealed in the press. They were not docked pay or suspended from their duties; they merely got letters of reprimand in their files.[40] Nixon's misbehaving subordinates were fired, and he was still impeachable.

This we know from the Rodino Report, assembled with the able assistance of Hillary Rodham and Bernie Nussbaum: Nixon was impeachable for the acts of his subordinates in *trying to do* what we know Clinton's subordinates *actually did.*

Chapter Twelve

Filegate:
A "Bureaucratic Snafu"

In one of the five federal investigations into the Travel Office putsch, one small fact slipped through the White House stonewall: White House officials had pulled Billy Dale's FBI file in an after-the-fact attempt to justify his firing. It is important to recall the scrolling series of excuses the Clinton administration issued for its inappropriate possession of Dale's file, ordered from the FBI seven months after Dale's abrupt termination.

First, the White House claimed Dale's records had been retrieved from the White House archives, where Dale's file had been left from an earlier effort to complete unfinished "background information folders." Then, when it turned out the White House had not requested Dale's file from the FBI until seven months *after* firing him, the White House said Dale's folder had been pulled at the request of the General Accounting Office (GAO), which was conducting an investigation of the Travel Office firings. In short order, however, the GAO denied having requested Dales's FBI file.

When those excuses turned out to be inoperative, the White House was forced to make a dramatic revelation: Dale's file had been part of a slew of FBI files mistakenly requisitioned by the White House as part of an effort to update the background files of White House employees. The White House admitted that it had improperly pulled the files on as many as three hundred former White House employees, including prominent Republicans, but wrote the incident off as a "bureaucratic snafu." As solid proof that there was no illegal, unconstitutional intent, the White House repeatedly pointed out that the names on the improperly pulled FBI files went up only to the letter G.

On the theory that enemies lists are not assembled in alphabetical order, the White House supposedly proved that it had no nefarious purpose. As one syndicated columnist wrote of the White House's possession of hundreds of extremely sensitive FBI files: "But a major scandal, no. [Anthony] Marceca [one of the government employees involved] says the search of the outdated lists halted at the letter 'G.' Real enemies lists don't run out of steam."[1]

Thrilled by the surprise news that the requisitioned files "stopped at G," the White House went in high dudgeon at the thought that anyone could have imagined that the files snafu demonstrated anything other than the White House's well-established incompetence. "This is proof positive that Billy Dale's file was not singled out," boasted White House Associate Special Counsel Mark Fabiani.

Ann Lewis, deputy manager for the Clinton-Gore reelection campaign, asserted that the fact that the file-gathering had stopped at the letter G conclusively established that there was no "sinister conspiracy" to create a White House enemies list, saying the files matter was "like *Sesame Street*": "[A] conspiracy-minded president who really wanted to misuse power for his own political ends does not stop part way through the alphabet."[2] Even Republican lawyer Joseph diGenova conceded, "That makes me doubt a major plot."[3]

George Stephanopoulos demanded an apology from Republicans for having suggested that the White House had obtained Billy Dale's file as part of a vendetta: "These guys should be apologizing.... The charge they made earlier was wrong."[4] When asked to comment on the investigations being undertaken by the FBI, the independent counsel, and House investigative committees, White House Press Secretary Mike McCurry dismissively sniffed, "Surprise, surprise. What else?"

And then it turned out that White House excuse #3 was not true. They had plenty of files on Republicans with names like "Brent Scowcroft" (President Bush's national security adviser). Marceca even had the chance to review his own file, presumably filed under "M." We know Marceca saw his file because of the astonishing fact that he later brought a lawsuit against two women, Lilly Stephenson and Joyce Montag, for their unflattering remarks about him recorded in his FBI file.

It also turned out that the White House held hundreds more files than it had initially owned up to. Week by week the number would grow—three hundred, four hundred, six hundred, seven hundred. The Clinton administration eventually admitted that it had pulled at least nine hundred raw files, most of which dealt with former White House employees from the Reagan and Bush administrations. And the files hadn't stopped at the letter G. Was *this* now an enemies list?

The known perpetrators of this abuse of power were Democratic dirty-trickster Craig Livingstone, director of personnel security, and his enemies list assistant, Anthony Marceca, a small-time private eye and Democratic operative.

THE "SNAFU"

When the other excuses had run out, the White House reverted to its massive incompetence defense; Clinton called it "a completely honest bureaucratic snafu." Livingstone's office, White House officials said, had pulled files on Republicans because he had been given an outdated employee list by the Secret Service. That, supposedly, made the foul-up inevitable: How were Livingstone and Marceca to know that prominent Republicans were not employees of the Clinton administration?

The rosters had such names as President Reagan's chief of staff Ken Duberstein, Reagan press spokesman Marlin Fitzwater, Reagan and Bush cabinet member James Baker, Brent Scowcroft, and Gingrich spokesman Tony Blankley. While no one has claimed Livingstone and Marceca are rocket scientists, they are political junkies, and in that capacity at least they ought to have noticed that the people whose raw files they were flipping through were probably not employees of the Clinton White House.

In any event, two Secret Service agents, John Libonati and Jeffrey Undercoffer, promptly contradicted the White House's claim that it relied on outdated Secret Service lists when requesting the sensitive files from the FBI. Libonati and Undercoffer testified—perhaps self-servingly—that such an error on the part of their agency was impossible.

Self-serving or not, the agents soon came under criminal investigation by the Treasury Department's Inspector General's Office for possible perjury in contradicting the official White House line. The criminal investigation was called off after one week, and eventually Inspector General Valerie Lau apologized before a Senate committee for this apparent attempt to interfere with the agents' testimony. Lau implausibly claimed to the committee that she had been unaware of the criminal probe being conducted by her own office—a probe that at least six other employees in her office knew about.

Other aspects of the Republican file gathering did little to bolster the White House's claimed innocence. The White House had, for example, called off the established practice of sending copies of all requests for background files or investigations to the FBI White House detail. "They basically told me to stay away from the file office," Agent Dennis Sculimbrene said.[5] This was not the sort of thing that tended to promote the appearance of innocent bungling.

In addition, a six-month gap in the log used to sign out the sensitive files from the White House Security Office was never explained. One page of the looseleaf log ends on March 29, 1994, and the next page picks up again with September 21, 1994.[6] In testimony before the Senate Judiciary Committee, Livingstone had no explanation for the gap. The committee then sought out Mari Anderson, who had been Livingstone's assistant at the time. Anderson evaded a Senate committee's subpoena by, as the chairman said, "in effect, go[ing] into hiding." Federal marshals were assigned to look for her. Anderson eventually told committee investigators that she had kept the file up to date, and that Livingstone sometimes removed files without making an entry in the log. Even Rose Mary Woods never went into hiding.

Indeed, if there was anything "innocent" about this snafu, the White House sure wasn't acting like it. Why, for example, would an innocent White House hide its acquisition of the FBI file on Billy Dale from the House Government Reform and Oversight Committee—yielding the file only after the committee threatened to hold the White House in contempt? Why would an innocent White House destroy FBI request forms and lists of files found in the White House vault? The White House discovered its files problem in the fall of 1994: Why weren't the files shipped back to the FBI then? Why did the White House turn the files over to the Records Management Office, instead of returning them to the FBI?

On June 28, 1996, the *Washington Post* editorialized:

> [T]he question of why hundreds of unjustifiably collected FBI
> reports on Republicans ended up in the Clinton White House

remains unanswered. But another mystery now looms even larger. How did Craig Livingstone end up on the White House payroll? No one professes to know....

At this stage, nobody at the White House will claim credit for Craig Livingstone. It gets you wondering... Are there no papers in the payroll part of the operation that indicate that Mr. Livingstone was actually hired or okayed by someone?

The FBI files affair raises serious questions. They deserve and require serious answers and real ones.[7]

Answers to these questions, however, never came.

Never in recent memory had any administration obtained background investigations of another president's political staff. Yet the White House never investigated the files "snafu" and never provided Congress with answers to many enduring mysteries about the files.

With every other excuse having proved inoperative, Clinton senior adviser George Stephanopoulos gave the amazing defense that no one whose dossier White House employees had pawed over had actually been blackmailed. "There hasn't been any evidence of political manipulation," said Stephanopoulos. (That's the thing about blackmail: the person being blackmailed usually doesn't want to talk about it.)

THE FILES

The material in raw FBI background files is not the stuff of nominating speeches or awards banquets. Quite the opposite. These files contain the raw sewage of background investigations.[8] White House appointees have to fill out questionnaire SG-86, which former White House Counsel A.B. Culvahouse describes as designed to "affirmatively encourage the furnishing of adverse or derogatory information." The FBI performs background checks on a whole host of potential government employees to screen out individuals who might be vulnerable to espionage, theft, blackmail threats, or simple political embarrassment.

The raw file is the comprehensive pool of evidence, including every unsubstantiated rumor that diligent field agents are able to rout. This can include helpful observations from bitter ex-beaus, people who are certifiably mad themselves, or who confused the candidate with someone else. Not infrequently, raw files contain demonstrably false information. Even the true information can be something less than bragging material. Divorce, family problems, visits to the psychiatrist, debts—it's all in there. FBI analysts with expertise in sorting out reliable evidence from the unreliable, and who are dulled to reading about other people's deepest secrets, will eventually go over what the field agents bring in. The final report on the candidate will discount the improbable, the atypical, the vindictive—and the irrelevant.

So it was just a little bit unnerving for many former Republican appointees to learn that their raw files had been pulled by the likes of Democratic operatives Craig Livingstone and Anthony Marceca. Further, while these files were in Livingstone's possession, they were handled quite casually, with no controls on how often they were copied, to whom they were faxed, or who took copies away.

Simply obtaining an FBI file without a proper purpose could be a violation of the Privacy Act. Giving information from the files to someone else with intent to silence or embarrass someone would be a clear-cut crime.

According to testimony by the elusive Mari Anderson, Livingstone's secretary, someone in the White House wanted to see Billy Dale's file around the time of the Travel Office firings. However, it was more than seven months after Dale and the others were fired, and their security clearances revoked, that Livingstone's office filled out a request for Dale's FBI file.

The nominal sender of the request was then–White House Counsel Bernard Nussbaum. Nussbaum has maintained that such forms, with his typed signature on the "from" line, were produced in bulk for the use of Counsel Office staffers. The person filling out the form used one word, ACCESS, to describe the reason for the request.

It has never been suggested that Billy Dale was being considered for any kind of return engagement at the White House that would have justified a review of his file; nor is there any apparent reason why, if Dale had been under consideration for a new White House role requiring clearance, the bureau's normal vetting process would not have been sufficient, especially given Dale's more than three decades of uncontroversial government service. Under the circumstances, the inference that the White House was seeking derogatory information for an after-the-fact justification of the firing is hard to repress.

THE MYSTERIOUS CRAIG LIVINGSTONE

Who is Craig Livingstone? What may loosely be called his political career goes back at least to 1984, when he worked on Senator Gary Hart's presidential campaign. Livingstone was in charge of spreading dirt for what must be a very bitter Gary Hart. Dennis Casey, a Pennsylvania political consultant who met Livingstone on that campaign, told the *Washington Post* in 1996 that Livingstone had urged the use of information about sexual peccadilloes of labor bigwigs who supported Walter Mondale to help persuade them to switch to Hart. "I just got a very bad taste in my mouth" about Livingstone, Casey said. "He felt it was my duty to go to these people and try to coerce them into supporting Senator Hart."[9] For the record, Livingstone disputes Casey's account. (For the record, Livingstone also doesn't know who hired him at the Clinton White House.) In 1988 Livingstone was a paid advance man for then-Senator Al Gore's presidential campaign.

Between working on losing Democratic campaigns, Livingstone worked at Washington, D.C., bars, including J. Paul's and Annie's in Georgetown, which would later earn him the omnipresent appellation "former bar bouncer." Livingstone was fired from two jobs for misconduct.[10]

When Livingstone signed up with the 1992 Clinton-Gore campaign, he had finally found an employer who would hang onto him. He was "senior consultant for counter-events"—in his own words—for the campaign.[11] This entailed dressing up as Pinocchio and "Chicken George" to disrupt Bush-Quayle events. Livingstone moved from his job with the Clinton-Gore campaign, to director of security for the Clinton-Gore inaugural committee, to security director at the Clinton-Gore White House.

Indeed, two years before the files story broke, Senator Dennis DeConcini (D-AZ), then chairman of the Senate Intelligence Committee, warned the White House about security problems at the White House and recommended appointing a "non-partisan individual responsible for overseeing all security-related functions within the office of administration."[12] The White House ignored DeConcini's advice, preferring to keep Craig Livingstone in charge.

Someone must have wanted him badly, because he beat out a better-qualified competitor. (Not that dressing up as a chicken wasn't apparently a strong qualification for the Clinton administration.) Of course, anyone who had formal security experience of any sort would be better qualified to head White House security than Craig Livingstone. Livingstone was chosen over Jacquelyn Dinwiddie,[13] who had held the White House security job during the Carter administration, had worked on the Clinton campaign, and had applied for the job in the Clinton White House.

Agent Sculimbrene said of Dinwiddie, "She had integrity, she was competent, and she ran a good shop." Another FBI agent,

Robert Cronin, told *Investor's Business Daily*, "She had common sense combined with political sense that would have kept her out of a lot of these troubles." Dinwiddie remarked without irony, "Obviously I was not the best person for the job, or I would have gotten it."

"HILLARY WANTS HIM"

Who hired Livingstone remains one of Washington's great mysteries. No one who could have hired him will admit to so much as knowing Livingstone prior to his showing up as White House security director. As far as the Clinton administration is concerned, Livingstone's tenure in that job was part of the Lockean state of nature, or the Rawlsian original position. Or perhaps an effect of El Niño.

In 1994 George Stephanopoulos said of Livingstone, "He does a terrific job. All I know is that anything that has anything to do with security or logistics—Craig's going to take care of it. You don't have to tell him how to do it, when to do it. Just that it needs to be done, and he does it. And he knows how to cut through the bureaucracy and get things done."[14] After Livingstone's demonstrated bureaucracy-busting skills came to light in the Filegate matter, Stephanopoulos said, "I don't know him that well. He's a guy that was around."[15]

The president and the president's men—including former White House Counsel Bernard Nussbaum, who was nominally responsible for the office Livingstone headed—have all taken the position that none of them hired Livingstone, and none of them knows who did. Apparently no one is capable of finding out who did either, so could we all please drop the subject? Such claims are, according to the Rodino Report, the reason for the constitutional impeachment power:

[U]nder the... Constitution, the President "is of a very different
nature from a monarch. He is to be... personally responsible for any
abuse of the great trust reposed in him.".... [T]he predominant prin-
ciple on which the Convention had provided for a single executive
was "the more obvious responsibility of one person." When there was
but one man... "the public were never at a loss" to fix the blame.[16]

What can be pieced together about Livingstone's hiring,
despite the best efforts of the president and his men, is this: One
former FBI agent says Nussbaum told him—in an official interview, in which lying would be a federal felony—that Hillary
Clinton had recommended Livingstone's hire.

FBI Special Agent Dennis Sculimbrene took notes of the background check that he conducted on Livingstone as part of his routine examination of all new White House employees. Sculimbrene
interviewed Bernard Nussbaum on March 13, 1993. According to
Sculimbrene's contemporaneous notes of the meeting:

Mr. Nussbaum advised... that he has known the appointee, Mr.
Livingstone, for the period of time he has been in the new adminis-
tration. Mr. Livingstone came highly recommended to him by Hillary
Clinton, who has known his mother for a longer period of time.[17]

Nussbaum has denied making such a statement, and Mrs.
Clinton has denied ever knowing Livingstone before he came to
the White House, for what that's worth.

Before producing Sculimbrene's notes to a House investigating
committee, the FBI warned the White House about the revelation
in the notes and sent two FBI agents to Sculimbrene's home to
have a little chat with him about how unhappy the White House
was with the notes taken years before. Sculimbrene was then pres-
sured out of the bureau, after serving in its White House detail for

almost twenty years. Then–FBI General Counsel Howard Shapiro
sent the agents, and he also warned the White House. Incidentally,
Shapiro left the FBI in June 1996 under heavy GOP fire from the
Hill because of his always-at-your-service posture toward the
Clinton White House. He surfaced in the news again in March
1998, as attorney for private investigator Terry Lenzner, who, the
White House admitted, is paid to gather dirt on perceived ene-
mies of the Clinton White House.

(Noting that the White House's earlier denial that "any private
investigator" had been hired to "look into the background of... prosecutors or reporters" seemed to conflict with the eventual admission
that Lenzner had been paid since 1994 to do just that—by collecting
"public information" on the backgrounds of Starr's prosecutors—
journalist Stuart Taylor explained that the "Clintonian reasoning was
that looking into public information about a person's background
was entirely different from looking into his background."[18])

Absurdly, the White House responded to Shapiro's warnings
about Sculimbrene's notes by issuing a letter from White House
Counsel Jack Quinn informing FBI Director Louis Freeh that the
White House was "troubled" by Sculimbrene's "false report."

Sculimbrene could have had no imaginable reason to falsify
notes taken in 1993 about who hired Craig Livingstone. There
was no possible way of predicting that the question of
Livingstone's sponsor would ever become an issue—much less a
matter of considerable embarrassment. Back in March 1993
Livingstone hadn't done anything wrong yet. He might have gone
on to perform heroic feats for the White House, leaving his supe-
riors vying for the claim of having discovered young Craig.
Indeed, over a year after Sculimbrene dutifully recorded in his
notes that Nussbaum said Hillary was responsible for hiring
Livingstone, George Stephanopoulos would still be telling the
press what a "terrific job" Livingstone was doing.

Even before Sculimbrene's notes became public in July 1996, another FBI agent, Gary Aldrich, had already written in his book *Unlimited Access*—released the previous month—that Associate White House Counsel William Kennedy told him the same thing. According to Aldrich's book, Kennedy told him it was Mrs. Clinton who had Livingstone hired. "It's a done deal," said Kennedy according to Aldrich's account. "Hillary wants him."

ANTHONY MARCECA: DIGGING IN LOW-GRADE DIRT

At least we know who hired Livingstone's file-gathering colleague, Anthony Marceca: Craig Livingstone. Marceca was an army investigator when Livingstone arranged for him to be detailed to the White House. Army Criminal Investigation Command spokesman Paul Boyce said the request from the White House was for Marceca by name, not simply for any staffer.[19] Livingstone had gotten to know Marceca on the 1984 Hart campaign. Marceca had also worked on the presidential campaigns of Edmund Muskie and George McGovern (1972), Ted Kennedy (1980), John Glenn (1984), and Al Gore (1988), and had volunteered on Clinton's inaugural staff (perhaps figuring his only way to work for a winning candidate was to wait until after the election).

Robert Smith, a primary challenger to Pennsylvania Senator Arlen Specter in 1986, recalls that Marceca approached him during the campaign, offering derogatory material on Specter. He had basically just low-grade dirt, Smith told the Associated Press: "A lot of it dealt with Arlen's personal life and his family. I found it deplorable."[20]

One can only hope Marceca had the foresight to preserve his personal letter from President Clinton, praising him for contributing to "the dedicated efforts of our great security team," and concluding, "Without your help, Craig might have been buried under the paperwork required to ensure White House personnel security…. Hillary joins me in wishing you every future success."[21]

SHAKY WHITE HOUSE EXCUSES

When all is said and done, we know this: two Democratic operatives with shady backgrounds—according to the various Democratic campaign officials who have employed the duo—were working for the president, on the White House payroll, in a chain of command that had them reporting to the president through the White House Counsel's Office. They collected files teeming with derogatory information on hundreds of former—and possibly future—Republican appointees. Given the record of these custodians, and the White House's laughably lax security around the files (Marceca even took some home with him), the nine hundred Americans whose raw files were obtained by the Clinton White House have little reason to suppose that their private file folders are not now swelling the cabinets of Democratic-aligned activist groups, awaiting confirmation hearings in future Republican administrations.

The *New York Times* editorialized in June 1996:

> *While it remains unclear whether White House aides were pursuing a political agenda in rummaging through the files, it is now apparent that there was a great potential for mischief. Both the White House and the FBI showed remarkably little regard for the privacy rights of Americans in their cavalier treatment of background files on more than 400 men and women who worked in recent Republican administrations…. [The White House's] explanation has not been discredited, but it is looking shakier.*[22]

"Shakier" indeed.

Recall that throughout Travelgate and Filegate, the FBI was

remarkably compliant with the White House: it investigated the Travel Office, sent over the files, cut its own White House detail out of the file-retrieval process, leaked to the White House an advance copy of Agent Gary Aldrich's book *Unlimited Access*, shook down Agent Sculimbrene, and so on. As noted, the general counsel of the FBI at the time, Robert Shapiro, ultimately left the FBI due to the heavy flak he received for his compliant attitude toward the Clinton White House.

Neither the press nor the Republican Congress has shown as much indignation about the files as have the citizens whose files were illegally obtained. No impeachment hearings were initiated— even to demand simple answers to the continuing Filegate mysteries. And the press has moved on.

FIGHTING BACK

Still haunted by the Ghost of Leaks Yet to Come are the citizens whose files were pulled. Many of these may be future Republican leaders. Or perhaps even present ones: nearly a dozen former Reagan/Bush White House staffers currently working on Capitol Hill were among those whose files were pulled.[23]

The citizens whose rights have been so egregiously violated brought a class action suit under the Privacy Act against President Clinton, Hillary Rodham Clinton, and former White House aides Bernard Nussbaum, Craig Livingstone, and Anthony Marceca.

U.S. District Judge Royce C. Lamberth has denied the defendants' motions to dismiss, holding that the Privacy Act, 5 U.S.C. 552, provides a basis for a civil suit against the defendants by Republicans whose files were pulled, noting that "[t]he Privacy Act was passed by Congress to prevent exactly this kind of behavior." The act was passed in 1974 following revelations about political spying by the FBI and other government intelligence agencies.

Lawyers for Mrs. Clinton had argued that "there is simply no precedent" for alleging an invasion of privacy for transferring personal data from the FBI to the White House. No controlling legal authority. Judge Lamberth rejected the first lady's arguments, curtly noting that "despite the characterization of Mrs. Clinton, this is not a case concerning the transfer of information from one part of government to another."

THE PRESIDENT'S RESPONSIBILITY

Can no one higher than Craig Livingstone, a.k.a. Chicken George, be held accountable for Filegate? Richard Nixon's men illegally obtained one person's security file; Chuck Colson did seven months as a result. Nixon—who did not know about the Daniel Ellsberg or Watergate break-ins beforehand—was forced out of office for creating an environment that encouraged such adventures.

A president whose aides pull such stunts can escape responsibility only by coming clean, as President Reagan did in the Iran-Contra matter. Reagan had his own attorney general break the news to the public; in the months that followed, he and his aides cooperated with Congress and the independent counsel, and he waived executive privilege for all Iran-Contra communications.

In contrast, the various Clinton White House players have denied, evaded, stonewalled, fled, taken the Fifth (in Livingstone's case), and made claims of ignorance. Claiming ignorance isn't enough.

In the 1974 Rodino report, the House Judiciary Committee made a persuasive case for impeaching President Nixon for having people like Craig Livingstone around him. The report noted that, following the end of the Commonwealth and the Restoration of Charles II (1660–1685), "a more powerful Parliament [than had existed under the Commonwealth] expanded somewhat the scope of 'high Crimes and Misdemeanors' by impeaching officers of the Crown for such things as *negligent discharge of duties* and improprieties in office" (emphasis added).

The second article of impeachment against Nixon charged that he had "misused" the FBI in violation of "the constitutional rights of citizens" by "directing" the FBI to wiretap or investigate individuals "for purposes unrelated to national security." At that time, it was not illegal for a president to authorize wiretaps without a court order—even "for purposes unrelated to national security." FDR had begun the practice of using the FBI to wiretap the press and investigate his enemies. This political skullduggery was expanded upon by Presidents Kennedy and Johnson.[24]

By contrast, Nixon had authorized FBI wiretaps exclusively for national security purposes. The FBI had installed a grand total of seventeen wiretaps, thirteen of which tapped the phone lines of government officials and four of which tapped reporters who had published classified national security information.[25] Several of the bugged government employees had been designated for wiretaps by their boss, Secretary of State Henry Kissinger, who had authorized wiretaps on all his aides "who had seen or handled various documents which had been leaked."[26] In neither intent nor execution were the wiretaps used against Nixon's "enemies." They were going after leaks of potentially damaging national security information.

On the other hand, the nine hundred FBI files ultimately discovered in the Clinton White House were certainly not being used to create a "friends" list. Unlike the Nixon administration wiretaps, the Clinton White House's possession of FBI raw files was against the law. Also unlike the Nixon administration wiretaps, there was no national security reason for the White House to have these files, as the Clinton administration has admitted, trying to portray the nefarious files business as a "snafu."

Indeed, the only rational explanation for the Clinton administration's possession of the files on many Republicans—and some prominent Republicans—was to harass Clinton's political enemies more easily. Recall that former Clinton adviser George

Stephanopoulos said that the "whisper[s]" around the Clinton White House were that Clinton's people were going to start blackmailing their political opponents to survive the Monica Lewinsky scandal—Stephanopoulos called it the "Ellen Rometsch strategy."

And we know the Clinton White House illegally sought the FBI file on at least one individual citizen "for purposes unrelated to national security," but whom the White House had a political interest in damaging. Perhaps there have been others.

Someone at the Clinton White House is responsible for hiring the men who implemented an unprecedented violation of nine hundred Americans' civil liberties. Someone at the White House is responsible for hiring the men who abused the powers of the executive branch to engage in political espionage against its presumed enemies, on a scale only dreamed of by the Plumbers, whose activities brought down Richard Nixon. According to this country's most recent precedent on impeachable offenses, that someone is the president.

Framer James Wilson noted that the Constitution provided the president with no "screen" from misconduct in the executive branch. The president would not be able to "act improperly, and hide either his negligence or inattention." Any attempt to do so, Wilson explained, would render the president impeachable.[27] Another participant at the Constitutional Convention, James Iredell, a strong proponent of the Constitution at the North Carolina ratifying convention, and later a Supreme Court justice, said that it was the president's personal responsibility that demonstrated the "very different nature" of the president "from a monarch." William Davie noted that the "predominant principle" of making a single president responsible for the entire executive branch was to establish "the more obvious responsibility of one person."

All these quotes from the framers were admiringly cited in the Rodino Report, which explained to the nation the grounds for impeachment the last time a United States president faced impeachment, just a quarter century ago.

Chapter Thirteen

Auditing the Enemy

The second article of impeachment against President Nixon charged him with "endeavor[ing]" to cause income tax audits, "in violation of the constitutional rights of citizens." A president's use of the IRS for political purposes is such a clear, egregious abuse of power that even *trying* to do it constitutes an impeachable offense. If success is any measure of effort, Nixon didn't try very hard. Not only was Nixon unable to trigger any political audits of his enemies, he was also unable to stop the IRS from auditing him while he was president.

Twenty-five years later, few critics of President Clinton seem to have escaped audits by the IRS.

BILLY DALE

The IRS audited beleaguered Travel Office head Billy Dale after the Clinton administration fired him. In addition, of course, Dale endured a full FBI investigation and prosecution and a review of his sensitive FBI file by political flacks in Clinton's White House months after he had been summarily fired.

You would think Billy Dale was Carlos the Jackal. Assorted

felons, hustlers, and bribe-takers had streamed through the Clinton administration, and high-level government officials, and Clinton himself, had always played the unwitting dupe. But the one executive branch employee who couldn't even jaywalk on Clinton's watch was Billy Dale. The reason was simple: Dale was an enemy of the administration. He had made them look bad by not having engaged in criminal conduct when they said he had.

And this time, not only was an enemy of the administration actually audited, but also there was a smoking gun indicating that the audit was political.

Congressional investigators looking into the White House Travel Office massacre uncovered that memo about Billy Dale written by White House lawyers that summarized Associate White House Counsel William Kennedy's remarks. Kennedy informed the lawyers that IRS Commissioner Margaret Milner Richardson was "on top of it."

Richardson was a political appointee, not one of those "career professionals" so often used as camouflage for the Clinton administration's misconduct. Recall that she was a friend of Hillary's at Yale Law School, had advised Clinton during his 1992 campaign, and had served on Clinton's transition team. While she was commissioner of the IRS, Richardson attended the 1996 Democratic National Convention.

What exactly might Richardson have been "on top of"? This was not a White House memo generally reviewing Richardson's job performance at the IRS. It was a memo about the Travel Office. It was written soon after the Travel Office firings, as Clinton's people were desperately investigating Dale for some sort of criminal conduct. And, of course, Billy Dale would eventually be personally audited.

That alone—the use of the IRS for a single political audit— would have been enough to call for the impeachment of any other president at any time in this nation's history. As the Rodino

Report explained, the president is "personally responsible for any abuse of the great trust reposed in him."[1] But, amazingly, nothing happened. President Clinton was never held accountable for this abuse of power so grand that Nixon was charged with impeachment for *thinking* about it.

And, recall, that wasn't the only smoking gun. According to the White House's own internal report on the Travel Office firings, Kennedy had informed an FBI agent that he would order the IRS to investigate if the FBI refused to start an investigation of Dale within the next fifteen minutes.[2]

And, of course, one week after Kennedy's warning, IRS officers burst into the offices of UltrAir, the charter airline used by the White House Travel Office.[3]

It is difficult to write off this unannounced visit by the IRS as a mere coincidence. Not only was there Kennedy's threat to call in the IRS to investigate the Travel Office, but also, as a newly formed company, UltrAir *had not yet had occasion to file a single tax return.*

It didn't stop with Dale and UltrAir. The evidence that Clinton used the powerful IRS as a political attack machine would begin to accumulate rapidly.

CAN'T WIN IN THE SUPREME COURT?
CALL THE IRS

Consider this: Which American citizen has caused Clinton more trouble than any other? That's easy: Paula Jones. Jones was the one "bimbo eruption" Clinton's attack squad couldn't squelch. No Paula Jones, and there would have been no Monica Lewinsky, no job offers from U.N. Ambassador Bill Richardson, no chauffeur-driven limousine with Vernon Jordan, no perjurious affidavit, no Linda Tripp subpoena, no talking points, no tapes—and no perjury by the president. Paula Jones was the one Clinton antagonist who was holding him responsible in a court of law.

Now, guess who got audited by the IRS. Paula Jones. Jones's audit letter arrived just a few months after Clinton lost his contrived "presidential immunity" claim in the Supreme Court. Not only that, but it arrived just days after settlement negotiations had broken down. Unless they reached a settlement, the Supreme Court's ruling meant Jones's lawyers could begin deposing other women immediately. Negotiations had collapsed on account of Jones's steadfast insistence on an apology from President Clinton. Overseeing the IRS means never having to say you're sorry.

Rejecting the White House's popular "bureaucratic snafu" excuse, Clinton spokesman Mike McCurry said of the Jones audit, "We do dumb things from time to time, but we are not certifiably crazy." The standard White House defense had transmogrified from *we're not evil, just incompetent,* to *that is too evil even for this administration, so don't even think about it.* But as a *New York Times* columnist said of another Clinton scandal—the fire sale on plots at Arlington National Cemetery—because it's Clinton, "the charge was plausible."[4] (And this was before Arianna Huffington established that what was plausible was actually true.)

After the Dale audit, replete with not one but two smoking guns, it would not be "certifiably crazy" for the White House to assume it could get away with anything.

The IRS audit of Jones, especially on the heels of her 9-0 victory over Clinton in the Supreme Court, was suspect on another count: Tax lawyers say that individuals who make less than $50,000 a year are more likely to be struck by lightning than audited by the IRS. Paula Jones is a housewife, and her husband earns less than $37,000 a year. According to *Investor's Business Daily,* the IRS's own data indicates that Jones and her husband "were part of the least audited income group." But during the Clinton administration, the chances of being audited by the IRS apparently turned more on politics than on income.

Paula Jones and Billy Dale had done more harm to the president's poll numbers than any other two individuals—with the possible exception of journalists covering the president's troubles with Jones and Dale. Both were in the least-audited income group. Both were audited by the IRS. If no other Clinton antagonists had been audited, if there had been no smoking guns, these two audits would be remarkable.

But there were other suspicious audits.

THE LIST GOES ON

Patricia and Glenn Mendoza became targets of the IRS soon after becoming a nuisance to the president. In July 1996 Mrs. Mendoza had expressed her opinion of the president as he approached her and tried to shake her hand. Mrs. Mendoza synthesized the opinions of millions of Americans with the succinct and punchy phrase, "You suck." This latter-day Patrick Henry was immediately pounced upon by Secret Service agents and, along with her husband, was held for twelve hours. (The Secret Service is another federal agency that has been in overdrive investigating critics of the Clinton administration.)

One month later the Mendozas received a letter from the IRS threatening to confiscate their property to satisfy an alleged $200 debt to the IRS. At first glance, that might seem insignificant. However, not only was there the Dale and Jones matter, and not only had the Mendozas been shaken down by the Secret Service like a couple of international terrorists, but also the charge turned out to be a mistake. As the IRS eventually explained, the letter was due to a "computer error." Oops, sorry, our mistake.

In the abstract, the Mendozas would seem to be too insignificant to inspire a political audit from any administration. But the Mendozas weren't too insignificant to be arrested and held for twelve hours by the president's Secret Service detail. Billy Dale wasn't too insignificant for the White House to demand a full FBI investigation and prosecution. Kathleen Willey wasn't too insignificant for the White House to try to smear.

As journalist Joe Sobran has said, it's the corner-of-the-eye facts that tell you what kind of man Clinton is. He's the kind of man who doesn't take on Saddam Hussein; he takes on Billy Dale.

Under Clinton, political IRS audits of every tobacco and firearm manufacturer in the nation would be less believable than political audits of these lone gadflies. (Another "little guy" audited by the IRS was Kent Masterson Brown. He brought the lawsuit that compelled Hillary's health care task force to reveal the names of its members.)

Still not convinced?

Consider this partial list of conservative groups that have been investigated by Clinton's IRS: *National Review, The American Spectator*, the Christian Coalition, Citizens for a Sound Economy, Oliver North's Freedom Alliance, the Heritage Foundation, the National Rifle Association, the Western Journalism Center, the National Center for Public Policy Research, Fortress America, and Citizens Against Government Waste.

And these are just the ones that are public knowledge. IRS audits are not a matter of public record, and most targets of an IRS investigation don't like to talk about it. But variations of this list have been published in numerous articles in a variety of newspapers, along with the claim that no comparable liberal groups have been audited. No one has disputed that claim. No liberal outfit has stepped forward to say that it is being audited, too. The IRS has not denied the charge.

Either President Clinton has abused the most fear-inspiring arm of the federal government, or there has been a mathematically improbable series of coincidences involving IRS audits under Clinton. It is difficult to brush off the accumulated evidence that the Clinton administration used the IRS to conduct politically motivated audits. But this is, after all, the Clinton administration.

Under the Clinton administration, the president's employees have audited Clinton's enemies (coincidentally or not); they have hauled secret Republican files from the FBI for inspection by White House employees; they have summarily fired the White House Travel Office staff and then brought criminal charges against the head of the office to cover the nepotism (criminal charges that were swiftly rejected by a jury); and they have interfered with an FBI investigation into Vince Foster's White House office—which contained the personal legal work Foster had been performing for the Clintons.

And that's just what they did in Clinton's first year in office alone. This omits the many other notorious Clinton administration officials who popped up after the most ethical president's inaugural year, such as convicted felon and former Associate Attorney General Webb Hubbell (*see* Chapter 16), Interior Secretary Bruce Babbitt (*see* Chapter 18), Agriculture Secretary Mike Espy (under investigation for taking illegal gifts), Housing and Urban Development Secretary Henry Cisneros (under investigation for false statements to the FBI about a mistress), and Vice President Gore (for felonious fund-raising calls from the White House). Bad apples just seem to gravitate to the Clinton administration.

But the president cannot surround himself with con men and criminals and then demand a signed confession or photographic evidence that he was directly responsible for their transgressions before he is held accountable. The whole idea of having a single president, subject to impeachment, Hamilton said, was to ensure that the president would not be able "to conceal faults and destroy responsibility."[5] If he gets away with this, Clinton will have accomplished precisely what the Constitution was designed to prevent.

ASSIGNING RESPONSIBILITY

As the Rodino Report noted, *"[T]he impeachability of the President* was considered to be an important element of his responsibility," so that "there should be a single object for the jealousy and watchfulness of the people."[6]

Clinton is president, and he is responsible. He is responsible for the politicization of the IRS. He is responsible for nine hundred FBI files illegally obtained by his White House. He is responsible for the abuse of the FBI for a political investigation. Yet he repeatedly acts as if he is just another White House employee, like Craig Livingstone. Outrageous abuses of power are constantly being unearthed in his administration, and he acts like he's just another cog in the wheel of some huge bureaucratic morass he doesn't understand himself.

It is true that an innocent president could have bad actors in his administration from time to time, but an innocent president would attempt to rout out corruption in his own administration rather than wait for the *Washington Post* to do so. An innocent president would promptly fire knaves in his administration, without waiting for his allies at the *New York Times* to demand their heads.[7] An innocent president would take steps to see that abuses do not continue. An innocent president would set a tone so that corruption and abuses of power do not become a pattern.

It is interesting that the Clinton administration's repeated "bureaucratic snafus" have not ordinarily come to light as a result of the administration's own internal investigation. Wrongdoing in the Clinton administration has almost invariably been exposed only through the media or congressional investigators—at which point President Clinton says he knows only what he reads in the papers. Contrast that with Iran-Contra in the Reagan administration. Iran-Contra was first disclosed at a press conference held by Attorney General Edwin Meese. He knew because of an internal investigation conducted by the administration.

President Clinton has fired wrongdoers only after a hue and cry has gone up in the friendly press. He has clearly failed to set a standard that prevents abuses from occurring, since they occur habitually. It is not enough to fire the wrongdoers once they get caught, if the president keeps filling his administration with a never-ending cast of scoundrels.

Nixon was almost impeached for thinking about political IRS audits. (Actual result: he himself got audited.) He was threatened with impeachment for thinking about trying to influence an FBI investigation. (Actual result: an FBI investigation was delayed for two weeks, until the president himself ordered that it be resumed.) He was threatened with impeachment because one of his aides misused one security file.

That's what it means to be president. Or that's what it used to mean. Now, the president can duck all responsibility for actual and repeated abuses of power by his administration and demand proof beyond a reasonable doubt in a court of law that he was responsible. But there doesn't need to be a jury trial to "fix the blame," as the Rodino Report put it; Clinton is responsible because he is president.

It is implausible that the administration of a blameless president would: use the FBI for a political prosecution, be caught with nine hundred FBI files in its possession, or use the IRS to audit the president's enemies. It defies logic that all three of these abuses of power could occur in one administration without the concurrence of the president. That much corruption can be the responsibility only of the man at the top—even under a less exacting standard for presidents than the one Hillary Rodham delineated for a different president in 1974.

PART THREE

Obstruction of Justice

Chapter Fourteen

Whitewater

This is the boring part. Whitewater gets interesting only when you understand why it is boring. It is boring by design, like a *New York Times* editorial. Don't skip to the next chapter! That's just what the Clintons want you to do.

The reason the constellation of crimes orbiting Whitewater seems tedious and complicated is the reason all pyramid schemes seem tedious and complicated: The fraudulent transactions are purposely structured in an extremely complex manner in order to keep government regulators in the dark for as long as possible. In the case of the "Whitewater" scandals there were multiple loans criss-crossing one another as down-payments. It is not necessary to comprehend the precise form these transactions took to understand the scandal known as Whitewater. In fact, it is probably an impediment.

Whitewater is about two very simple things: stealing and lying—stealing from taxpayers and lying to prosecutors, judges, and juries. The "failed land deal" that Whitewater Independent Counsel Kenneth W. Starr has supposedly spent $40 million investigating has already led to the convictions or plea agreements of fourteen people, including the Clintons' partners in Whitewater—James and Susan McDougal, and the former sitting governor of Arkansas, Jim Guy Tucker, who succeeded Bill Clinton.

The heart of Whitewater is Madison Guaranty Savings and Loan, operated by the Clintons' friend and business partner James McDougal, and insured by the government. The Madison-McDougal-Tucker-Clinton scandals are collectively known as "Whitewater" because the shady Whitewater land deal happened to be the first of the overlapping scandals that directly implicated the Clintons to surface in the news. But, as with Copernicus's discovery, the Whitewater universe makes sense only when it is understood that Whitewater revolved around Madison, not Madison around Whitewater.

McDougal was looting the federally backed Madison Guaranty he is said to have called his "candy store."[1] McDougal used Madison depositors' money to gamble on high-risk real-estate ventures such as Whitewater. In case his real-estate gambles didn't pay off, McDougal also directly defrauded his own S&L in a variety of sham transactions to ensure that he and his friends would make money out of his operation of Madison Guaranty.[2] He made bad loans to friends, business partners, and other insiders, knowing the loans would not be repaid, and knowing that the government, through deposit insurance programs, would be left holding the bills.

Everyone involved in these deals benefitted, save the American taxpayers—who were still on the hook for the $60 million McDougal had given away. Eventually, the government caught up with McDougal and shut down Madison Guaranty.

McDougal and his wife, Susan, were, it seems, crooks. On May 28, 1996, James McDougal was convicted on eighteen felony counts related to bad loans by Madison, including conspiracy, fraud, and making false statements. That same day, Susan McDougal was convicted on four felony counts, including mail fraud, making false statements, and misapplication of funds. He was sentenced to three years in prison, she to two years in prison, plus community service. Between them they were ordered to pay more than $4.5 million in restitution and fines, still far short of the $60 million they stole.

But James and Susan McDougal, of course, weren't the president and first lady. Associating with crooks may have been enough for James Madison to impeach a president, but it is unlikely to be enough today. The Clintons' apparent wrongdoing stemming from the McDougals' $60 million swindle, however, goes deeper than mere friendship. There are reasons to believe that the Clintons may have been among the friends who benefitted from McDougal's crimes, whether or not those reasons rise to the level of proof beyond a reasonable doubt.

OVERVIEW OF CLINTON CONNECTIONS
TO MCDOUGAL'S CRIMES

The Clintons deny any role in Madison Guaranty's fraudulent loans. In the abstract, it might have been just a coincidence that Mr. Clinton was governor and Mrs. Clinton performed legal work for Madison while McDougal was looting the S&L. But both of the Clintons have more direct involvement in some of the known crimes surrounding Whitewater.

- First, the Clintons were equal partners with James and Susan McDougal in Whitewater, the failed Arkansas land deal. Some of the fraudulent loans issued by McDougal on behalf of Madison went to prop up the ailing Whitewater Corporation. The Clintons and their flacks repeatedly note that they "lost money" on the Whitewater land deal.[3] While it is possible the Clintons were completely innocent of criminal intent with regard to the Whitewater venture, the fact that they lost money on the deal has absolutely nothing to do it. McDougal was stealing from Madison to prop up Whitewater: If Whitewater had succeeded, the Clintons stood to make a large profit, having put little of their own money down. Mrs. Clinton's defense—repeated incessantly—that they "lost money" is the equivalent of stealing money to buy a lottery ticket and then saying no theft occurred because the lottery ticket didn't win.

■ Second, wherever the Clintons' full share of Whitewater payments were coming from, they were not coming from the Clintons. Even if the Clintons knew nothing of McDougal's financial double-dealing with Madison, they had to know they were not paying their fair share in the Whitewater partnership, raising the possibility that McDougal was using his Whitewater partnership with the Clintons to bribe the young attorney general and then sitting governor. There is a reason the thieving owner of a corrupt S&L might have wanted to bribe the governor.

The Clintons have maintained that they were merely passive investors uninvolved in the day-to-day details of the Whitewater venture. Thus, their story is, if they were being bribed, they didn't know it.

At least one Resolution Trust Corporation (RTC) officer investigating Whitewater doubts the Clintons' purported naivete. And, as the *New York Times* has noted, Mrs. Clinton must have been at least vaguely familiar with the workings of Madison Guaranty since she was one of its lawyers.[4]

■ Third, if McDougal thought he was paying bribes, he got all he could have wanted out of Clinton. The Senate

Whitewater Committee turned up a series of favors Mr. Clinton performed for Madison Guaranty while he was governor of Arkansas, concluding that "substantial evidence supports Mr. McDougal's claims that he had 'clout' with the governor." These included sending valuable state leases to Madison, and signing special interest legislation intended to benefit Madison. While back-scratching is nothing new to politics, most politicians could expect to see their presidential aspirations dashed for such back-scratching with a crook.

Governor Clinton cast a crucial veto in June 1987, striking down legislation that was designed to help Madison Guaranty, Jim Guy Tucker, and Tucker's business partner.[5] But prior to casting the veto, Clinton was unaware of the bill's intended effect on Madison. Members of his "political family" did not waste time in bringing this detail to the governor's attention by leaving a message for Mr. Clinton, asking whether the veto would stand and "mention[ing] a meeting between [Clinton], Tucker, and Jim McDougal a couple years ago which involved $33,000."[6] As the governor's secretary noted on the phone message, the caller was "pretty cryptic." A few weeks later, Clinton reversed his veto, and the bill became law.[7]

At one point, the governor's wife was lobbying the governor's appointee on behalf of Madison—a matter in which the governor had a financial interest. The Clinton-appointed securities commissioner, Beverly Bassett Shaffer, approved some of Mrs. Clinton's requests on behalf of Madison, though apparently not for any nefarious purpose. Interestingly, however, top White House aides were not confident about that. According to notes taken by then–White House Communications Director Mark

Gearan at a January 1994 White House meeting on Whitewater, Clinton's top aides were extremely concerned about what Shaffer might say. Harold Ickes, Clinton's deputy chief of staff, was quoted in the notes saying: "Bassett is so f—ing important, if we f— this up, we're done."

Of course, as Clinton would later say of shady contributors to his presidential campaigns, "I don't believe you can find any evidence of the fact that I had changed government policy solely" out of political patronage.

■ Fourth, Madison's legal work was performed by the once prestigious, now infamous, Rose Law Firm. McDougal said that, under pressure from the governor, he arranged for his S&L to pay the Rose Law Firm a monthly retainer simply as a personal favor to Hillary. He admitted this even while still trying to "protect" the president, on cross-examination during his 1996 trial. McDougal's claim is supported by contemporaneous notes James Blair took of a conversation with Mr. McDougal in 1992. Blair is the longtime Clinton back-scratcher who helped Mrs. Clinton place her fabulously lucrative cattle futures trades. The Clintons deny McDougal's claim.

■ Finally, whether or not McDougal's retainer payments to the Rose Law Firm were intended as a bribe, the arrangement led to the peculiar situation of the governor's wife lobbying the governor's appointees on behalf of Madison Guaranty. The retainer also gave Hillary the opportunity to perform much of the legal work that enabled McDougal to pass bad loans, bankrupting the S&L and costing the taxpayers $60 million. The transaction at the heart of Castle Grande—one of Madison's most fraudulent schemes—hinged on a legal document drafted by Hillary Clinton.

As we will see, it is undisputed that Mrs. Clinton drafted a document used to defraud the RTC. But a prosecutor would have
to prove that she did so knowing that the document would be
used to defraud. The only thing that stands between Hillary
and a prison cell for her work on this document is the possibility that instead of being a criminal lawyer, she is an incompetent lawyer.

That's "Whitewater" without the bank ledgers. But two
Whitewater-related deals involving the Clintons deserve closer
review: Castle Grande and FOB David Hale's Small Business
Administration (SBA) loan.

CASTLE GRANDE

Castle Grande was one of McDougal's most corrupt Madison ventures, becoming the fulcrum of his last loan-swapping fraud in
the dying days of Madison Guaranty. Mrs. Clinton drafted one of
the documents central to the Castle Grande fraud.

McDougal had been looting Madison Guaranty for years. By
1984 federal regulators were nipping at his heels. As part of a
scheme to pad Madison's accounts in order to keep bank examiners at bay a little longer and to keep the inside deals flowing,
McDougal hired Seth Ward, Webb Hubbell's father-in-law, to
scout out new deals that would pump up Madison's books.
(Hubbell—Bill's friend and Hillary's law partner—served in
Clinton's Department of Justice before going to jail.)

Ward recommended "Castle Grande," as McDougal would later
christen a thousand acres of swampland south of Little Rock. In an
intentionally complex transaction, Madison bought the land, using
Ward as the purchaser on paper, or the "straw man" purchaser.
Castle Grande was then used as a huge Ponzi scheme, benefitting
Ward, McDougal, Jim Guy Tucker, and various other Madison

insiders—everyone involved except the U.S. taxpayers, who were left to pay the bill once the government caught up with McDougal.

The pyramid scheme consisted of McDougal issuing risk-free loans from Madison Guaranty to friends and insiders to buy lots on Castle Grande. The loans, often far exceeding the purchase price of the lots, were secured only by the land itself, and were not expected to be repaid.[8] In any event, the details of the pyramid scheme are not as important as the fact that it was a pyramid scheme.

The Castle Grande deals alone looted more than $3 million from Madison Guaranty. Ward walked off with $300,000 in phony sales commissions related to Castle Grande, other insiders with $460,000.[9]

The Castle Grande transactions managed to fool federal regulators for a while by listing each sale of a Castle Grande plot as a profit for Madison Financial, a subsidiary of Madison Guaranty. But the profits were bogus, because the plots had been purchased with bad loans from Madison Guaranty. The subsidiary seemed to be taking in huge amounts of money with each sale of a Castle Grande plot, but its parent, Madison Guaranty, was the only entity actually forking out money for the plots—money insured by the taxpayers.

Still, since the lots were sold by a subsidiary of Madison, the purchases were listed on paper as profits for Madison Guaranty, thus artificially inflating Madison's net worth by about $1.5 million.

MRS. CLINTON DRAFTS
THE FRAUDULENT OPTION AGREEMENT

The original sham transaction that made the rest of the Castle Grande pyramid schemes possible was an agreement between Seth Ward and Madison Guaranty making Ward the straw man purchaser. The document intended to deceive federal regulators as to the nature of the fraudulent scheme was drafted by Hillary Clinton.

On paper Ward had purchased the lion's share of Castle Grande for $1.15 million in October 1985. Madison Financial

Corporation, the Madison subsidiary, bought the rest for $600,000. In fact, Ward paid nothing for the land. Madison Guaranty paid the entire purchase price with a risk-free loan to Ward, secured only by the land itself. Madison needed to use Ward as a straw man purchaser because rules governing savings and loan institutions prohibited it from buying the entire property itself. But this is exactly what Madison had done.

This raw transfer of money to Ward in the form of an unsecured loan would be difficult to explain to federal bank examiners. To disguise the true nature of the transaction—Madison using Ward as a straw man purchaser—Madison needed to cook up some phony debt it owed Ward. An option agreement dated May 1, 1986, described the cooked-up debt; the agreement gave Madison Financial an option to buy from Ward 22.5 acres of Castle Grande land—a portion of his total share—for $400,000, a grossly inflated price. Madison Financial paid Ward $35,000 for the option.

Again, the details of the option agreement, titled "Option to Purchase Real Estate," are not particularly important, beyond the fact that it was used to deceive federal regulators.

The federal examiner who reviewed the May 1, 1986, option agreement has expressly found that the option was used to deceive him when he reviewed Madison's transactions that year. The examiner, Jim Clark, said that the option agreement was "deceptive on its face,"[10] and "was created in order to conceal" the fact that Madison was the real purchaser.

But it was not until Mrs. Clinton's billing records surfaced in the White House residence on January 4, 1996, that the lawyer who drafted the option agreement was conclusively established. The drafter was none other than Hillary Clinton.

Though Mrs. Clinton drafted the option agreement that incontrovertibly was used to deceive federal regulators, it is possible that she did not have the requisite criminal intent to be guilty of any crime herself. The woman who was named one of the nation's top one hundred lawyers in 1988 and 1991 by *The National Law Journal* may have simply been hornswoggled by Jim McDougal.

MRS. CLINTON ACTS LIKE A GUILTY PERSON

A number of odd events somewhat undermines the theory that Mrs. Clinton was an unwitting cat's paw for McDougal's criminality.

First, in 1988, Mrs. Clinton directed the Rose Law Firm to destroy her files on Castle Grande. This was not illegal, but it was unusual, especially because of the irregular banking practices engaged in by this particular client. In another year, Madison's Castle Grande project would itself be the focus of a criminal investigation against James McDougal. The remaining Rose Law Firm records of Mrs. Clinton's work on Castle Grande vanished from the firm during Clinton's 1992 presidential campaign, only to materialize in the White House residence four years later.

Also raising questions about the first lady's self-portrait as an unwitting dupe are her unequivocal denials that she had performed any work on Castle Grande—until her billing records materialized in January 1996.

Until the billing records surfaced, the RTC had been completely in the dark about Mrs. Clinton's involvement with Castle Grande. One RTC officer testified in 1995, for example: "We have no evidence that [Mrs. Clinton] worked on Castle Grande."[11] This is hardly surprising. On May 24, 1995, Mrs. Clinton had given a sworn statement to the RTC saying, "I do not believe I knew anything about any of these real estate parcels and projects"—specifically including Castle Grande.[12] Indeed, Mrs Clinton had stated in two separate federal investigations that she had had absolutely nothing to do with Castle Grande.

It was peculiar that she had been unable to recall her work on Castle Grande. Her billing records revealed that she had been the billing partner for Madison Guaranty generally, and on Castle

Grande in particular. She had billed the bulk of her work for Madison Guaranty to Castle Grande.[13] In fact, she had billed more time to Castle Grande than had any other partner at the Rose Law Firm for the period of time leading up to the Castle Grande option.[14] Most significantly, of course, she had drafted the sham option agreement used to defraud the federal regulators in Castle Grande, according to her own billing records.

The FBI tested the billing records for fingerprints in early 1996 and found Mrs. Clinton's fingerprints on two pages: the page summarizing all her work for Madison, and the page giving a detailed account of her work on Castle Grande exclusively.

After her billing records mysteriously surfaced in the White House—about two years after they had been subpoenaed by congressional investigators—she had some explaining to do.

Mrs. Clinton clarified her earlier denials by saying she had known Castle Grande by another name—"IDC." This was the Rose Law Firm's internal billing code for the matter, referring to the company that sold the property to McDougal. Mrs. Clinton said she believed "Castle Grande" referred exclusively to a trailer park called "Castle Grande Estates" that was to be located on "Castle Grande"—or "IDC," in her lexicon—and she had done no work on the trailer park.

There would be no reason, however, for federal officers to be asking Mrs. Clinton about "Castle Grande Estates," the trailer park. That was not a part of any fraudulent transactions. By contrast, Castle Grande the development had been the focus of James McDougal's first trial in 1990, and would soon form the basis of criminal fraud convictions against the McDougals and Arkansas Governor Jim Guy Tucker. Mrs. Clinton's explanation for previous denials would be on the order of O.J. attempting to revise earlier responses to investigators about a certain "Nicole," on the grounds that he had understood "Nicole" to refer exclusively to his manicurist, not his murdered wife whom he called "Honey."

Moreover, if Mrs. Clinton knew Castle Grande only as "IDC," she was the only person involved in the project who did.[15] Madison's senior loan officer said, "[I]t was known as Castle Grande by everyone that was involved within thirty days of the purchase."[16] The development was referred to as Castle Grande in minutes of a board meeting at Madison. A document prepared in 1986 by government officials from the Federal Home Loan Bank Board described the development as the "Castle Grande project."[17]

Mrs. Clinton would also have been the only person in all of Little Rock who would not have recognized the Castle Grande development as "Castle Grande." During Jim McDougal's first trial for fraud involving Castle Grande in 1990, news accounts of the trial referred to the development only as "Castle Grande."[18] Even if Mrs. Clinton drew no connection between the trailer park "Castle Grande Estates" and the "Castle Grande" it was located on, it is difficult to understand how she could not have known that others called the entire development Castle Grande, including "everyone... involved," Arkansas newspapers, and government officials.

Despite the evidence of Mrs. Clinton's own entries in the long-lost billing records, Mrs. Clinton continued to attempt to minimize her role in Castle Grande. Various witnesses, however, directly contradicted the first lady. Mrs. Clinton testified, for example, that it was not she, but lawyer Richard Massey, who was responsible for bringing Madison in as a client to the Rose Law Firm. Testifying before the Senate Whitewater Committee, Massey denied Mrs. Clinton's effort to thrust Madison Guaranty at him. At the time Mrs. Clinton claims Massey was the rainmaker on the Madison business, he was a first-year associate.

The third piece of evidence establishing either Mrs. Clinton's criminal intent or her incompetence as a lawyer is the testimony of H. Don Denton, a senior officer at Madison Guaranty. Denton has testified that he specifically warned Mrs. Clinton about the dubious legality of the option agreement she was drafting.

In a deposition taken by the Federal Deposit Insurance Corporation, Denton said Mrs. Clinton had called him to ask for notes when she was drafting the option agreement. Denton testified that at that time he raised the legal problems of such an option agreement with Mrs. Clinton, noting that the notes "constituted in effect a parent entity fulfilling the obligation of a subsidiary."[19] Mrs. Clinton "summarily dismissed" his concerns, he told investigators. He recalled that she said something to the effect that "he would take care of savings and loan matters, and she would take care of legal matters."[20] She was, after all, one of the country's top one hundred lawyers.

As she had once denied performing any work on Castle Grande, Mrs. Clinton denied having any such conversation with Mr. Denton. Perhaps she knew him by a different name.

The White House immediately questioned Mr. Denton's motives, fingering him as a political enemy of the White House. But, as the *New York Times* has noted (prominently on page B-9), this "was the first time a figure not under threat of indictment or imprisonment ha[d] given such damaging information" against the Clintons. As such, the article observed, it was a "further dent" in the White House incompetence defense portraying Mrs. Clinton as "a mere technical adviser, not an insider in the deal."[21]

THE GOVERNOR'S ALLEGED PARTICIPATION IN DAVID HALE'S CRIME

In May 1996 an Arkansas jury returned a series of guilty verdicts against Jim and Susan McDougal and Governor Jim Guy Tucker, finding that they had defrauded not only Madison Guaranty but also the federal SBA. The guilty counts involving the SBA found that the three conspired to get a $300,000 loan for Susan McDougal through a small business investment company owned by David Hale. Some of the money from that fraudulent loan ended up in Whitewater accounts.

The prosecution's chief witness at trial was former municipal judge David Hale, who had already pleaded guilty to the loan fraud in 1994. Hale accused Mr. Clinton of pressuring him to make the incontrovertibly fraudulent $300,000 federally-backed loan to Susan McDougal in 1985. The loan was made to Mrs. McDougal's front company, Master Marketing, in order to comply with SBA requirements that borrowers be "socially or economically disadvantaged."

Hale testified that Clinton asked him to make the loan "for Jim [Guy Tucker] and the governor," in Hale's words.[22] McDougal explained to Hale that the loan was necessary to "clean up some members of the political family," a reference Hale took to mean that the loan was intended to help Mr. Clinton. (Though the White House would later denounce Hale as an enemy of the Clintons, at the time he was active in Democratic politics in Arkansas.) At the meeting in a trailer at Castle Grande, Hale testified, Clinton explicitly warned him, "My name cannot show up in this," at which point McDougal assured Clinton that he had "already taken care of that."[23]

Almost $50,000 of the $300,000 loan made to Susan McDougal's front company found its way to the ailing Whitewater venture.[24] Most of the rest of the fraudulent loan went to pay for Mrs. McDougal's personal expenses. The loan was never repaid. (Clinton's interest in the loan to Susan McDougal may have been unrelated to Whitewater. James McDougal suspected that his wife had had an affair with the governor.)

Mrs. McDougal served eighteen months in prison rather than tell a grand jury what she knows about the Clintons' business dealings. When this civil contempt sanction expired she still wouldn't talk and was indicted for criminal contempt of the grand jury. Mrs. McDougal simply refuses to state under oath whether the president lied in his testimony about the SBA loan.

Of course, if she could answer "no," there would be no reason for her to refuse to answer. If she ever did stop defying the court, one thing the grand jury might want to know is what she meant when she wrote "Payoff Clinton" as a notation on a check.

In videotaped testimony shown at the trial, Clinton denied ever discussing the loan with Hale. At trial James McDougal supported the president's denial. McDougal attacked Starr's prosecutors and said he would never cooperate because they were "Republican gangsters" pursuing a "political prosecution."

One year after his conviction, however, McDougal changed his tune. He said he lied when he testified that Clinton did not pressure Hale to make the fraudulent loan. In an interview with NBC, McDougal said he had been present when the president met with Hale to discuss the loan, just as Hale had described in his testimony. McDougal explained that he had corroborated the president's denials at trial because "I was trying my best to protect him."

McDougal admitted that since he had lied at his trial, people would "have every right to be suspicious" and think that he was lying again. But this time, McDougal said, everything he had to say "was very well documented," and Clinton "should be deeply concerned" about what McDougal was going to say about the meeting.

If David Hale told the truth at trial, and McDougal told the truth after the trial, the president committed perjury in his testimony for the McDougal-Tucker trial. Admittedly both McDougal and Hale are convicted felons, but that's just the price of having to call Clinton's friends and associates to testify.

Chapter Fifteen

Fostergate

White House Deputy Counsel Vincent Foster, Jr., was found dead in Fort Marcy Park in northern Virginia on Tuesday, July 20, 1993, shortly after 5:30 PM. The death was reportedly a suicide, a single gunshot through the head. He was the first top executive branch official to kill himself since Secretary of Defense James Forrestal committed suicide in 1949.

For White House cover-ups, almost nothing beats the case of Vince Foster. Not of how he died—that, Independent Counsel Ken Starr established, was clearly a suicide—but of what Foster was working on in his White House office. (Points to ponder: If Starr is part of the vast right-wing conspiracy, why did he conclude Foster's death was a suicide? If conspiracy theorists on the right are supposed to accept his conclusion that Foster's death was a suicide, conspiracy theorists on the left ought to show a little respect for Starr's determinations of malfeasance by the Clinton administration.)

FOSTER'S ROLE

Vince Foster was a longtime Arkansas friend of Bill and Hillary Clinton, having attended kindergarten with the future president and with future Chief of Staff Mack McLarty. Foster was a partner in the Rose Law Firm with Webster Hubbell, William Kennedy III, and Hillary Clinton. As deputy White House counsel as well as the Clintons' personal attorney, Foster knew more about the first couple and their political and legal machinations than perhaps any other individual.

In addition to being the taxpayer-supported deputy White House counsel, Foster performed personal legal work for the Clintons regarding their Whitewater and tax problems. Performing personal legal work for the first couple was an improper role for a public servant, to say the least. That, however, does not seem to be what troubled Foster. Nor, obviously, did it trouble the president. In almost any other administration, a taxpayer-supported public servant performing legal work on the president's personal affairs would have been a scandal by itself.

It was Foster who was constantly submitting corrected tax forms to the IRS on behalf of the Clintons, such as when he discovered the Whitewater partnership—of which the Clintons were half-owners—had neglected to file corporate tax returns for three years.[1] Foster himself referred to the first couple's tax issues as a "can of worms." As Special Prosecutor Robert Fiske determined in his report on Foster's death, the May 1993 sacking of Billy Dale and the rest of the Travel Office staff had troubled Foster. But White House Counsel Bernard Nussbaum dismissed Foster's worries and disagreed with his view that the Travel Office matter merited an independent counsel.

White House efforts to cover up whatever it was Foster was working on would eventually lead to interference with an FBI investigation, resignation of a top Justice Department appointee, attacks of amnesia—so peculiar as to suggest perjury—by top White House officials before Senate and House investigative committees, and completely frivolous assertions of privilege by the White House that were thrown out by the courts. If the White House wasn't trying to hide something in Foster's office, it didn't act like it.

The White House's secretive actions could not help but create the impression that there was something worthy of being kept secret. As the Clinton-appointed deputy attorney general, Philip Heymann, said to Bernard Nussbaum when he learned that Nussbaum had refused to allow federal investigators to search Foster's office, "Bernie, are you hiding something?"

THE TIMELINE

The White House was first notified of Foster's death at around 8:30 PM on the night of July 20, 1993, when the Secret Service contacted David Watkins, assistant to the president for management and administration. Over the next forty-eight hours, there would be a flurry of activity by the first lady and her close aides and advisers— a search of Foster's office, scores of phone calls that none of them would later remember, moved files, and rebuffed federal investigators.

About an hour after the Secret Service telephoned Mack McLarty, he called First Lady Hillary Rodham Clinton in Little Rock to tell her the news. At 9:45—five minutes after her phone call from McLarty—Mrs. Clinton called her chief of staff, Maggie Williams. After receiving Mrs. Clinton's call, Williams headed to the White House—to Foster's office.

Park Police Major Robert Hines called the White House sometime between 9:45 and 11:00 PM that night to ask that Foster's office be secured. Hines said he made his request to White House aide Bill Burton. In addition, Park Police Sergeant Cheryl Braun told the Senate Whitewater committee that she spoke to David Watkins within hours of Foster's death and asked him to make sure Foster's office was secured, so that the Park Police could search for a suicide note or other evidence of suicidal disposition. But during those critical early evening hours of July 20, the security Sergeant Braun asked for was breached by a sort of *ad hoc* White House political search team, comprised of Nussbaum, Maggie Williams, and Patsy Thomasson.

Instead of sealing the office, Watkins asked his deputy, Patsy Thomasson, to go into Foster's office to look for a suicide note.[2] As White House administrator, Thomasson had the combination to Foster's office safe. Soon, Nussbaum and Williams would join Thomasson.

Nussbaum later testified that he and the others present that evening opened a drawer or two but that "no one, no one looked through Vince's files."

Patsy Thomasson later testified that she spent at least ten minutes searching for a suicide note in Foster's office on the evening of July 20, 1993.[3] Thomasson, by the way, did not receive her security clearance until March 1994. During her testimony before the Senate Whitewater committee, Senator Lauch Faircloth (R-NC) wondered why the security clearance–challenged Thomasson was allowed to rifle through Foster's papers but Justice Department and Park Police officials were not allowed to touch anything in the room that night. "If this isn't a total contradiction," said Faircloth, "I don't know what it is."[4] Thomasson's security problems may have been related to her former boss, Little Rock investment banker Dan Lasater, a Clinton friend and campaign contributor, who was convicted of cocaine distribution in 1986. The Drug Enforcement Administration had identified him as a drug dealer as early as 1983.

Eighteen-year veteran Secret Service agent Henry O'Neill testified that he saw Maggie Williams walk out of Foster's office that night with a stack of folders about three to five inches thick—a claim Williams would later deny.

O'Neill's story was detailed and unshakable—despite four hours of testimony and detailed cross examination by Senate Democrats trying to raise doubts about his credibility. (O'Neill was asked, for example, "In July of '93, was there a sofa against that wall?")

O'Neill had arrived at the White House in uniform around 10:30 PM, he said, and began his office rounds, unlocking office doors in the West Wing for the White House cleaning crew and disposing of "burn bag" documents. When O'Neill first went by the counsel's office he chanced upon Evelyn Lieberman, Maggie Williams's aide, who asked him to be sure to lock up the counsel's suite. On returning to the office a little while later, O'Neill said he saw a woman sitting at Foster's desk reading something. He assumed the woman was Foster's wife, so he left. In fact, he later learned, the woman was Patsy Thomasson. Returning to the office a third time to lock up, O'Neill said he saw Lieberman leave the office followed by Nussbaum, and then Maggie Williams, who was carrying a stack of documents.

Williams, according to O'Neill, put the documents in her office down the hall and then went down to the first floor. "I'm not in any doubt about it," O'Neill testified. Lieberman identified Williams to O'Neill as "the first lady's chief of staff." At 11:41, O'Neill said, he locked up the counsel's office and took the elevator down with Lieberman and Williams.

Williams, however, denied that she removed anything from Foster's office that night. As she testified before the Senate Whitewater committee, "I took nothing from Vince's office.... I did not look at, inspect, or remove any documents.... That evening was not about documents." Williams explained that she had gone to the White House after the first lady called her at home, and when she saw a light on in Foster's office, she decided to go in, propelled by the "this hope, albeit irrational, that I would walk in and find Vince Foster there."[5]

Williams was ultimately forced to plead to having a very poor memory regarding a number of events surrounding Foster's death. In particular, Williams had no recollection of the frenzy of phone calls between Hillary and her advisers in the forty-eight hours between the discovery of Foster's body and the White House's decision not to allow investigators access to Foster's documents.

"BERNIE, ARE YOU HIDING SOMETHING?"

Those forty-eight hours comprise the crucial time period during which Bernard Nussbaum first agreed to give the FBI access to Foster's office and then reneged.

The day after Foster's death, July 21, 1993, Nussbaum and Deputy Attorney General Philip Heymann discussed how to proceed with the investigation of Foster's office. According to Heymann, at 5:00 PM that day Nussbaum agreed to allow senior Justice Department officials and FBI agents to examine Foster's office the next day at 10:00 AM.

But when the FBI agents showed up the next morning, Nussbaum said he had changed his mind: the investigators would be permitted only to watch Nussbaum perform his own search. (It was when Heymann later found out about this that he asked Nussbaum if he was "hiding something.") Nussbaum assistant Steve Neuwirth testified that he understood Nussbaum to say the policy reversal was made at the request of Susan Thomases, Hillary Clinton's close friend and Whitewater adviser, to accommodate Mrs. Clinton's concerns about investigators having "unfettered access" to Foster's office. This was denied by the first lady, Thomases, Nussbaum, and Williams.[6] But Nussbaum admitted he had spoken with Thomases—contradicting Thomases.[7]

When first asked about her telephone conversations with Hillary Clinton and Susan Thomases in the period leading up to when Nussbaum rebuffed the federal investigators, Williams said she had talked with the first lady about three times and Thomases, once.

But then the phone records, which were subpoenaed by a Senate committee, suggested that Maggie Williams had a very bad memory indeed. Thomases phoned or paged Williams nine times during that period, including five times on July 22 alone—just up to the time the Justice Department officials were turned away from Foster's office.[8] Even if—as Williams noted—that doesn't prove Thomases actually spoke with Williams on each of those occasions, Williams's recollection of a single conversation with Thomases during that period strains plausibility.

Williams's ear wasn't the only one Thomases wanted. She paged Nussbaum once and talked to him at least once, and she called Mack McLarty three times. In all, phone records showed that Thomases had made seventeen telephone calls to the White House in a forty-three–hour period following Foster's death.

In the early morning hours before Nussbaum reneged on his deal with Justice, a flurry of phone calls established a daisy chain from the first lady to Nussbaum. First, at 7:44 AM, Maggie Williams called Mrs. Clinton at her mother's home in Arkansas. Presumably, Williams would have known of Nussbaum's agreement with the Department of Justice from the night before. Williams and Clinton spoke for seven minutes. One minute after that phone call ended, the first lady placed a three-minute phone call to Susan Thomases, who had come to Washington. One minute after that call, Thomases was on the horn to Nussbaum.

And a couple of hours later, of course, Nussbaum was rebuffing Justice Department investigators. Just minutes after the investigators left, Nussbaum and Williams were back in Foster's office themselves, conducting their own search.[9]

Susan Thomases—mad phone-caller in the forty-eight hours after Foster's death—had also handled the Clintons' rapid response work on Whitewater during the 1992 campaign. As *New York Times* reporter Jeff Gerth was hot on the trail of the Clintons' Whitewater and tax problems, Thomases flew to Little Rock, at the first lady's request, and performed her own investigation in order to defend the Clintons from Gerth's persistent questions. And Vince Foster had taken over both issues from Thomases.

Nussbaum did allow FBI agents and Park Police investigators into Foster's office—but only to observe him search the office. Nussbaum refused to let them examine the files and leapt up at investigators when they tried to approach documents on their own. Instead, he let them watch from a distance as he separated the documents into three piles: personal, government, and the Clintons. It can no longer be determined exactly which files went where. Only Nussbaum knows—possibly Maggie Williams too, and possibly the Clintons.

Deputy Attorney General Heymann criticized Nussbaum's performance art investigation as failing to constitute an "acceptably trustworthy and reliable process." Heymann, who resigned about six months later, explained, "A player with significant stakes in the matter cannot also be referee."[10]

In any event, even this limited access ultimately proved problematic for the White House. Five months later a Park Police investigator who had observed Nussbaum's search recalled having seen Whitewater-related files among Foster's papers. This forced the White House to admit that Whitewater files, as well as personal tax returns for the Clintons, had been turned over to the Clintons' personal attorney, Robert Barnett. But as Senator Richard Shelby (R-AL), then a member of the Senate Whitewater committee, told Nussbaum, "You did it your way and the American people will never know really what was in there."[11]

THE ODDITIES PILE UP

Maggie Williams herself has even admitted that she removed documents from Foster's office. Williams testified that on the afternoon of July 22—just two days after Foster's death—Bernard Nussbaum called her into Foster's office and instructed her to take a box of files related to the Clintons' legal matters, including Whitewater, and deliver them to Robert Barnett.[12] (When Barnett's wife, Rita Braver, became a White House correspondent for CBS about a month later, one of Barnett's partners, David Kendall, replaced him as the Clintons' personal lawyer.[13]) But, after consulting with Mrs. Clinton by telephone, Williams took the files to the family residence of the White House and placed them in a locked closet. Williams said she did not send them immediately to Barnett because she was exhausted and wanted to get home.[14]

It was a strange course of action: why not either let the files stay in Foster's office until the next day or place them in her own office? Even Senator John Kerry (D-MA), who had been a Clinton loyalist throughout the hearings, said Williams's explanation seemed to defy common sense.[15] And, in fact, two White House aides testified that Williams had told them that the first lady had requested that the files be moved to the White House so that she could review them.[16] Williams said that she herself had decided to put the files in the Clintons' personal White House quarters on a temporary basis, and that the first lady never reviewed them.

Williams testified that when Robert Barnett came to look at the documents in the White House residence five days later, on July 27, she merely bumped into him. Barnett stated in a letter to a congressional committee that Williams led him to the files and did not leave his side as he examined them.[17]

There are other oddities surrounding the White House's actions in the wake of Foster's suicide. After the suicide note was discovered on July 26, 1993, for example, Mrs. Clinton directed Mack McLarty and others not to inform the president about the discovery. She asked Bernard Nussbaum and Steve Neuwirth to research whether executive privilege could be asserted to cover the suicide note. Consider that there was nothing exceptional about the note—apart from the delay in its discovery. The note defensively denounced the press for its interest in the White House's actions in the Travel Office firings, and famously asserted that in Washington "ruining people is considered sport." Still, no one called Mrs. Foster the evening the note was discovered, and President Clinton did not learn of it until after Mrs. Clinton met with Nussbaum and Neuwirth to discuss their research on invoking executive privilege to cover the suicide note. No smoking gun, certainly, but it *is* damned peculiar.

Throughout the Clinton scandals in which he was involved, Nussbaum has taken the position that there is no legally relevant distinction between the interests of the president as president and the interests of the president as citizen and defendant (a view President Clinton clearly shares, having employed Foster as his personal tax and Whitewater lawyer). On this view, a publicly salaried White House counsel has the same duties as a privately paid outside counsel. But few legal experts other than Richard Nixon have agreed with this view.

For instance, the *New York Times* editorialized on March 4, 1994, while Nussbaum was still White House counsel:

> *It is, of course, long past time for Mr. Nussbaum to be dismissed. He seems to conceive of his being the President's lawyer as a license to meddle with the integrity of any federal agency.... When Vincent Foster, the deputy counsel, committed suicide, Mr. Nussbaum interfered with the investigation by the National Park Service and transferred secret files to Mr. Clinton's private lawyer. All this paints a picture of a White House dedicated to short-cutting justice if that is what it takes to shield the financial affairs of Mr. Clinton and his wife from scrutiny.*[18]

As Clinton's deputy attorney general asked, "[A]re you hiding something?"

THE WHITE HOUSE HIDES THE TRUTH

Foster's death occurred during the period when the Whitewater investigation was heating up. Foster had been heavily involved with Madison's affairs at the Rose Law Firm; at the White House he had been the designated water-carrier on the Whitewater/Madison issue. After his death—and by the White House's own admission—tax and business files pertinent to the Clintons were removed from his office.

Indeed, some months after Foster's death, Associate White House Counsel William Kennedy and Clinton adviser Bruce Lindsey met with Clinton's personal lawyer, David Kendall, and his staff to bring them up to speed on Whitewater. At first the White House asserted attorney–client privilege to protect notes taken by taxpayer-funded White House lawyer Kennedy at the November 5, 1993, meeting. When the twelve pages of notes were finally produced, the reason for the White House's reluctance became clear. Among other intriguing entries, Kennedy had written: "Vacuum Rose Law Firm files. Never know go out. Quietly." The White House tried to explain that "Vacuum Rose Law Firm files" simply referred to an existing vacuum in the files. And oral sex is not adultery.

Secrecy, blocking official investigative work, phone calls involving Mrs. Clinton, executive privilege research, failing to call Mrs. Foster, delivering files to the family quarters of the White House— all these suggest, at a minimum, a panicked effort to suppress incriminating documents, possibly on Whitewater, possibly on Travelgate, possibly on both, or on other scandals. Congressional committees, and later Special Prosecutor Robert Fiske and Independent Counsel Kenneth Starr, would have had a legitimate interest in these documents. Deliberately preventing their discovery is an act of obstruction of justice.

Of course, it's hard to prove documents have been destroyed once they've been destroyed. Or vacuumed. It is evident that officials high in the Clinton White House hierarchy at least wanted to make sure that reliable political spear-carriers—not law-enforcement agents— took the first cut at Foster's papers. This suggests an interest in obstructing justice, or at least in taking a peek to see if there was any justice there that needed obstructing.

There is a reason the law imposes severe penalties for obstruction of justice. Criminals have incentive enough to destroy incriminating documents. The law needs to create a strong counterweight.

Members of Clinton's splinter party of defenders continually insist that they do not believe the president should be above the law, *but he shouldn't be below the law either*. Well, other citizens can't turn the FBI away when it drops in for an investigation. Other citizens go to jail for carting off documents from an office subject to an investigation. Other citizens apparently do not have as much to hide as the president.

The president and first lady, it seems, wanted to obscure something about Foster's work on Whitewater, which may have revealed presidential corruption, or Foster's work on the Travel Office firings, which may have revealed presidential abuse of power. But now "the American people will never know really what was in there." Their abuse of power in permitting the White House counsel to repel FBI investigators and spirit documents out of Foster's office is itself an abuse of power, a "high Crime and Misdemeanor."

Chapter Sixteen

Webb Hubbell:
Friend of the Voiceless

After the 1992 election Webster Hubbell joined his close
friends and law partners, Hillary Clinton and Vince Foster, in the
move from Little Rock to the nation's capital, to take a job with
his golfing partner, President Clinton. Hubbell assumed the number three position at the Department of Justice, associate attorney
general. Just a little more than a year after moving to Washington,
Hubbell was forced to resign because of a criminal investigation
into his billing practices at the Rose Law Firm, charges that eventually led to his guilty plea and prison sentence.

On the occasion of his resignation, Attorney General Janet Reno
heaped praise on her felonious associate attorney general as a friend
of the underdog. Hubbell helped those, she said, "whose voices have
not always been heard." Soon, Hubbell's efforts on behalf of those
"whose voices have not always been heard" would include such
major corporations as MacAndrews & Forbes and Sprint, as well as
the multibillion-dollar conglomerate the Lippo Group. Perhaps out
of empathy, Hubbell would soon become voiceless himself.

He would also become a wealthy man. Clinton friends and
administration officials arranged for Hubbell to receive more than

$500,000 in "consulting fees" in the eighteen months following his resignation. This turn of events couldn't help but suggest the possibility that Hubbell's profitability and voicelessness were connected.

A FELON IN THE DEPARTMENT OF JUSTICE

In early 1994 Special Prosecutor Robert Fiske had been nosing around the prestigious Rose Law Firm trying to locate certain records from Mrs. Clinton's work on various disputed land transactions for Madison Guaranty Savings & Loan. In stirring up Rose billing records, Fiske unearthed billing records that indicated Hubbell had bilked his former partners out of about half a million dollars.

With his indictment imminent, Hubbell resigned from the Department of Justice on March 14. He was looking at a long prison sentence. The special counsel would have a strong hand if he offered Hubbell leniency in return for cooperation on the scandals collectively known as Whitewater. The question was: Who at the Rose Law Firm had done what to enable James McDougal to loot the taxpayer-backed S&L for his personal Rube Goldberg investment schemes? Hubbell would know. (As we now know, the missing Rose Law Firm documents discovered in the White House residence in January 1996 revealed that none other than Hillary Rodham Clinton had authored the fraudulent Castle Grande document. But back in 1994 the only possible lead the prosecutors had was Webb Hubbell.)

Hubbell had been close to the late Vince Foster and Hillary Clinton and, more importantly, had worked with Mrs. Clinton on some of the transactions at the center of the independent counsel's investigation. In particular, Hubbell had worked with Mrs. Clinton on the fraudulent Castle Grande land deal and had done work at the law firm for Madison. Indeed, Hubbell's father-in-law had been the phony "purchaser" in that deal. Consequently, part of any plea agreement with Hubbell would have to include his pledge to cooperate in the Whitewater inquiry.

On December 6, 1994, Hubbell pleaded guilty to two felony counts of tax evasion and mail fraud for stealing from the Rose Law Firm. The court sentenced Hubbell to eighteen months in prison and ordered him to pay $135,000 in restitution to the Rose Law Firm for the $484,000 he admitted stealing. On April 24, 1995, the man who had been the third highest-ranking lawyer at the Department of Justice had his license to practice law revoked.

Hubbell's plea agreement seemed to spell trouble for the Clintons. Their Whitewater partner, James McDougal, certainly thought so. Years later, on *Larry King Live*, McDougal had this exchange with a caller:

CALLER: Mr. McDougal, of all the characters associated with Whitewater—Hillary and Bill, Webb Hubbell, Kennedy, Foster, Nussbaum, some of the other legal guys—who do you think holds to a large degree the key to unlocking the prosecutor's case, not only with their knowledge, but with documents they might have?

MCDOUGAL: Webb Hubbell. Webb Hubbell is a person who had all the documents in his personal possession when they cleaned out the Rose Law Firm to come to Washington. He knows all the twists and turns.... And to sum it up, he knows where the bodies are buried. Webb Hubbell is the guy they have to get to talk.

(McDougal also remarked during the interview that if Hillary is "saying in the grand jury what's she's saying publicly about the circumstances [that] led to my hiring her as an attorney, then she's perjured herself."[1])

But despite the plea agreement, Hubbell never gave the prosecutors any useful information in their investigation. (By the time the plea agreement was struck, Ken Starr had been appointed independent counsel, replacing Robert Fiske.[2])

Just three months after his resignation, however, Hubbell began receiving a series of lucrative job offers from various FOBs, who had been alerted to Hubbell's need for "consulting fees" by top Clinton staffers. It looked a lot like someone was trying to buy his silence. People who don't have anything incriminating to say tend not to increase their market value as a result of a criminal indictment.

Though Hubbell wouldn't talk to the prosecutors, he did talk to his wife—in taped telephone conversations from prison. He knew his conversations were being taped, and curtly informed his wife of that when she probed him for information about the first lady's legal vulnerability. Still, even knowing that his every word on that phone could be heard by Independent Counsel Ken Starr, Hubbell and his wife exchanged some intriguing remarks:

SUZANNA HUBBELL: I'm the one that has to try and explain to Marsha [Scott, longtime Arkansas FOB and chief of staff in the White House personnel office]. She said you're not going to get any public support if you open up Hillary. Well, by public support I know exactly what she means. I'm not stupid.

WEBSTER HUBBELL: And I sat there and spent Saturday with you saying I would not do that. I won't raise those allegations that might open it up to Hillary, and you know that. We talked about that.

SUZANNA HUBBELL: Yes. But then I get all this back from Marsha, who's ratcheting it up and making it sound like, you know, if Webb goes ahead and sues the firm back, then any support I have at the White House is gone. I mean I'm hearing the squeeze play.

WEBSTER HUBBELL: So I need to roll over one more time.[3]

What might that mean?

Some of Mr. Hubbell's remarks on the tape-recorded phone conversation are seemingly self-serving, to say nothing of demonstrably false. For example, after he mentions that "most of the articles are presupposing that I—my silence is being bought," Mr. Hubbell launches into a soliloquy—to his wife—about how broke they are. In case his wife was unaware of the family's finances, he says, "[W]e're dead solid broke and getting broker, you know?"[4]

In fact, in the eighteen months following his resignation, amazing amounts of money came Hubbell's way, mainly in the form of "consulting fees" arranged by various Clinton administration officials and advisers. In all, Hubbell was paid about half a million dollars by friends of the Clintons, more than he had ever earned for a comparable period in his life—and this was when he was facing a criminal indictment. There is no evidence, apart from a few phone calls, that he performed any work for these generous payments. Hubbell refuses to discuss any aspect of the nature of the work he allegedly performed for the more than half-a-million dollars on the grounds of attorney–client privilege.

Within a few months of resigning, Mr. Friend-to-the-Voiceless was suddenly flying first class and taking golf vacations in exotic locales such as Bali and Indonesia. This is when Hubbell not only was facing a criminal indictment, but also had no visible means of support.[5] While in prison he would effortlessly foot the bill for his children's college tuition.

THE WHITE HOUSE ACTS SUPPORTIVE

It would not be revealed until three years after Hubbell resigned that on March 13, 1994, the day before Hubbell was to announce his resignation, there had been a high-level meeting at the White House regarding the Whitewater investigation. Present at the meeting were the president; the first lady; White House Chief of Staff Mack McLarty; Deputy Chief of Staff Harold Ickes; the first lady's chief of staff, Margaret Williams; and David Kendall, the Clintons' personal lawyer.

According to the administration's account of what happened, as the meeting was breaking up McLarty informed Mrs. Clinton that efforts would be made "to try to help" Hubbell and to be "supportive" in his time of need. Mrs. Clinton expressed her approval and perhaps gave thanks. McLarty said he told the first lady this out of earshot of the rest of the group. The administration could not confirm or deny whether McLarty had a similar conversation with the president. As Lanny Davis reported, McLarty "thinks he might have also mentioned it to the president, but his memory is less clear about that."[6] Remember, this is what the White House has admitted to.

In fact, top administration officials did spend that spring diligently fishing for lucrative "consulting" fees for Whitewater target Hubbell. The massive undertaking to be "supportive" of Webb included the efforts of then–White House Chief of Staff McLarty, soon-to-be White House Chief of Staff Erskine Bowles, U.S. Trade Representative Mickey Kantor, and informal Clinton adviser Vernon Jordan.

Impressively, Webb's little helpers managed to get him more money than he had ever earned in a single year of his life. This is not the typical effect of coming under a criminal indictment.

THE LIPPO GROUP CHIPS IN

The most curious "consulting fee" paid to Hubbell came from a subsidiary of the Lippo Group, an Indonesia-based conglomerate owned by the Riadys, the ethnic Chinese family at the heart of many Clinton campaign fund-raising scandals.

A little more than three months after Hubbell resigned from the Clinton administration under threat of indictment, James Riady of the Lippo Group was particularly anxious to talk consulting fees with Hubbell. Riady did so between his numerous telephone calls and visits to the White House. Riady had already been to the White House about two dozen times since Clinton had become president, but Riady's flurry of White House meetings the week of June 20 may have set new records.

Riady met with President Clinton himself at the White House on Tuesday, June 21, 1994. That Thursday, June 23, Riady had a 7:00 AM breakfast meeting with Hubbell. A few hours later, Riady attended a White House meeting. Immediately after his White House meeting, he repaired to the Hay Adams hotel, across the street from the White House, for his second meeting of the day with Hubbell.

By Saturday negotiations had concluded. Two days after Riady had been shuttling between meetings with Hubbell and the White House, a Lippo subsidiary paid Hubbell $100,000. Before Hubbell received the Lippo payment, he was down to $6,780 in his bank account.[7]

Little was expected of Hubbell in return for these payments, according to unnamed sources cited by the *Washington Post*.[8] The $100,000 payment was arranged by John Huang, who attended the June 23 meeting with Riady at the White House. (Huang is also responsible for raising about $3 million for the Democratic Party during the 1996 campaign, of which over half had to be returned.) The following month, the Clinton administration granted the Riadys' long-standing request that Huang be given a post at the Commerce Department.

President Clinton later said he knew nothing about the Riady payments to Hubbell until 1996, when he "read about it in the press."[9] Lanny Davis loyally supported his leader, saying Clinton "did not know about any business relationship between Lippo and Mr. Hubbell until he read about it in the newspapers."[10]

It's funny that James Riady would have neglected to mention that he was hiring Clinton's former number three man at the Justice Department during his June 23, 1994, White House meeting— squeezed in between breakfast and lunch meetings with Hubbell. It's also funny that Riady would forget to say anything about it during any of the other visits he would pay to the White House every day that week, leading up to the June 25 $100,000 payment.

During the period of his amazingly profitable consulting fee racket, Hubbell played golf with Clinton on at least one occasion and went to Camp David with the Clintons twice. He also had numerous meetings with White House officials and played golf with Vernon Jordan. Hubbell donned his prison blues in August 1995. In his waning days as a free man, White House aides threw him a party, attended by Bruce Lindsey, among others. But in all this time Hubbell's financial situation never came up.

In late 1997 lawyer and FOB Douglas Buford stepped forward to tell House investigators that he, and he alone, had been responsible for arranging the $100,000 Lippo payment to Hubbell. Buford is a partner at Wright, Lindsey & Jennings, where Bruce Lindsey was a partner, and where Clinton had worked for two years after losing the governorship in 1980. In an October 23, 1997, deposition, Buford said that Hubbell had called sometime after resigning in disgrace from the Justice Department, and asked Buford to propose that the Lippo group—a Buford client—hire him as a consultant. Buford said he passed the suggestion along to John Huang, and the rest is history.

Buford insisted in his deposition that, despite his "frequent contact" with both Lindsey and the president himself, the White House was completely in the dark about Buford's efforts on Hubbell's behalf. These he made strictly "as a friend."[11] "I wanted to make sure," he explained, "that nobody would confuse the message." One person who might have confused the message was James Riady, who visited the White House every day for a week before granting Hubbell the $100,000 lump sum payment. Another person who may have confused the message is President Clinton, who one month later acceded to Riady's request to have Huang placed at the Commerce Department.

MONEY, MONEY

Lippo's $100,000 "consulting fee" was only the beginning of Hubbell's post-resignation profits. After the March 13 Whitewater meeting at the White House, Clinton's subordinates managed to scare up all manner of "consulting fees" for Hubbell.

Just days after that meeting, McLarty began calling potential Hubbell benefactors from the White House. Among McLarty's solicitees was Truman Arnold, an FOB in Arkansas. McLarty "expressed his concerns about Webb," asking Arnold "whether Webb might be useful to Arnold in any of his business enterprises or to any of his associates." This, again, is the White House's own account, offered up years later, in response to inquiries from an impertinent press.

Arnold put Hubbell on the payroll and prevailed on others to do the same, including Democratic donor and Texas businessman Bernard Rapoport, who put Hubbell on a $3,000-a-month salary for six months. Hubbell's work assignments for Arnold and Rapoport were unspecified. Lanny Davis insisted that "any suggestion there was a linkage in Mr. McLarty's mind between Whitewater-related issues and his call to Mr. Arnold is without foundation."[12]

Vernon Jordan lined up consulting fees for Hubbell in 1994 at two major corporations—MacAndrews & Forbes Holdings, Inc., and Time Warner. MacAndrews owns the cosmetics company Revlon, where Jordan sits on the board; Jordan is also close with MacAndrews owner Ronald Perelman. MacAndrews paid Hubbell more than $60,000 in fees. Time Warner put Hubbell on the payroll at $5,000 a month—a job that lasted only one month.[13] Jordan told the House Government Reform and Oversight Committee under oath, "I told the president in an informal setting that 'I'm doing what I can for Webb Hubbell,'" and "the president said, 'Thanks.'" (Would discussions of hush money ordinarily take place in a *formal* setting?)

The fast-rising head of the SBA, Erskine Bowles, called at least three men to seek consulting fees for Hubbell: Will Dunbar of Allied Capital Corporation, as well as Sam Poole and Reef Ivy, both attorneys at North Carolina's Sanford Law Firm. Hubbell got a meeting with Dunbar but no payments from any of Bowles's contacts. The Sanford Law Firm was no Rose Law Firm.

Mickey Kantor has strenuously denied arranging any "consulting fees" for Hubbell. But he admits that he did create a trust fund to pay for Hubbell's children's educations (one of three private funds set up for Hubbell[14]), hitting up Democratic donors for contributions. He also gave Hubbell's son a job in the U.S. Trade Representative's office, and then helped him get his next job.[15] In addition, Kantor stepped in to ensure that the city of Los Angeles paid Hubbell his $24,750 "consulting fee," despite the inconvenient discovery by City Controller Rick Tuttle that Hubbell had performed little or no work for the payment.

The inspector general of the Department of Transportation (DOT), Mary Schiavo, confirmed Tuttle's conclusion, finding that Hubbell's work for Los Angeles consisted of one or two five-minute phone calls to the DOT general counsel. Hubbell had apparently been recommended for the $2,000-a-minute lobbying job by then–Deputy Mayor Mary Leslie. Leslie had been a political appointee at the SBA under Erskine Bowles.

But Los Angeles got off easy. Some of Hubbell's other post-resignation jobs defy a straight-faced description.

The Consumer Support and Education Fund, a private foundation in California, gave Hubbell a $45,000 grant to write a report on the scandal-mongering media's oppression of government officials. (Hubbell never wrote anything, so the man who had recommended Hubbell for the project, lawyer John Phillips, ended up reimbursing the fund out of his own pocket.)

SunAmerica, Inc., owned by major Democratic donor Eli Broad, paid Hubbell undisclosed sums of money "to generate public interest in a national policy to encourage saving for retirement," as the *Washington Post* put it.[16]

The Pacific Telesis Group (Pac-Tel), a telecommunications company, paid Hubbell undisclosed amounts of money at the same time that Sprint—a competitor—also had Hubbell on its payroll for undisclosed amounts of money and for undisclosed services. Lobbyist Jack L. Williams had arranged the Pac-Tel payments to Hubbell. In March 1997 Williams was convicted for making false statements in the federal investigation into whether former Agriculture Secretary Mike Espy and his aides accepted illegal gratuities from agricultural companies. Williams had also arranged payments to Hubbell from the Mid-America Dairymen's Association.

THE PRESIDENT EXPLAINS EVERYTHING

As late as April 1997 President Clinton was maintaining that any help administration officials were providing Hubbell was entirely innocent because "no one had any idea" of the seriousness of the criminal allegations against him: "Everybody thought there was some sort of billing dispute with his law firm." In a dogged attempt to get the truth out, Lanny Davis recited the White House line almost verbatim, also in April 1997, saying, "[L]ots of people believed that Webb Hubbell had done nothing wrong… that he was involved in some type of billing dispute with his former law partners."

That still wouldn't have explained why Hubbell was being paid enormous amounts of money for so little work[17]; but the explanation wasn't true, anyway. On May 4, 1997, the *New York Times* reported that two of Clinton's closest advisers had, after all, explained unequivocally to President Clinton back in March 1994 that Hubbell was in serious trouble. Oops.

The trouble was serious, in fact, that both advisers told Clinton that Hubbell was going to have to resign. Arkansas lawyer James B. Blair told the Clintons that the law firm had "pretty strong proof of wrongdoing," and that Hubbell would have to resign immediately. President Clinton's personal lawyer, David Kendall, had flown to Little Rock to investigate the allegations. He seconded Blair's conclusion and facilitated Hubbell's resignation.[18]

So really, everybody didn't think it "was some sort of billing dispute," as the president had claimed before the evidence indicated otherwise.

HELP ON THE WAY

When the Monica Lewinsky story broke, it did not pass unnoticed that one of the same Clinton friends who had arranged "consulting fees" for Hubbell had arranged a job in New York for young Monica. Vernon Jordan had set up a job for Monica with Revlon—whose parent company had seen fit to hire Hubbell as a consultant for $60,000. Remarking on the similar pattern of career assistance bestowed on both Hubbell and Lewinsky, one former White House official admitted, "these are people Bill Clinton is worried about, and he's trying to keep them happy."[19]

In fact, the president's concern about the former intern's job search grew to a fever pitch just about the time it became evident that Paula Jones's lawyers were going to seek Lewinsky's testimony. But Lanny Davis soon clarified things: "This does not sound to me like a pattern of people being paid off. You could find numerous instances of Bill Clinton helping his friends get jobs."[20]

Bill Clinton has, in fact, tried to help many friends get jobs, frequently jobs with the government. Friends such as Gennifer Flowers, the Arkansas troopers, Kathleen Willey, and Monica Lewinsky. But they're not friends, really—they're witnesses.

Flowers, with whom Clinton has finally admitted to an affair, leap-frogged over more qualified applicants for a job with the state of Arkansas, despite scoring ninth out of the eleven applicants on a merit test. According to Flowers, she told Clinton, "get me a job," and he did.[21] Clinton sent a state employee to coach her for the job interview, and changed the job description to better suit Flowers's skills. Charlette Perry, a long-time state employee who had applied for the position, filed a grievance when she lost out to Flowers. Though the grievance committee ruled in Perry's favor, the Governor's Board of Review overturned the decision.[22] And, of course, on the tapes she secretly recorded, Flowers can be heard telling then-Governor Clinton, "The only thing that concerns me, where I'm, where I'm concerned at this point, is the state job." Clinton responds, "Yeah, I never thought about that.... If they ever ask if you've talked to me about it, you can say no."

Independently corroborating Flowers's story, Arkansas Trooper Larry Patterson said, "I was in the governor's car when he made the call on the cellular phone... I remember Clinton was insistent. He finally said something like, 'Do whatever it takes... get her a job.'" The state official Patterson says Clinton was haranguing admitted that he recommended Flowers for the job, but has denied that he did so because of a call from Clinton. Must have been her score on the merit test.[23]

Patterson himself, along with another state trooper, became the sort of "friend" Clinton likes to help when they started blabbing to reporters in late 1993. While the troopers were still waffling on whether to allow their off-the-record recollections to go on record, Clinton called Trooper Danny Ferguson to offer them federal jobs, either in Washington or in Arkansas. According to Ferguson, Clinton specifically mentioned openings with the Federal Emergency Management Administration or the U.S. Marshals Office. One of Clinton's White House aides called Ferguson's wife the next day to offer her a job in the White House.[24]

To their financial detriment, the troopers opted against the jobs, and for the truth—not only about Clinton's use of the troopers as his sexual escort service but also about Clinton's offers to trade government jobs for silence. Betsey Wright, who had been Governor Clinton's chief of staff and had supervised Clinton's "bimbo eruption" response team during the 1992 campaign, promptly flew to Little Rock to have a chat with Trooper Ferguson. According to witnesses, Wright said to Ferguson, "This infidelity stuff we can handle—don't worry. But... this jobs for silence allegation could get the man impeached."[25] Back in 1993, that kind of thing could get you impeached.

On December 22, 1993, Clinton said, "The allegations on abuse of the state or the federal positions I have—it's not true. That *absolutely* did not happen." The word "absolutely" seems to be the president's secret little code word meaning he or his men are lying. During the 1992 campaign, when he denied having an affair with Gennifer Flowers, Clinton said, "I have *absolutely* leveled with the American people."[26] Clinton lawyer Bob Bennett said Kathleen Willey had "*absolutely* no knowledge or information of any relevance" to the Paula Jones case, and that Monica Lewinsky swore that "there is *absolutely* no sex of any kind in any manner, shape, or form, with President Clinton." And Mrs. Clinton said of the Lewinsky allegations, "I believe they are false—*absolutely*."

In any event, the troopers didn't sell their silence and, consequently, didn't get jobs with the federal government—or half a million dollars in "consulting" fees. They didn't even get a book deal with a $400,000 advance, as Webb Hubbell did. (Hubbell's book was fittingly titled *Friends in High Places*.) The troopers' only financial "gains" were (1) not being fired from their state jobs, though they were forced to give up their moonlighting jobs, and (2) patching together a few thousand dollars from conservative groups.

PRISONER BLUES

We aren't waiting for any new facts to come out. It is a known fact that Webb Hubbell could not possibly have done anything on his own to earn half a million dollars in consulting fees after a disgraceful resignation and impending criminal indictment.

The first article of impeachment against President Nixon charged him with obstruction of justice. Most seriously the article accused Nixon of "approving, condoning, and acquiescing in, the surreptitious payment of substantial sums of money for the purpose of obtaining the silence or influencing the testimony of witnesses, [or] potential witnesses."

Even with the release of the Nixon tapes, and his complete perfidy laid bare, the worst that can be said about Nixon is the least that Clinton is willing to admit. Nixon can be heard on the tapes discussing the possibility of raising money for the Watergate defendants. The Clinton administration had a full-court briefing in the White House on the subject of paying Hubbell.

After Nixon discusses the idea of paying the Watergate burglars, however, *no money was ever paid*. Hubbell actually got paid—more money, in fact, than he had ever earned in a single year of his life, before being indicted. Both Nixon and Clinton maintained that they never thought of the payments—conceptual in Nixon's case and actual in Clinton's case—as "hush money."[27] Both said they only wanted to help defray the living expenses of the defendants and their families. Both said they expected nothing in return.

What might either president have sought in return?

The Watergate defendants could not have implicated Nixon in the break-in, for the simple reason that Nixon had nothing to do with that. What they could have done is ratted out the president for trying to prevent national security leaks. After secret security codes in the Pentagon Papers had been leaked to the *New York Times*, Nixon had hired his private band of "Plumbers" to plug the leaks. He paid the Plumbers through donations funneled through his campaign committee. That's what Nixon wanted to hide.

This time, not only were payments actually made, but they were made to a defendant who, according to Clinton's Whitewater partner, James McDougal, "knows where the bodies are buried."[28]

If Nixon talking about paying living expenses—or "hush money"—amounted to "a violation of his constitutional oath faithfully to execute the office of President of the United States,... and [a] violation of his constitutional duty to take care that the laws be faithfully executed,"[29] what is more than half a million dollars in "consulting fees" that was actually paid to a witness against the president?[30]

PART FOUR

Corruption

Chapter Seventeen

White House Coffees

Back in 1992 Clinton promised America "the most ethical administration in the history of the Republic." Of course, he also promised a middle-class tax cut.

In any event, having warmed to the theme that he, Clinton personally, was virtue and goodness personified, his 1996 campaign ran a commercial that oozed, "As Americans, there are some things we do simply and solely because they're moral, right, and good." His campaign could afford slapstick commercials like this one because of the extensive White House coffees and Lincoln bedroom sleepovers for major campaign donors during his first term in office.

THE PLAN

The impetus to put the president's time on the auction block came from an understandably panicked reaction to the 1994 election by leading Democratic Party officials. On February 28, 1997, Bob Woodward of the *Washington Post*, speaking on *Larry King Live*, noted, "There was such a money frenzy…. Clinton began this process in '95 when it looked like he was dead, that the Republicans were going to elect a president. The Republicans had

213

taken over Congress, and there was a kind of panic that overtook the White House."

In fact, the plan was hatched on Christmas Day 1994, and apparently Clinton himself was the ringleader. "It was Christmas 1994. Hillary and Chelsea were in New York on a holiday jaunt. The president was home alone, feeling blue. The Democrats had lost badly, and were blaming him."[1] So to "cheer up" the commander in chief, his deputy chief of staff, Harold Ickes, presented Clinton with Democratic National Committee (DNC) finance chief Terry McAuliffe.

McAuliffe proposed that Clinton start selling access. He was the president, the leader of the free world, commander in chief— a money magnet. By making himself available to deep-pocket supporters he could raise enough money to ward off primary challengers and bury the Republicans. "It was the first positive news he'd had," McAuliffe told *Newsweek*. McAuliffe concluded the breakfast meeting with the famous words, "Mr. President, this is the last discussion you'll ever have to have about money."[2]

Just eleven days later, on January 5, 1995, McAuliffe sent Clinton's secretary, Nancy Hernreich, a memo slotting three days that month for Clinton to meet twenty "major supporters for breakfast, lunch, or coffee." Another ten people, wrote McAuliffe, could be invited on golf outings or morning jogs with the president. The purpose of these meetings would be to "offer these people an opportunity to discuss issues and exchange ideas with the president," wrote McAuliffe. "This will be an excellent way to energize our key people for the upcoming year." Not a bad way to pull in the dough either. Hernreich passed the memo on to Clinton with the query, "Do you want me to pursue?"

Clinton's response will someday appear in the anthology of famous Clinton quotes alongside "kiss it." He wrote: "Yes, pursue all 3 and promptly. And get other names at [$]100,000 or more,

[$]50,000 *Ready to start overnights right away.* Give me the top 10 list back, along w/the 100, 50,000" (emphasis added). The "overnights" were Clinton's own little brainstorm; "It was not anyone else's idea; it was mine," Clinton told the *National Journal.*[3]

THE WHITE HOUSE EXPLANATION

Clinton's explanation for the note was: It was taken out of context. This, despite the fact that the entire memo had been produced, handwritten notes and all. It seems the proper "context" is that Bill and Hillary Clinton just happen to be friends with a lot of people who happen to make large donations to the DNC. And his mother died that year.

> *I think that first of all, if the note is understood in its accurate and proper context, there's nothing wrong with it…. I think what I was telling her is that, you know, we've been out of touch with a lot of these people for two years and we've had a lot of work going on in Washington and we've had, both of us had lost a parent, and we just hadn't kept in touch with people like we should have, and that's what I was saying.*[4]

Classic Clinton. He needed to start selling the Lincoln bedroom because both he and Hillary had "lost a parent" that year.

Before Clinton offered this telling explanation, the White House press office had released a list naming 831 of the overnight guests, thus far, and divided them into various make-believe categories having nothing to do with their status as prospective campaign donors: 370 Arkansas "friends," 155 longtime non-Arkansas "friends," 111 "friends and supporters" the Clintons had met since 1992, 128 "public officials and dignitaries," and 67 representatives from the world of "arts and letters."

This self-released White House list did not mention the large-donor, soon-to-be-friends category, whose names were forwarded to the White House by then–DNC Finance Chairman Marvin Rosen. Documents made public months later would reveal, as one fundraiser said, that "Marvin Rosen had the final say over who would stay in the Lincoln Bedroom. The decision was usually based on how much money people had given or were willing to give later on."[5] *"[W]hat I was telling her is that, you know, we've been out of touch with a lot of these people for two years and… both of us had lost a parent…."*

When these other internal White House lists appeared, some of Bill and Hillary's "friends" had asterisks by their names—indicating payments were being made in installments.[6]

In fact, at least 938 people stayed overnight at the White House during Clinton's first term, according to documents released by the White House in February 1997.

THE SHOPPING LIST

Even before the 1994 Republican sweep of Congress—and before Bill and Hillary had each "lost a parent"—a memo had circulated through the DNC to Harold Ickes at the White House proposing the sale of various White House perks to raise campaign cash. The April 1994 memo, written by an unidentified Democratic staffer, was addressed to Martha Phipps, a top DNC aide. The shopping list proposed selling seats on Air Force One and Two, as well as "[b]etter coordination on appointments to boards and commissions" as some of the ways "to reach our very aggressive goal of $40 million this year." Phipps faxed a copy of the memo to Ickes.

The proposed shopping list of the president's perks to lure large contributions included:

- Two seats on Air Force One and Air Force Two trips
- Six seats at private White House dinners
- Six to eight seats at all White House events, such as Jazz Fest, official visits, and ceremonies

- Places on official delegations abroad
- Better coordination on appointments to boards and commissions
- The right to eat in the White House mess
- Visits to the White House residence and overnight stays
- Guaranteed Kennedy Center tickets
- Six spots in the audience for the president's weekly radio address
- Photo opportunities with "principals"—that is, President and Mrs. Clinton and Vice President and Mrs. Gore

This memo might have been written off as the fantastical scribblings of an exuberant (and irrelevant) campaign staffer—if some of the anonymous staffer's ideas had not eventually been implemented with gusto. By the fall of 1995 the DNC had begun assembling complicated budgets for "fund-raising events"at the White House—including the White House coffees. They methodically listed the amount "projected" to be raised from each event, and the cash each eventually took in.

Long before the threat of Newt Gingrich was there to justify any maniacal fund-raising events in the White House, Clinton was hosting breakfasts at the White House for the express purpose of raising money to promote Hillary's health care plan.[7] (Ironically, just the thing that led to the Republican takeover of Congress.) The "friends" invited to the health care breakfasts contributed about $50,000 to $100,000 a piece, raising about $1 million in all.[8]

"POLITICAL FUND-RAISING IS CRITICAL"

There is no question that the president and vice president were intimately involved in the use of the White House for fund-raising purposes. Clinton, Gore, and senior White House staff were kept personally abreast of each month's fund-raising intake and projected tallies for future events.[9] White House officials met weekly with DNC officials to plan White House fund-raising events. Harold Ickes forwarded status memos to the president and vice president on these strategy sessions. Clinton often handwrote comments and suggestions on the memos.

The Clinton fund-raising coffees were strictly private and were never listed on the president's public itinerary, despite Clinton's after-the-fact declaration at a March 7, 1997, press conference: "I almost wish that one of you [reporters] had been in all of these coffees...."[10]

The coffees were supposedly scheduled to allow people to talk about things and share their convictions, the president said on March 7, 1997, after the story had come out when a subpoena forced Harold Ickes to hand over documents to House investigators.

Monthly schedules of coffees and their projected revenue were compiled and continually updated—and reviewed by Clinton and his top White House staff. Anticipated revenues, respectively, included for example: January 17, 1996, $400,000; January 25, 1996, $400,000; January 26, 1996, $400,000; and February 6, 1996, $400,000. In some cases the documents amount to precise spreadsheets with running totals breaking out projected total revenue and total funds in hand, reported the *New York Times*.[11] In a July 14, 1996, memo on raising $3.2 million, Clinton-Gore campaign manager Peter Knight states that just one coffee would bring in approximately $350,000 and another coffee, $600,000.[12]

Besides many coffees marked as being attended by POTUS (President of the United States), documents show others denoted as FLOTUS (First Lady of the United States), VPOTUS (Vice President of the United States), MEG (Mary Elizabeth Gore, a.k.a. Tipper Gore), and SHALALA (Donna Shalala, secretary of Health and Human Services). The latter's projected contribution intake was $100,000.

A January 19, 1996, memo by White House aide Evelyn Lieberman to then–Chief of Staff Leon Panetta and Harold Ickes stated: "[T]he political staff implored the schedulers to add a series of small coffees… to the president's schedule…. They believe there is considerable urgency to their request. Attached is their proposed list of 27 coffees…. Political fund-raising is critical…." Lieberman concluded the memo by stating that its recommendations would require approval from the president. Evidently such approval was, as they say, not unreasonably withheld.

In 1995 and 1996 alone, the White House, in cooperation with the DNC, held at least 103 coffees for 358 selected guests. These meetings, held in the White House Map Room, generated $27 million for the Democratic Party (that's an average of more than $75,000 per attendee). Typically, each coffee was budgeted to raise $400,000 in contributions.

At least four Democratic fund-raising officials have revealed that former DNC Finance Chairman Marvin Rosen explicitly advocated selling access to the president through the $50,000-a-head coffees. "I can't count the number of times I heard, 'Tell them they can come to a coffee with the president for $50,000,'" one official who worked under Rosen told the *Los Angeles Times*. "It was routine. In fact, when staffers said, 'This is all I can raise,' they were told, 'Keep selling the coffees.'"[13]

Prominent New York City attorney and Democratic fund-raiser Melvyn Weiss said that offering coffees to potential contributors was part of the Democrats' strategy. Weiss further said, "I brought people down and I would say, 'I really think that you should consider helping the party.' They would say, 'What kind of contribution would be appropriate?' And I would say, 'We have a trustee program, and if you want to give $50,000, it's up to you.'"[14]

A DNC fund-raiser told Nynex Corporation executives that they would receive invitations to White House coffees if they joined the DNC's "Managing Trustees" program and agreed to donate $100,000 to the Democrats. Nynex sent a $35,000 check to the DNC on August 21, 1995, and on September 5 Nynex President Donald Reed attended a coffee. "I think it is fair to say that there was an understanding that if we became a trustee member [by donating $100,000 to the DNC], there was going to be an invitation to a White House coffee," said Nynex Executive Vice President Thomas Tauke, a former GOP congressman from Iowa. Elaborating on his description of the DNC fund-raising approach, he added only that Nynex was a longtime Democratic supporter.[15]

Both Alexis Herman, then–director of Public Liaison and current secretary of Labor, and President Clinton attended a coffee on May 13, 1996, at which top banking executives got to chat with Treasury Secretary Robert Rubin, DNC officials Donald Fowler and Marvin Rosen, and Comptroller of the Currency Eugene Ludwig. After news of this meeting made it into the press, both Herman and Clinton acknowledged that the event was inappropriate and should not have occurred. Yet neither Clinton nor Herman saw fit to cancel the meeting at the time. The bankers gave $332,654 to the DNC around this time.[16]

WHITE HOUSE SPIN

When Clinton's deceased-parents excuse for turning the White House into a very pricey bed-and-breakfast disintegrated under a mound of White House memos, damage control from the White House was just as frantic as the fund-raising had been. (Maybe it was all that coffee.) White House Deputy Counsel Lanny Davis said, "We don't sell access." In point of fact, Davis elaborated, no one had been actually "required" to write a check in order to attend the coffees.

Davis did allow that it was "[in]appropriate" for the president to be entertaining a two-time convicted criminal, Eric Wynn, just months after his second conviction.[17]

DNC spokesperson Amy Weiss Tobe said there "were no price tags for White House coffees" but conceded that "it appears that some may have tried to put a price tag on coffees at the White House."[18] Technically, that's true. The price tag varied.

That is precisely the aperçu that Clinton administration spokesmen have been at pains to avoid. Mike McCurry promoted the theory that it's not a fund-raiser unless tickets are sold, even if the event is an element in a campaign-related financial program. He said in late February 1997 that the coffees were "technically not used for fund-raising, but they became an element of the financial program that we were trying to pursue in connection with the campaign." Expanding on this interesting new distinction, McCurry explained: "…I've been to [fund-raisers]… you buy a ticket… you have to buy a ticket to get in. These were not events in which you had to buy a ticket to get in, nor was there any solicitation of funds made by the president at the occasion, and that's why they were not fund-raisers."

Of course, you don't really need the standard ticket-takers when you have a complement of Secret Service officers at the gate.

The White House Counsel's Office claimed it was completely unaware of the coffee "fund-raisers" or Lincoln bedroom sleep-overs—which is probably true. Abner Mikva, former Clinton White House counsel, was asked by *Newsweek* if there had been any White House "finance-related events" on his watch. He said if he had known about the coffees or sleep-overs he "sure as hell would have been upset about it—and we would have put a stop to it. Any Philadelphia lawyer knows you don't raise money in a government building. And if they were budgeting money for them, that's raising money."[19]

THE LAW

Federal law—if not the Clinton administration—seeks to separate political fund-raising from public policymaking. It is a federal crime to solicit or receive campaign contributions on federal property. In observance of this policy, some care is usually taken to avoid involving White House staffers directly in fund-raising matters. But such precautions were thrown to the wind as Alexis Herman and Harold Ickes played active roles in organizing coffees and other events requested by the DNC.

Fund-raising events on federal property would, as Mikva says, violate a federal felony statute. Theoretically, Clinton has also opened himself up to a conspiracy charge under Section 371 of Title 18. The conspiracy statute criminalizes a conspiracy to commit any offense against the United States—such as soliciting contributions on federal property. The draw of the White House coffees to potential donors was not the opportunity to meet with DNC officials; it was the opportunity to meet with the president, the vice president, or the first lady. Though mere presence during the commission of a felony is not itself a felony, in the case of the coffees, an understanding that one of the executive branch luminaries would attend each coffee was a central element to the fund-raising scheme. DNC Chairman Don Fowler may be a charming fellow, but he wasn't the reason people were paying an average of $75,000 for a cup of coffee. A jury could thus find a conspiracy to violate Section 607 of Title 18, the statute prohibiting solicitation on federal property.

In addition, Section 4 of Title 18, "Misprison of felony," seems designed for such situations as this. That section of the federal criminal code provides: "Whoever, having knowledge of the actual commission of a felony cognizable by a court of the United States, conceals and does not as soon as possible make known the same to some judge or other person in civil or military authority under the United States, shall be fined under this title or imprisoned not more than three years, or both." President Clinton is legendary for his ability to pass the buck to others whenever "mistakes were made." If he knew of the mistake the DNC was making in holding fund-raising events at White House coffees, with himself as the star attraction, the misprison statute passes the buck back to him.

The currently available facts could also—again theoretically—form the basis for an extortion charge under the Hobbs Act, 18 U.S.C. 1951. Significantly, in a 1992 opinion, the Supreme Court confirmed that the "passive acceptance of a benefit by a public official is sufficient to form the basis of a Hobbs Act violation if the official knows that he is being offered the payment in exchange for a specific requested exercise of his official power. The official need not take any specific action to induce the offering of the benefit."[20] It is difficult to avoid surmising that Clinton's agreement to listen to hundreds of large donors "share their convictions" with him during 103 coffees was implicitly predicated on their making contributions to his campaign or to the DNC. President Clinton's passive acceptance of this benefit in exchange for listening to the donors could constitute extortion—even if Clinton never acted on the convictions shared by the donors.

If—as appears to be the case—these donors were contributing more than the average American's annual income *not* merely for an opportunity to shake the president's hand, but to influence the president in some official action, a series of federal bribery laws would also come into play. The federal bribery law, 18 U.S.C. 201, provides that a public official faces criminal penalties if he "directly or indirectly, corruptly demands, seeks, receives, or agrees to accept anything of value personally or for any other person or entity, in return for... being influenced in the performance of any official act...." The courts have interpreted "corruptly" to mean a *quid pro quo*. But this does not mean that envelopes stuffed with cash need to change hands. The statute is written broadly to encompass certain direct and indirect efforts at selling or buying influence.

Clinton said on March 7, 1997, "I don't believe you can find any evidence of the fact that I had changed government policy *solely* because of a contribution" (emphasis added). According to

224 HIGH CRIMES AND MISDEMEANORS

bribery statutes, it is not necessary for the official to act *solely* because of the bribe; it's still a crime to be partially influenced by a bribe. Also, to be convicted under the gratuity statute, the official does not have to be influenced by the gratuity at all. Clinton's statement is remarkable because, by negative implication, it's a confession. It's just like, "There *is* no improper relationship."

And yet no action was ever brought to determine whether Clinton broke the law. To determine, that is, whether there was "any evidence of the fact that [Clinton] had changed government policy" *in part* "because of a contribution." Only Michael Kelly ever understood this point in the mainstream print, writing in his first satirical "I Believe the President" column, "I believe that it is proper to change government policy to address the concerns of people who have given the president money, as long as nobody can find evidence of this being the sole reason."

MEDDOFF

Though no coffee was served, one potential donor has already provided evidence of palpably illegal conduct by the Clinton administration. A federal grand jury in Washington, D.C., heard testimony from Florida businessman R. Warren Meddoff on March 26, 1997. Meddoff testified that he had a conversation with President Clinton at an October 22, 1996, fund-raiser, at which Meddoff gave Clinton a business card with a note stating that he had a friend, Bill Morgan, who wanted to make a tax-deductible donation of up to $5 million to the DNC. Instead of leaping back in horror and loudly proclaiming, "Sir, that would be improper!", Clinton turned back to him and asked him for another card.

Subsequently, Harold Ickes telephoned Meddoff, leaving a message on his office answering machine "saying that he was calling on behalf of the president from the White House, and would I please contact him."[21] Ickes later faxed a three-page memo to Meddoff from the White House on October 31. The memo suggested that Morgan's proposed donation be contributed in the form of $540,000 to three pro-Democrat tax-exempt groups and another $500,000 go directly to the DNC. (One allegedly tax-exempt organization had the unlikely name "Defeat Proposition 209.") Ickes included the bank account numbers for the DNC and the other organizations and stressed that Morgan should make the payments.

That would seem to be sufficient to convict Harold Ickes for soliciting contributions on federal property, in violation of Section 607 of Title 18. Ickes even told Meddoff to shred the fax-memo; as Meddoff testified, "Anytime an individual asks me to shred a document, there's a problem." Moreover, Meddoff said negotiations broke down when Morgan requested a thank-you note from the president. Ickes clearly committed a felony when he followed up on the offer of a $5 million donation. Unless both Ickes and the donor are lying—and what Clinton really said to Ickes was "please give this card to someone at the DNC immediately"—Clinton did, too.

SLEAZE AND CORRUPTION

If you're going to take bribes as president, it helps if you fire all the United States attorneys, replacing them with your own people upon taking office. President Clinton is the first president to have done this, at least in recent memory.

Relying on his own appointees not prosecuting him, Clinton lives in the interstices of the law and the proof-beyond-a-reasonable-doubt standard. Perhaps there wouldn't have been sufficient evidence to convict him. The difference between a "fund-raising" event and the president having coffee with his new rich "friends" is admittedly tricky to establish under the law. But there is still the little matter of political ethics, involving the wholesale auctioning off of the president's time.

As Clinton lawyer Bob Bennett reminded the Supreme Court in attempting to block Paula Jones from having her day in court, the president's time is extremely valuable. The president's day is parceled out to various duties by a small army of timekeepers and schedulers. The president simply does not have time to absorb every input that might conceivably lead to a better policy decision on a particular matter. For better or worse, he must depend for advice on the advisers he has chosen, and who are known or knowable to the public (and confirmed by the Senate, in the case of higher-ranking executives), and on a paper flow that is tightly regulated by those same advisers.

There are some minor and unavoidable exceptions to this rule. A president may unilaterally override his advisers and take in a source of advice on which he particularly depends. Or he may talk to his personal friends: no posse of advisers and schedulers can keep him from doing that. But these are trivial exceptions to the general rule that the president's time, and his radar screen, are public trusts.

Of course, the term "Gucci Gulch" had to come from some-place. The lobbying business does seem to be a profession precisely designed to circumvent prohibitions on selling access to government officials. But lobbyists are also heavily regulated by law. And whenever there are *quid*s discernably matching up with *quo*s, both the lobbyist and lobbied can be in trouble.

Noticeably, fund-raising letters from both parties purporting to offer special briefings with high-ranking officials in return for high-dollar contributions are like letters from Ed McMahon. Typically, they clarify in the fine print that what is being offered is a "briefing," in which the senator or the cabinet secretary briefs you—not an unstructured shmooze session in which you get to brief him. There is no prohibition on this—provided those letters are written on party stationery and at party expense, no public-salaried officials help set up any of the briefings, and the briefings take place at clubs or restaurants and not federal property.

An occasional White House coffee with large donors or

Lincoln bedroom sleep-over by a large donor would not implicate any criminal statutes. What sets the Clinton coffees and sleep-overs apart is this: the DNC documents referring to them as "fund-raisers"; the DNC charts—reviewed by Clinton—listing anticipated revenue streams from each coffee; Clinton's hand-written note, *Ready to start overnights right away*; the presence of DNC officials at the coffees; the existence of large contributions from the attendees the day of, or soon after, meetings with the president; and the sheer number coffees and sleep-overs. Clinton has been shown to have used the White House as the command center for his presidential campaign, with DNC Headquarters being used "as little more than a checking account," as former Bush administration White House Counsel C. Boyden Gray has observed.

So what you're left with in the White House coffees is an administration that defends itself by saying, *We didn't break the law, we're just sleazy*. For columnist William Raspberry, the apparent sale of the Lincoln bedroom was the last straw. He professed himself not all that upset about Paula Jones or about anything that had come out in Whitewater. But, he wrote, "the selling of nights in the White House is so crass a thing, so close to the possibility and appearance if not the actuality of corruption—and such god-awful judgment on Clinton's part—that I cannot imagine any defense for it."[22]

Chapter Eighteen

Wampumgate

Secretary of the Interior Bruce Babbitt's transformation from potential Supreme Court nominee to potential highest member of the Clinton administration to be indicted calls to mind Mark Shields's line that Clinton could drive a convertible through a car wash with the top down and only Al Gore would get wet. Babbitt's getting wet, too.

Mr. Integrity has been accused by the Chippewa Indian tribe of trading a decision on a government casino license—worth about $80 million—for hefty donations to the DNC.

THE CHIPPEWA CASINO

In October 1993 three northern Wisconsin bands of the Chippewa tribe made the fateful decision to apply to the Department of Interior for a permit to run a casino on the St. Croix Meadows Greyhound Racing Park track in Hudson, Wisconsin. The federal government, through the Interior Department, exercises extensive jurisdiction over Indian territories, arising out of various nineteenth-century treaties. This includes approving or disapproving Indian-run gambling casinos. In recent years, the gambling business has been seen by some tribes as a rags-to-riches formula. But, as the Chippewa would soon find out, it is also a business that leads to conflict with other tribes over government-granted monopolies.

About one year later, in November 1994, the regional Bureau of Indian Affairs (BIA) office in Minneapolis approved the Chippewa's application and forwarded its recommendation to the Department of the Interior in Washington for final approval.

A coalition of five rival tribes—all much wealthier than the Chippewa, since they already had their casinos—was not keen on the idea of another casino in the area. In January 1995 the coalition retained the Washington lobbying firm O'Connor & Hannon to help it persuade the administration to reverse the BIA decision.

Patrick J. O'Connor, a name partner of O'Connor & Hannon and former DNC treasurer, raised the issue directly with President Clinton at a reception in Minneapolis on April 24, 1995. O'Connor spoke with Clinton and then, at Clinton's direction, with White House adviser Bruce Lindsey, complaining that the White House aide on Indian Affairs, Loretta Avent, had not been returning his calls.[1]

That day Lindsey called the elusive Loretta Avent from Air Force One and asked her to investigate the Chippewa's casino application at Interior. Avent responded to Lindsey's call that very day by sending a memo to Harold Ickes, White House deputy chief of staff, curtly informing him that "the legal and political implications of our involvement in the Hudson casino case would be disastrous."[2] Also on that day, Michael Schmidt in the White House's Domestic Policy Council sent a memo to the same effect to the White House Counsel's Office stating that O'Connor "must stop telling others that he had access to the White House" on the Chippewa casino issue. Schmidt's memorandum said O'Connor's boasts would be "political poison" for the president.[3]

Ickes was unmoved by Avent's and Schmidt's concerns. Between April 25 and 28, 1995, Ickes repeatedly left messages for

O'Connor. On May 8 O'Connor replied to Ickes's phone calls in a letter: "I appreciate your calling me concerning the above subject on Tuesday, April 25, and again on Wednesday, April 26. I assume these calls were prompted by my discussions with the president and Bruce Lindsey on April 24 when they were in Minneapolis."

O'Connor wrote that he wanted "to relate the politics involved in this situation" to Ickes, and proceeded to tick off the Republicans and Democrats arrayed on either side of the casino project: "Governor Thompson of Wisconsin [a Republican] supports this project." He continued, "Senator Al D'Amato [a Republican] supports this project." In addition, he noted, "[t]he chairman of the [Chippewa] Indian tribe in the forefront of this project is active in Republican party politics." On the other hand, referring to an April 28 meeting between DNC Chairman Donald Fowler and the representatives of the anti-Chippewa tribes, O'Connor noted, "[a]ll of the representatives of the tribes that met with Chairman Fowler are Democrats and have been so for years. I can testify to their previous financial support to the DNC and the 1992 Clinton/Gore Campaign Committee."[4]

Similarly unconcerned with—or unaware of—the resistance by some White House staffers to becoming involved in the Chippewa casino issue was a lobbyist from O'Connor's firm, Thomas Corcoran. On April 25, the day after O'Connor's little chat with Clinton and Lindsey, Corcoran called Babbitt's office and talked to aide Heather Sibbison. He informed her that she would soon be hearing from Loretta Avent at the White House. Bruce Lindsey, he told her, was on the case.[5]

Meanwhile, the rival tribes opposed to the Chippewa casino were working on a parallel track. On April 28, 1995, leaders of the objecting tribes smoked the peace pipe with Chairman Fowler of the DNC.[6] In explaining the purpose of the meeting, the executive director of the Minnesota Indian Gaming Association, John McCarthy, wrote to the leaders on April 25, saying: "A meeting has been set… with Mr. Don Fowler, the head of the Democratic National Committee, a top-level

White House staff member, and [others].... *The people we will be meeting with are very close to President Clinton and can get the job done*" (emphasis added).[7] Wampum is the mother's milk of politics.

Soon thereafter Fowler began lobbying Ickes himself. "I called Mr. Ickes, explained to him the nature of the situation, and I called someone at the Department of the Interior," Fowler told Senator Fred Thompson's Senate Governmental Affairs Committee on September 9, 1997.[8] On May 5, 1995, Fowler wrote a letter to Ickes, requesting his assistance on the casino issue.

On May 15, 1995, Babbitt attended a political meeting at the White House. After the intimate, one-hour meeting, Babbitt attended a DNC dinner thrown by Fowler at the Hay Adams hotel for various cabinet secretaries.[9]

Two days later, on May 17, 1995, Chippewa lobbyist Paul Eckstein and his clients met with the Interior Department's head of Indian gaming. Eckstein emerged from the meeting confident that the casino proposal would be approved. But he did not realize the fix was in: that very evening, Babbitt's senior Interior Department aides decided they should reject the Chippewa's casino application, putatively on the grounds of local opposition, which is practically inevitable with all casino applications.

Babbitt's attorney, Washington super lawyer Lloyd Cutler, explained that it was "just coincidental"[10] that the decision came so soon after the DNC dinner, and after Fowler's lobbying campaign.

Wasting no time in spreading the good news, Heather Sibbison was on the horn to the White House the next day, May 18, informing them that the Chippewa's application would probably be denied. The career official at Interior who made the decision— or thought he was making the decision—testified that he did not "make up [his mind]" about the Chippewa casino until June.[11]

The decision to reject the Chippewa casino application was formally announced on July 14, 1995. Later that very day Paul

Eckstein met with his friend, former partner, and law school class-
mate, Secretary Babbitt. The testimony of Eckstein becomes crucial at this point. According to Eckstein's amazing testimony
before the Thompson committee on what Babbitt had said:

> *Harold Ickes had directed him to issue the decision that day…. The*
> *Secretary said, at some point, when we were standing up, asked me,*
> *rhetorically, "Do you know how much"—I believe it was these tribes but*
> *it is not clear to me what these tribes referred to—"had contributed to*
> *either the Democratic Party or the Democratic candidates or the DNC?" I*
> *can't be certain of that, but I am certain he asked me the general rhetori-*
> *cal question. I said I don't have the slightest idea. And he responded by say-*
> *ing, "Well, it's on the order of half a million dollars," something like that.*

Also on the day the decision was formally announced—it was a busy
day all around—Pat O'Connor, lobbyist for the triumphant tribes,
made a notation in his calendar to discuss "fund-raising strategies" with
Ickes and Fowler. Whether he did so or not, on September 14,
O'Connor sent a Democratic fund-raising letter to his client tribes
reminding them of the favorable decision he had just won for them
from the Interior Department. Over the course of the next eighteen
months, the rival tribes contributed $286,000 to the Democratic Party.[12]

THE LAWSUIT

The casino-less Chippewa—whose leader was known to have been
"active in Republican party politics," according to O'Connor's letter to Ickes—sued the Interior Department in December 1995.
Not without reason, they alleged that campaign contributions had
colored the Interior Department's decision-making process. (The
judge overseeing the case, U.S. District Judge Barbara B. Crabb,
said she "believe[d] there is a distinct possibility that improper
political influence affected" the Interior Department's decision.[13])

Unfortunately for Babbitt, Eckstein was no Susan McDougal. Consequently, in the summer of 1996 the Senate Committee on Indian Affairs began an inquiry into the Chippewa casino rejection, particularly Eckstein's claim that Secretary Babbitt had blurted out the decision was based on the rival tribes' generous contributions to the Democrats. Senator John McCain, chairman of the committee, sent a letter to Secretary Babbitt on July 19 requesting an explanation.

In a letter dated August 30 Secretary Babbitt replied to Senator McCain, "I must respectfully dispute Mr. Eckstein's assertion that I told him that Mr. Ickes instructed me to issue a decision in this matter without delay. I never discussed the matter with Mr. Ickes; he never gave me any instructions as to what this department's decision should be, or when it should be made."

More than one year later, Babbitt's memory of his conversation with Eckstein would markedly improve.

On October 10, 1997, Babbitt wrote a letter to another committee, the Thompson committee, which was investigating campaign finance abuses. This time Babbitt recalled that he had mentioned "something to the effect that Mr. Ickes wanted a decision" after all. But, he claimed, he was lying when he said this. *It was only as an awkward attempt to get Eckstein out of his office.* Babbitt denied that he mentioned the rival tribes' campaign contributions to the DNC, and maintained that political contributions and White House pressure had not improperly influenced his department's decision.

The Thompson committee made a criminal referral to the Justice Department for perjury on the basis of Babbitt's testimony on this point.

THE CASE AGAINST BABBITT

Obviously, Babbitt's testimony is irreconcilable with Eckstein's. It is also in conflict with reams of other evidence, to say nothing of common sense.

On February 11, 1998—the day Attorney General Janet Reno

decided to seek an independent counsel to investigate whether Secretary Babbitt lied to Congress—Babbitt, relying on a modified version of the Clinton "He said/She said" defense, said, "This is a disagreement between two people about the exact words spoken in a meeting they had alone two years ago. We've each told our version and we disagree. There's nothing else to say about it. My attorneys say it can't possibly form the basis of any legal charges."[14] And Monica's lawyers told her perjury doesn't count in a civil case.

But it's not as simple as that. There may not be more than twenty hours of tape, but there is substantial evidence that makes Eckstein's version of events much more credible than Babbitt's.

To begin with, in order to believe Babbitt's recollection—his October 30, 1998, recollection, not his August 30, 1996, recollection—one would have to believe that Babbitt lied to Eckstein, an old friend, about a very serious matter just to get Eckstein out of his office. Claiming he was under pressure from Ickes is not just an awkward white lie. It is an allegation of conduct that is certainly improper, and possibly illegal under the federal bribery statute, 18 U.S.C. 201 (criminalizing the receipt of anything of value in exchange for the performance of any official act). So Babbitt's improved recollection to the Thompson committee asks us to believe that he gravely slandered Harold Ickes just to get an old friend out of his office, when a glance at his watch and a remark about a meeting in five minutes, *Love to talk, really jammed this week*, would have done the job just as well.

And why would Ickes's name have sprung to mind in the first place? Even if we assume Babbitt had to allege federal crimes in order to make Eckstein leave, there seems to be no reason why he would instantly choose Ickes for his culprit—unless, as suggested by Patrick O'Connor's May 8, 1995, letter to the deputy chief of staff, Ickes had become crucial to what would ordinarily have been a routine Interior matter.

Ickes, for his part, tepidly endorsed Babbitt's assertion that the Clinton administration was *not*, in fact, selling government policy decisions to the highest bidder. Ickes testified, "I don't have any recollection of it, [of] talking to Interior about this."[15]

Babbitt aide Heather Sibbison also somewhat corroborated her boss's recollection that the casino rejection was not bought and paid for by the rival tribes. Sibbison stated under oath that she was completely unaware of any lobbyists' contacts with the White House, and that the decision was made on the merits, not politics.[16] Sibbison was, of course, directly contradicted on this point by lobbyist Thomas Corcoran, who said under oath that he told Sibbison his firm was lobbying the White House, and that she should be expecting a call from White House Indian Affairs aide Loretta Avent.

In addition, there is evidence that Sibbison was, in fact, keeping the White House aware of progress on the Chippewa's application, which would seem strange unless she had some reason to believe the White House was interested in this one little government decision. A White House memorandum dated May 18, 1995, from a White House aide to Harold Ickes, states that "Heather Sibbison" at Interior had relayed the datum that the Department had concluded that the Chippewa casino was "probably a bad idea."

Moreover, then-Chairman Dan Burton's House Government Reform and Oversight Committee went over the bills that O'Connor & Hannon sent to the anti-Chippewa tribes whom they represented, and found charges for the following items that seem to suggest that the DNC was involved in the casino issue. The invoices included the following:

- Meeting at DNC with Truman Arnold [high-profile Texarkana businessman and FOB] and Chairman Don Fowler.

- Calls to the White House and the DNC regarding tribes meeting with Don Fowler.
- Appointment at White House with Harold Ickes.
- Calls to DNC regarding White House appointment.
- Report to L. Kitto [Larry Kitto, a Wisconsin-based lobbyist who worked for the anti-Chippewa coalition] regarding President Clintons [*sic*] comments about "our friends and racetrack issue" [racetrack may refer to the fact that one of the properties that the Chippewa entrepreneurs wanted to turn into a casino was a dog racetrack].
- Memorandum to T. McAuliffe of Clinton/Gore Re-Elect Committee [Terry McAuliffe, finance chairman of that committee].
- Long distance telephone conference to T. Corcoran [Thomas Corcoran of O'Connor & Hannon] regarding Terry McAuliffe arranging appointment with Harold Ickes.
- Discussions with several aides on the White House staff, including aides to [then–Chief of Staff] Leon Panetta and Harold Ickes.
- Discussion regarding necessity to follow-up with Harold Ickes at the White House, D. Fowler at DNC and Terry Mac at the Committee to Re-Elect, outlining fund-raising strategies.[17]

Why would lobbyists who were retained for the purpose of influencing an Interior Department decision bill the clients for so much time related to DNC and Clinton-Gore fund-raising?

THE INDEPENDENT COUNSEL

As noted, on February 11, 1998, the fleet-footed attorney general decided to seek an independent counsel to investigate whether Interior Secretary Bruce Babbitt lied to Congress about how well-heeled Indian tribes managed to reverse a government decision that would have allowed a much smaller tribe to compete with them in the casino business. On March 19, 1998, Carol Elder Bruce was chosen for the assignment.

Reno has reportedly asked that the new independent counsel's mandate be confined to whether Babbitt lied when he told a Senate committee that campaign contributions played no role in the Indian casino decision. Theoretically, Reno's limitation would insulate Ickes and Lindsey, various DNC officials, and perhaps other Clinton acolytes who sold administration decision-making for campaign cash. (And how about the guy who steered lobbyists with bulging checkbooks, such as O'Connor, toward aides who could gin up the process, such as Lindsey?)

In any event, under the independent counsel statute, the investigation cannot be so circumscribed as Reno would like. The investigation could well spill over into what is obviously the question of broader public significance: did the Clinton administration sell a government-enforced monopoly to a group of tribes in return for campaign cash?

As mentioned, the Supreme Court has held that passive acceptance of a benefit by a public official is sufficient to form the basis of a Hobbs Act violation if the official knows that he is being offered the payment in exchange for a specific requested exercise of his official power. The official need not take any specific action to induce the offering of the benefit. In applying this to Clinton administration officials in the Chippewa case, much would depend on whether they knew that O'Connor or O'Connor's clients were not making a request with empty hands—that they would pony up to the DNC in exchange for the action they desired.

In addition to the Hobbs Act, there is the bribery statute, which prohibits, on pain of a fifteen-year prison sentence, seeking anything of value in return for the performance of any official act. The thing of value need not be for the official himself: it could

before any other person or entity—such as, for instance, the
DNC. Here, proving intent would be difficult in the case of
Clinton, somewhat less so in the cases of Ickes or Lindsey.

Chapter Nineteen

The Manchurian Candidate

The Chinese money scandal is for people too squeamish to face the perjury about oral sex charges. If the president's "sex life" is no one's business—as if we were talking about what Bill and Hillary do in the privacy of their bedroom—how about treason? Concerns about treason sound so much more high-minded than concerns about the president having a sexual relationship with an intern and then lying about it under oath. The framers did expressly set forth "treason" as one of the grounds for impeachment. They neglected to do the same for "having an oral-sex affair with White House interns and then lying about it baldly and repeatedly under oath." Clinton's defense to impeachment on the sex scandals is essentially that he has engaged in conduct so reprehensible that James Madison couldn't have imagined it.

The problem with the Chinese money scandal is that Clinton was right when he tauntingly announced to reporters, "I don't believe you can find any evidence of the fact that I had changed government policy solely because of a contribution." That is basically a confession: Clinton has admitted that he did change government policy—in part—because of a contribution.

241

But, on the other hand, it remains true that some plausible alternative explanation can always be dreamed up for policy changes. His statement is a reminder that it is going to be very difficult to prove that, like everything else in the Clinton administration, foreign policy was sold.

What makes the idea of national security being traded for campaign dollars so arresting is that we're talking about Clinton. As columnist Maureen Dowd said of another Clinton scandal that turned out to be false—and then turned out to be true—"What you need to know about Bill Clinton is that the charge was plausible."[1] With the exact same money trail followed by the exact same policy changes in a Carter White House, illegal donations to the DNC would be a minor incident. But with a White House "where everything is political and everything is for sale," it does not take a fevered conspiracy theorist to think that foreign policy was on the block. As Dowd said about other "despicable" charges against the Clinton White House, "it sounded so plausible."[2] And that was before what sounded plausible turned out to be true.

As we go to press, the public information about the Chinese money scandal has gaping holes. There is "strong circumstantial evidence," according to a Senate report, that various individuals with close ties to the People's Republic of China (PRC) were funneling money to American political campaigns during the 1996 campaign.[3] Several of these individuals had extraordinary access to the president. Many small, and some large, Clinton policies coincided with the desires of some of these individuals. But that doesn't add up to evidence that Clinton changed government policy because of a contribution. And, if the new Clintonian standards for American presidents are to be accepted, it does not amount to evidence that Clinton "changed government policy *solely* because of a contribution."

THE LIPPO GROUP

Mochtar Riady and his son, James, control the Lippo Group, a $6 billion conglomerate based in Indonesia. They have been friends and supporters of President Clinton since at least the early 1980s, when the Lippo Group acquired a minority interest in the Arkansas-based Worthen Bank, and James had moved to Little Rock to learn the banking business.

The Riadys also had a "long-term relationship with a Chinese intelligence agency," according to a report by the Thompson committee.[4] The report, which reveals only unclassified information, does not claim that Clinton knew of the relationship between the Riadys and the PRC, nor is that relationship explained.[5]

This much is known: On November 7, 1992, two days after Bill Clinton was elected president, China Resources Holding Company, a Beijing government–owned corporation known by U.S. intelligence to provide cover for Chinese intelligence-gathering operations, purchased 15 percent of the Hong Kong Chinese Bank (HKCB), a subsidiary of the Riady family–controlled Lippo Group. The Riadys sold the 15 percent interest to China Resources for $2.10 a share at a time when the public stock was trading at $2.62 per share—a 20 percent discount. As the *South China Morning Post* noted, "It was essentially a private placement… structured in such a way as to circumvent having to secure the approval of the Hong Kong stock exchange."

On June 17, 1993, Lippo announced that it had sold an additional 35 percent of HKCB to China Resources, giving the Beijing government–owned espionage front half ownership. This time, instead of getting a discount, Beijing paid a 50.7 percent premium on HKCB stock. According to the *Morning Post*, the "deal will also bring a profit of about $164.8 million to HKCB holding"[6]—that is, to the Riady family.

According to a summary prepared in December 1996 for

House investigators examining the Lippo-China connection, "under Hong Kong law, China Resources [Holding] Company's 50 percent share in the bank provided it with access to all [Lippo] corporate information."

Thus, as of July 1993, every time Riady or Huang met with Clinton, the president was dealing with the partners of a Chinese government–owned organization known by U.S. intelligence agencies to provide cover for Chinese intelligence-gathering operations.

During the 1992 presidential campaign—about the same time the Red Chinese were acquiring an interest in the Riadys' Lippo Group—James Riady and his wife contributed $200,000 in "soft money" to the DNC. In January 1993 Lippo executives James Riady and John Huang gave a joint $100,000 contribution to the Clinton inaugural fund. By the end of Clinton's first term John Huang would be at the center of the Democratic Party's fund-raising scandal.

Soon the Riadys were enjoying extraordinary access to President Clinton. Huang and the younger Riady began a series of Oval Office meetings with the president. In briefing selected news agencies on November 15, 1996, White House spokesman Mike McCurry admitted that in the first Clinton administration Riady met with Clinton at least six times in a minimum of twenty separate White House visits, and Huang met with Clinton at least fifteen times in ninety-four separate White House visits.

Indeed, when the Indonesian ambassador sought a meeting with President Clinton, he went to James Riady to arrange it.[7]

There is little doubt that President Clinton changed government policy because of campaign contributions from the Riady family, though we cannot be certain he changed policy "solely because of a contribution." At least not as we go to press.

In a confidential letter dated March 9, 1993, Mochtar Riady asked the president to extend Most Favored Nation (MFN) status to

China.[8] (That same month, the elder Riady flew into Little Rock from Indonesia for a March of Dimes banquet for First Lady Hillary Rodham Clinton, and donated $50,000 in Mrs. Clinton's honor.[9])

Reversing his campaign stance against MFN—and his insistence that he would not deal lightly with the "butchers of Beijing"—Clinton did extend MFN to China on May 28, 1993. Soon the president was enthusiastically lobbying Congress to grant MFN *permanently* to China.

In May 1993 Clinton met with Indonesian official B.J. Habibie, over the objections of the president's foreign policy advisers. Riady had requested the meeting. At the meeting Habibie pled his case for President Clinton to meet with then-President Suharto of Indonesia. Habibie must have been persuasive.

Shortly thereafter, Clinton gave a speech to the Export-Import Bank, where Habibie was in the audience. To the surprise of Clinton's foreign policy advisers, Clinton at one point diverged from his prepared remarks—and his foreign policy aides' advice—to discuss Indonesia and declare his intention to meet with Suharto. Referring to Habibie, Clinton said, "I know we have someone here from Indonesia.... We have enormous opportunities there.... I'm going to meet with the president of Indonesia [in Tokyo] to send a signal to the... emerging nations of the world that the United States wants to be their partner in new trade relations."[10]

One of Clinton's foreign policy advisers later said, "We never figured out how the promise to meet Suharto got in there."[11]

And in fact in July 1993 President Clinton did meet with Suharto in Tokyo. He did so, he later told the *New York Times* with refreshing candor, because, among others, Mochtar Riady had "encouraged me to see President Suharto."[12] One of Suharto's top priorities at the meeting was to ask Clinton to preserve Indonesia's trade preferences with the United States. Since 1992, the year before Clinton took office, the United States had been reexamining Indonesia's trade preferences under the Generalized System of Preferences in light of that country's abominable treatment of workers.

In February 1994, in the midst of a formal governmental review of whether to permit Indonesia to continue to receive trade benefits, U.S. Trade Representative Mickey Kantor abruptly terminated the review process and formally announced that the administration was allowing Indonesia to keep its trade privileges, valued at more than $600 million a year to Indonesian companies.[13]

Indonesian workers might suffer, but the Lippo Group would benefit.

COMPANY MAN JOHN HUANG

At the Riady family's urging, Lippo executive John Huang joined the Commerce Department in the summer of 1994, leaving his position as vice chairman of the Lippo Bank to become deputy assistant secretary for International Economic Policy at Commerce. According to sources "who asked not to be identified," the Riadys boasted that they had won the position for Huang on account of their campaign contributions to President Clinton. Just before leaving for his job at Commerce, Huang received close to a million dollars in salary and bonuses from Lippo as well as another $700,000 from another Riady company.

While maintaining his ties to Lippo, Huang attended 109 Top Secret briefings at Commerce, involving classified information. Huang repeatedly called Lippo following the meetings.[14] Huang's logbooks recorded weekly meetings with Commerce's Central Intelligence Agency (CIA) liaison officer, which were weekly intelligence briefings on the PRC. Any materials related to the briefing were under the control of the CIA.[15]

In response to congressional inquiries, a Commerce Department official stated, "Mr. Huang received routine intelligence briefings, including intelligence reports. The office that handles intelligence matters does not make a record of each briefing or item provided in the course of briefings. Available records indicate that 37 intelligence briefings were scheduled. Available records show that Mr. Huang saw 15 classified field reports... [and] received 12 finished intelligence reports."[16]

On January 31, 1994, six months after Lippo became full partners with China Resources, the Clinton Commerce Department granted a Top Secret security clearance to Lippo executive John Huang. The normal background investigation required of candidates for Top Secret clearances was waived. Commerce Department security official Paul Buskirk signed a memo stating that the "request for a waiver of background investigation prior to appointment for Huang" had been approved. "Huang has been granted this waiver due to the critical need for his expertise in the new administration for Secretary [Ron] Brown."[17]

During the six months before he formally joined the government on July 17, 1994, as a principal deputy undersecretary of Commerce, Huang simultaneously held a United States government Top Secret clearance and the vice presidency of an Indonesian corporation that was partners with a Chinese company known to provide cover for Chinese intelligence-gathering operations.

Despite the fact that he was born in mainland China, was educated in Taiwan, had served in the Taiwanese military, had worked in Hong Kong, and was employed by a foreign company, Huang was never given a full field FBI background check prior to receiving, or while holding, a Top Secret security clearance. Instead his interim background check was conducted by the Office of Personnel Management. It did not involve checking his overseas contacts.[18]

Commerce Undersecretary for International Trade Jeffrey Garten tried to prevent Huang from dealing in U.S.-Chinese relations. He assigned Huang to work with Assistant Secretary of

Commerce Charles Meissner on boosting U.S.-Taiwanese trade. Garten explained his decision: "Neither Meissner nor Huang have traveled to Beijing nor have they played a high profile role in the JCCT [U.S.-China Joint Commission on Commerce and Trade] process. We plan to keep this separation of function."

Although Huang was supposed to promote U.S.-Taiwanese trade, he tried to spike action on a strategy to do just that out of concern for the reaction of the Chinese government. In a hand-written memo attached to his draft "Proposed Country Strategy for Taiwan," Huang said, "Anything we need to do to delay pro-gram with Taiwan, we should do it (to protect what we have accomplished so far in China). Regardless, we need to take a low-key approach with Taiwan at least before the spring [is] over. We have so much planned with China during this period of time."[19]

According to his appointment logs, the day after returning from a January 1995 trade trip to Taiwan, Huang had dinner with Beijing's ambassador to Washington, Li Dao.

Even though Undersecretary Garten had assigned Huang to work a Taiwan portfolio because Huang had never traveled to Beijing and was not expected to, Huang planned a trip to China in the spring of 1995. According to Commerce Department documents released to House Rules Committee Chairman Gerald Solomon (R-NY), this trip was abruptly canceled the same week Huang submitted the South Korean and Chinese visa applications on which he certified a birth-date different from the one on his security clearances.[20]

On September 13, 1995, Clinton met with James Riady, presi-dent of Lippo; John Huang, former Lippo employee; and Joseph Girior, FOB and then–Lippo consultant. The Riadys and Huang lobbied the president for a transfer from the Commerce Department to a senior fund-raising position with the DNC. Clinton accommodated the request, directing Bruce Lindsey and Harold Ickes to work out the details.

The White House repeatedly described the September 13 meeting as a "meet and greet" social visit, neglecting to mention that it was decided at the meeting that Huang would become a DNC fund-raiser.[21]

On December 3, 1995, one day before Huang left Commerce for the DNC, his boss, Charles Meissner, formally requested that Huang be retained at Commerce as a "consultant" even while he worked for the DNC. Meissner also requested a new Top Secret clearance for Huang for his consultancy. Huang never became a consultant, but on December 14, 1995, the Defense Industrial Security Clearance Office approved his new Top Secret clearance. It was not terminated until December 9, 1996, after numerous stories had been published about Huang's fund-raising activities.[22]

In the 1996 election cycle John Huang raised approximately $3 million for the DNC, about $1.5 million of which the DNC has deemed questionable or improper and has returned. Huang even took the Fifth Amendment, refusing to cooperate with congressional investigators.

President Clinton has defied subpoenas from the House Government Reform and Oversight Committee asking him to turn over government documents detailing his dealings with Riady and Huang. The president is claiming that "attorney–client" privilege exempts him from fulfilling these congressional subpoenas.

CHINA CAT JOHNNY CHUNG AND COSCO

"*I see the White House is like a subway:* You have to put in coins to open the gates," Johnny Chung, a Taiwan-born international businessman, told the *Los Angeles Times* in a July 1997 interview.[23]

Despite being described as a "hustler" by one of Clinton's own National Security Council advisers, Chung was granted a meeting with President Clinton in March 1995. By coincidence, the meeting came just two days after Chung had handed a $50,000 check to Maggie Williams, the first lady's chief of staff. Chung brought five Chinese businessmen to meet with Clinton.

One of Chung's "friends" was Zheng Hongye, a representative of the China Ocean Shipping Company (COSCO), which had a strong interest in leasing the Long Beach Naval Station.

Soon after chatting and picture-taking with the COSCO representative, Clinton met with Long Beach officials in the White House to encourage them to lease the station to COSCO. Several months later, Clinton flew to Long Beach himself to lobby for the COSCO deal. Finally, the day before the November 1996 election a Clinton administration official placed a "highly unusual" call to local officials in Long Beach stating that lease of the terminal to COSCO "was the preference of the White House" and not something "the White House wanted studied further," according to one Long Beach official quoted in the *New York Times*.[24]

YOU GOT ME

By early February 1997 FBI Director Louis Freeh had assigned twenty-five agents to a special task force to investigate espionage against the United States, including the Lippo Group's partnership with China Resources, and the close linkage in time between intelligence briefings Huang received from the CIA while at Commerce and calls he made to the Lippo Group from his Commerce Department telephone.[25]

When the FBI investigation came to light, the White House immediately requested information from the FBI about what federal investigators knew or suspected about Chinese attempts to influence American politics. Then–White House Counsel Charles F.C. Ruff sought the sensitive counterintelligence information in a February 18 letter to Deputy Attorney General Jamie S. Gorelick, but Director Freeh intervened from abroad to block release of the information to the White House. Freeh was concerned, his spokesmen said, that the White House would leak the information and he would come under attack for having passed on sensitive intelligence to the president of the United States.[26]

The most interesting aspect of this episode is that the president did not kick up a huge fuss. Rather, the White House response was not unlike Clinton's response, about one year later, to Wolf Blitzer's famous question about Monica: *Okay, you got me.*[27]

In fact, President Clinton had admitted in 1996 that he knew that things he said to James Riady might be passed back to the Chinese government. Despite that, he said there were no notes of any of his meetings with Riady. "I don't have any notes or anything from the conversations [with Riady], but I think I have reasonable memory of it," Clinton said.[28] The president did not, however, have a "reasonable memory" of at least one meeting with Riady—the September 13, 1995, meeting when Clinton acceded to Riady's request that Huang be moved from Commerce to the DNC.

THOMPSON COMMITTEE

Senator Thompson, chairman of the Senate Government Oversight Committee, dramatically opened the hearings on campaign finance abuses referring to allegations of "a plan hatched during the last election cycle by the Chinese government and designed to pour illegal money into American political campaigns."[29]

Soon Thompson would be ridiculed for overreaching. Senator John Glenn of Ohio, the committee's ranking Democrat, promptly declared he did not believe there was "any real evidence" that China had carried out such a plan. One columnist gave a typically ironic title to his piece on the hearings, "The Chinese Commies Are Coming!" and termed Thompson's opening gambit a "wonderful ploy."[30]

All this was difficult for the public to evaluate. In the months-long investigation, the committee had access to classified FBI and CIA intelligence information, but the classified information could not be made public. Remarking that he had "read the same material," Senator Glenn announced, "I refuse to play around with intelligence information loosely," and said Senator Thompson's remarks went "beyond what I can say."[31]

On the other hand, Democratic Senator Joseph Lieberman of Connecticut had essentially concurred with Thompson's approach and conclusions throughout the investigation. But the normally nonpartisan Senator Glenn had been at loggerheads with Thompson from the very inception of the investigation. Glenn had vigorously objected to the breadth of the investigation and the amount of money being spent. Senator Glenn was a former astronaut: he had been the first American to orbit the earth. He wanted to go to space again.

As the Thompson committee was putting the finishing touches on its report in January 1998, the Clinton administration announced that it was granting Senator Glenn's long-hoped-for request to fly on a space-shuttle mission scheduled for later in the year. At $10,000 a pound, just adding Glenn to a previously scheduled mission would cost about $2 million. The entire launch would cost taxpayers half a billion dollars.[32] The theory for sending Glenn into space was that it would help scientists look at the effects of space travel on the elderly. Many scientists questioned the value of NASA's foray into gerontology.[33]

Then in May 1998 inside sources at the Pentagon began leaking information to Jeff Gerth at the *New York Times*. American intelligence sources had intercepted phone calls indicating that China had been interested in influencing American elections. Then "hustler" and FOB Johnny Chung admitted his own role. Chung had been the conduit for tens of thousands of dollars to the Democrats directly from the Chinese military.[34]

LORAL

Interestingly, one of Clinton's most alarming foreign policy decisions happened to coincide with campaign contributions from
American capitalists, rather than from the Red Chinese.

In 1996 the Pentagon began investigating two U.S. firms suspected
of giving vital missile technology to China. The technology would
be a great help to China, particularly for the twelve ballistic missiles
China had targeted at the United States. After a one-year investigation,
the Pentagon issued a report in 1997, concluding that "United States
national security has been harmed." The Justice Department
impaneled a grand jury.

Then the commander in chief stepped to the plate. President
Clinton derailed Justice's investigation, giving the firms, in the
words of one Senate aide, "a get-out-of-jail-free card."[35] The firms
at issue, it seems, were major campaign contributors to Clinton.

Jeff Gerth of the *New York Times* broke the story on April 4,
1998.[36]

Gerth's breathtaking story was that in 1996 the Chinese
launched a rocket carrying a commercial satellite owned by an
American company, Loral Space and Communications. The rocket, designed by a Chinese company, crashed and burned shortly
after take-off, killing hundreds of Chinese. (Consistent with its
human rights record, the Chinese government denied the death
toll.) This opening permitted sensitive rocket-guidance technology to be transferred to the "butchers of Beijing," as Clinton called
them back when he was campaigning.

Two U.S. aerospace companies, Loral and Hughes Electronics,
a General Motors subsidiary, rushed in to review the problem.
They concluded that an electrical problem had caused the crash.
In the review process they turned over two hundred pages of sensitive data to the Chinese, including information that would help
the Chinese with rocket guidance and control.

The guidance technology used for satellites is the same technology required to launch multiple warheads from a single missile. Loral and Hughes were handing over just the technology China needed to perfect its intercontinental ballistic missiles.

The State Department immediately ordered the Pentagon to review the incident. The Pentagon issued its report in May 1997, concluding that Loral and Hughes had given China "crucial assistance in improving the guidance systems" of its intercontinental ballistic missiles. The companies, the Pentagon found, had "turned over expertise that significantly improved China's nuclear missiles." U.S. national security had been harmed. And not just with regard to the "butchers of Beijing": China had already been caught selling nuclear weapons and missile technology to Iran and Pakistan.

In February 1998, just as the Department of Justice was gearing up to prosecute the companies, Bill Clinton granted Loral a waiver from the sanctions imposed after the Tiananmen massacre. The waiver gave the firm permission to launch another satellite from China and, consequently, to continue helping the Chinese beef up their rocket technology. This was also just at the time the commander in chief was weighing whether to risk American lives to prevent Iraq from acquiring weapons that would be launched on Scud missiles. A Scud does not have a fraction of the range of these Chinese rockets, nor, for that matter, did Iraq have any weapons targeted at the United States.

On February 18 President Clinton signed the waiver to allow Loral to launch its satellite, stating that the deal was "in the national interest."[37] The waiver expressly permitted Loral to do again that which had brought it under criminal investigation for having done once. To grant the waiver, Clinton had to ignore the advice of his own Justice Department, not to mention the concerns the Pentagon had already expressed.

But President Clinton did not turn a deaf ear to all advice. He was apparently following the advice of two major campaign contributors.

Since 1991 Hughes and Loral had contributed $2.5 million to the Democratic Party. Loral CEO Bernard Schwartz had personally contributed over $1 million; in 1997 Schwartz was the largest single contributor to the Democrats. Hughes CEO C. Michael Armstrong had been lobbying Clinton since 1993 to ease export limits on sensitive technology such as Hughes satellites. In one of Armstrong's letters to Clinton, he used the magic words: he reminded Clinton of his past political support.[38] What had the Pentagon done for Clinton?

In 1995 Armstrong and Schwartz had sent a joint letter to Clinton requesting that the president transfer satellite export controls from the national security–minded State Department to the acquiescent Commerce Department.[39] (Presumably, Commerce officials such as John Huang would be more open to sensitive technology transfers to China.) In 1996 Clinton did so.

Soon after Gerth's story broke, the *New York Times* pointedly editorialized, "Control of these sensitive technologies is too important to sacrifice for commercial gain, much less campaign contributions…. The White House should not relax export control rules either to improve relations with China or to accommodate generous donors."[40]

Obviously, the *Times* is right. Selling national security for campaign donations is treasonous. If true this is the biggest scandal of the Clinton presidency. But so far, there is no "evidence of the fact that [Clinton]… changed government policy solely because of a contribution." So at least it can be said Clinton has met the low standard of probity he has set for himself—much as he kept all the "promises he meant to keep."[41]

But the argument Clinton's defenders had made throughout the "bimbo" scandals blew up in their faces with the China scandal. They had essentially conceded that Clinton has no character, no morals, and that he lies a lot. Their argument was that it didn't matter because the president's low morals and perjury had to do with sex. (Those who believed the president was telling the truth belonged to a splinter party.) Well, here it mattered. Here national security was at stake, and the question was treason.

If all this were known about a Carter or Reagan administration no one would think "treason." "Stupid" or "sloppy" maybe, but not treason. "What you need to know about Bill Clinton is that the charge was plausible."[42] Clinton is to Carter what Aldrich Ames is to George Kennan.

As the *New York Times* story was breaking, Clinton had his own big trip ahead of him. Ironically, he was headed to China. Jay Leno's joke about Clinton being the only man who could distract attention from one scandal by starting another scandal had come full circle: In attempting to divert attention from the Monica scandal by planning a string of international junkets, Clinton had dropped himself right into the middle of his Chinese money scandal.

In Federalist No. 64 John Jay explained that there would be little danger of the country entering into unfavorable agreements with other nations because of the president's presumed "honor, oaths, reputations, conscience, the love of country, and family affections and attachments." The Constitution, Jay wrote, had "taken the utmost care" to ensure that the president would be a man of "integrity." But if a man like Bill Clinton ever worked himself into the White House, the impeachment clause of the Constitution would suffice "so far as the fear of punishment and disgrace can operate."[43]

Chapter Twenty

High Crimes and Misdemeanors

James Madison said the "first aim" of the Constitution was to ensure wise and virtuous rulers and to prevent "their degeneracy":

> *The aim of every political constitution is, or ought to be, first to obtain for rulers men who possess most wisdom to discern and most virtue to pursue the common good of the society; and in the next place, to take the most effectual precautions for keeping them virtuous whilst they continue to hold their public trust.*[1]

For that reason, the Constitution provides for impeachment.

The requirement of virtue went for the president most of all. John Jay said, for example, "there is reason to presume" the presidency would fall only to those "who have become the most distinguished by their abilities and virtue." He imagined that the electors would not "be deceived by those brilliant appearances of genius and patriotism which, like transient meteors, sometimes mislead as well as dazzle."[2] He did not imagine Clinton.

The third and final author of the Federalist Papers, Alexander Hamilton, praised the method for selecting the president[3] as likely

257

to ensure that the office will be "filled by characters pre-eminent for ability and virtue": "Talents for low intrigue, and the little arts of popularity, may alone suffice to elevate a man to the first honors in a single State," but, Hamilton wrote, "other talents," including virtue, would be required to win the presidency.[4]

Talents for "low intrigue" may be enough for Arkansas, but they were not expected to be enough to win the presidency. The entire system is constructed to ensure that the office will be filled by "some fit person."[5] At a bare minimum, this suggests that the president must have virtues beyond not being a convicted criminal. Implicit in everything the framers say is that the president cannot be fooling around with interns. If we can't trust him with Girl Scout troops visiting the Oval Office, he's not fit for the office.

That's where impeachment comes in. The whole reason for including an impeachment procedure was to provide a backup mechanism for removing rogues when the selection process itself had failed to produce "some fit person" with "ability and virtue"—not merely some person who, thus far, has managed to escape a finding that he is guilty beyond reasonable doubt in a criminal prosecution.

VIRTUE MEANS MORE
THAN NOT BEING A FELON

Clinton's few remaining defenders exult that he is not guilty of a crime—or at least, not clearly, beyond a reasonable doubt. This is (a) almost certainly false and (b) completely irrelevant to the question of whether he has committed impeachable "crimes." Though it may sound like it to the untutored ear, "high Crimes and Misdemeanors" need not be crimes at all.

It is absurd, in fact, to think that a constitutional system carefully calibrated to elevate men of "virtue" would permit removal of the man occupying the presidency only upon proof beyond a reasonable doubt that the president had committed a crime. The historical evidence "establishes that the phrase 'high Crimes and Misdemeanors'—which over a period of centuries evolved into the English standard of impeachable conduct—has a special historical meaning different from the ordinary meaning of the terms 'crimes' and 'misdemeanors.'"[6]

But with self-government a background fact rather than a brave new experiment, twentieth-century Americans seem no longer to expect their rulers, even presidents, to be "characters pre-eminent for ability and virtue." The charges against Clinton are discussed only in terms of the criminal law, as if Clinton were a common criminal rather than the elected leader of a self-governing nation. Elmer Gantry has somehow worked himself into the presidency, and congressional Republicans are sitting on their hands, saying they're waiting to see all the evidence.

Surely one reason for the modern confusion between impeachable offenses and criminal offenses is the odd phrase, "high Crimes and Misdemeanors." This is a mistake; the phrase "high Crimes and Misdemeanors" has nothing to do with the criminal law. High crimes and misdemeanors are completely different from criminal offenses in purpose, scope, consequence, and meaning. One telltale fact is that there is *no such thing* as a "high crime" in the criminal law. Though there are "crimes" and there are "misdemeanors," there are no "high crimes" or "high misdemeanors."

After surveying the etymological history of the phrase "high Crimes and Misdemeanors," constitutional scholar Raoul Berger concluded:

> *In sum, "high Crimes and Misdemeanors" appear to be words of art confined to impeachments, without roots in the ordinary common law, and which so far as I could discover, had no relation to whether [the act constituted a crime].*[7]

Likewise, the Rodino Report observed that "[s]ince the fourteenth century the phrase 'high Crimes and Misdemeanors' had been used in English impeachment cases to charge officials with a wide range of criminal and non-criminal offenses.... There is evidence that the framers were aware of this special, noncriminal meaning of the phrase 'high Crimes and Misdemeanors' in the English law of impeachment."[8]

The first-ever impeachment was of the king's chancellor, Michael de la Pole, in 1386. Of the charges against him, the Rodino Report observes: some "may have involved common law offenses," but others "plainly did not." One of the common law offenses was defrauding the king—and the realm—in a land deal by arranging a false appraisal.[9] (The "realm" was not defrauded of $60 million, but in other respects de la Pole's get-rich-quick scheme was not unlike the various Whitewater land deals, one hardly need add.)

Another of the charges against de la Pole's impeachable offenses was simply that he had promised Parliament to carry out the advice of a parliamentary committee on improvements to "the estate of the king and the realm," and then had not done so.[10] This, of course, was not a criminal offense, but it was an impeachable offense.[11]

Quite noticeably, the Constitution's many references to criminal proceedings and criminal judgments do not apply to impeachment. The president has the right to grant pardons for all "offenses against the United States," for example, "except in the case of Impeachment."[12] Similarly, impeachable "crimes" are excluded from the right to a trial by jury.[13] Though impeachment is expressly excluded from these criminal procedures, impeachment is not mentioned in the Sixth Amendment to the Constitution. The Sixth Amendment requires, among other things, a trial by jury for all "criminal offenses." Adopting this amendment would have directly abrogated the impeachment power of the House and the removal power of the Senate if an impeachable act were considered a "criminal offense."[14] But it is not.

While a "showing of criminality is neither necessary nor sufficient for the specification of an impeachable offense,"[15] any "*significant* breaches of criminal law*" are clearly among the grounds
for impeachment.[16] As the Rodino Report puts it, the impeachment device is not "limited to" criminal acts.[17] Rather, "high
Crimes and Misdemeanors" encompasses a "wide range of criminal and non-criminal offenses" against the state.[18] The whole point
of having a unitary executive subject to impeachment was to
throw out rogues and incompetents, not just convicted criminals.

Impeachment requires completely different types of offenses
and standards of proof. Indeed, the Rodino Report explicitly
rejected the idea that any aspect of a criminal prosecution should
be carried over to the impeachment process, including "the various elements of proof, defenses, and other substantive concepts
surrounding an indictable offense."[19] Impeachment should not be
undertaken lightly, but there seems no reason to expect the pre-
sumption of innocence in a criminal proceeding to carry over to
an impeachment proceeding. It's one thing to say we won't put
you in prison except on a beyond-a-reasonable-doubt standard.
But surely a lesser standard is required for the country to say: You
shouldn't be the fellow with his finger on the nuclear button.

Even on a preponderance-of-the-evidence standard, it is not
easy to obtain an impeachment conviction. The constitutional
check on whimsical impeachments is the hurdle of a two-thirds
vote in the Senate for conviction. James Madison explained: "As
the concurrence of two thirds of the Senate will be requisite to a
condemnation, the security to innocence, from this additional
circumstance, will be as complete as itself can desire."[20] (If
Madison could have foreseen today's Congress he might have
said, "as the Republicans are abject cowards, the security to innocence, even of the manifestly guilty, will be as complete as itself
can desire.") It was just that supermajority requirement for

removal that saved President Andrew Johnson from being removed after he was impeached by the House.

As James Wilson—the framer often called the "father of the presidency—said, "Impeachments… come not… within the sphere of ordinary jurisprudence. They are founded on different principles, are governed by different maxims, and are directed to different objects; for this reason the trial and punishment of an offense on impeachment, is not bar to a trial of the same offense at common law."[21]

IMPEACHMENT
IS THE MOTHER OF ACCOUNTABILITY

The "objects" to which impeachment would be directed in a constitutional Republic would be different from those under a monarchy. The president would have to be a virtuous man, for example, because he was not king. Having just fought the revolutionary war to throw off a monarchy, the framers of the Constitution were rather clear about the president not being a king. In fact, it was precisely to avoid such claims as are being made today—that the president is above the law or somehow special in any way because he is the sole repository of the entire executive branch authority—that the framers toyed with the idea of creating a committee of presidents. That idea was, obviously, rejected.

But the reason it was rejected was not to make the president more powerful, but to make him more accountable.

The idea was not even to have a series of kings with limited, four-year terms. Indeed, throughout the constitutional conventions and later ratifying conventions, the framers obsessively discussed the checks on the power of the president, so averse were they to recreating a monarchy. At the Pennsylvania ratifying convention, for example, James Wilson extolled the citizen stature of the president: "[N]ot a *single privilege* is annexed to his character; far from being above the laws, he is amenable to them in his private character as a citizen, and in his public character by *impeachment*."[22]

Still and all, the creation of a president was one of the most contentious points in the proposed Constitution. The anti-Federalists argued that the presidency would soon replicate the very thing the Revolutionary War had been fought to end. Caricaturing the anti-Federalists' portrayal of what the president would become—"[c]alculating upon the aversion of the people to monarchy"—Hamilton writes:

> *He has been shown to us with the diadem sparkling on his brow and the imperial purple flowing in his train. He has been seated on a throne surrounded with minions and mistresses, giving audience to the envoys of foreign potentates in all the supercilious pomp of majesty.*[23]

If he had been really prescient, Hamilton might have added, *He has been shown surrounded by interns, providing him with oral sex.* This was not the president envisioned by the framers, but a "counterfeit resemblance."

Methodically disputing this portrait, Hamilton compares the relative powers of the president, the king of England, and the governor of New York, concluding it "would be difficult to determine" whether the president or the governor of New York possessed more power.[24] It was certainly clear that the man filling the office of the presidency would have nothing resembling the king of England's powers. In any event, James Wilson pointed out that the president would have no proprietary claim on the office, but could be impeached for acting "improperly."[25]

And not only for acting improperly himself, but for suffering his subordinates to act improperly. This is why there is only one president, rather than a board of presidents.

One of the "weightiest objections" to vesting all the executive power in a committee rather than a single man, Hamilton said, was that a single executive would not be able "to conceal faults and destroy responsibility." The legislature's power to impeach the man in charge of the entire executive branch would make him responsible for the misconduct of his subordinates:

> *It often becomes impossible, amidst mutual accusations, to determine on whom the blame or the punishment of a pernicious measures, ought really to fall. It is shifted from one to another with so much dexterity, and under such plausible appearances, that the public opinion is left in suspense about the real author.*[26]

Placing all the executive power in a single man would lodge all the responsibility in a single man. The president would not be able to hide behind the decisions of others. All the blame for any wrongdoing within the executive branch would necessarily fall on the president.

Consequently, and as it turns out wholly theoretically, the unitary president would thereby be inhibited from engaging in bad acts. He would not be able to pass off his bad acts as the work of his subordinates because he would be held accountable for their misdeeds. And if the president did not orchestrate their misconduct, but merely failed to root out corrupt subordinates, he would still be held accountable for their actions. The people would not have to search for the wrongdoer, but rather would have, in Hamilton's words, "the opportunity of discovering with facility and clearness the misconduct of the persons they trust, in order either to their removal from office or to their actual punishment in cases which admit of it."[27]

The principal architect of Article II of the Constitution, James Wilson, exulted that the president would not be able to "act improperly, and hide either his negligence or inattention," and thus would have no "screen." The Rodino Report provides a series of quotes from founding luminaries showing that one important purpose of a unitary executive was to more easily—as the report puts it—"fix the blame."

> *James Iredell, who played a leading role in the North Carolina rat-*
> *ifying convention and later became a justice of the Supreme Court,*
> *said that under the proposed Constitution, the President "is of a very*
> *different nature from a monarch. He is to be... personally responsible*
> *for any abuse of the great trust reposed in him.".... William Davie, who*
> *had been a delegate in Philadelphia, explained that the "predominant*
> *principle on which the Convention had provided for a single executive*
> *was "the more obvious responsibility of one person."*[28]

MASTERPIECE: THE CONSTITUTION

The framers' particular enthusiasm for impeaching presidents lacking the requisite virtue is reflected in the Constitution. For openers, the impeachment clauses in the Constitution specifically cite the president and vice president as subject to impeachment:

> *The President, Vice President, and all civil Officers of the United*
> *States, shall be removed from Office on Impeachment for, and Conviction*
> *of, Treason, Bribery, or other high Crimes and Misdemeanors.*[29]

Despite the fact that "all civil officers"—as distinct from military officers—are subject to impeachment, the president and vice president are the only impeachable officials specifically identified in the impeachment clause. Senators, congressmen, judges, and random government bureaucrats are all liable to being impeached. But the framers' simply assumed that presidents would be the focus of most impeachments—as they were during the debates at the Constitutional Convention on the impeachment clauses. There is even a special procedural twist for the impeachment of a president: the chief justice of the United States presides at the Senate trial.

Congressmen and senators are referred to in the impeachment clauses only indirectly as composing the bodies that are to conduct impeachment trials. While Article II—which defines the

powers and duties of the president—sets forth the characters subject to impeachment, Article I—creating the legislative branch—
mentions impeachment only to describe the procedures.

The procedure provided is this:

> *The House of Representatives… shall have the sole Power of*
> *Impeachment.*

*   *   *

> *The Senate shall have the sole Power to try all Impeachments.*
> *When sitting for that Purpose, they shall be on Oath or Affirmation.*
> *When the President of the United States is tried, the Chief Justice*
> *shall preside: And no Person shall be convicted without the*
> *Concurrence of two thirds of the Members present.*[30]

Though the language is of trials and convictions, a conviction of
impeachment by the Senate is completely different from a criminal
conviction in a court of law. Unlike the English practice, no criminal
penalty attaches to an impeachment conviction, and therefore no
double jeopardy problem arises. This the Constitution makes explicit:

> *Judgment in Cases of Impeachment shall not extend further than*
> *to removal from Office, and disqualification to hold and enjoy any*
> *Office of honor, Trust or Profit under the United States: but the Party*
> *convicted shall nevertheless be liable and subject to Indictment, Trial,*
> *Judgment and Punishment, according to Law.*[31]

The penalty for personal crimes is punishment—execution or
imprisonment; the penalty for committing high crimes and misdemeanors is simply removal from office, and may include disqualification from holding in the future any position of "honor"
or "Trust" with the United States.

Some have interpreted the statement that "the Party *convicted* shall nevertheless be liable and subject to Indictment, Trial, Judgment and Punishment," to mean an impeachment "conviction" *must* precede a criminal indictment. That obviously is absurd. Since every civil officer of the United States is subject to impeachment, that would mean that thousands upon thousands of civil officers would have carte blanche to commit rape, murder, mayhem—without the possibility of facing a criminal prosecution, until after the House had impeached and the Senate removed the officer from his federal job.

The reference to "the Party convicted" reflects the framers' natural assumption that Congress would impeach and remove long before a "civil officer" might become vulnerable to a criminal indictment. The threshold for being merely unfit for office is substantially below the threshold for a criminal indictment. As Hamilton put it, "Men, in public trust, will much oftener act in such a manner as to render them unworthy of being any longer trusted than in such a manner as to make them obnoxious to legal punishment."[32]

Just because removal from office ought logically to precede a criminal indictment doesn't mean the Constitution requires it. In fact, the only three impeachment convictions in the last half century were preceded by criminal trials.

Whatever the order, an impeachment trial in the Senate is no substitute for a judicial proceeding in a court of law: the Constitution expressly separates the two procedures. At the end of an impeachment there is no other punishment but removal from office and the possibility of being disenfranchised from holding any other federal office.

It didn't have to be this way: the English system, from which the framers borrowed, attached criminal penalties to impeachment convictions. The framers simply took for granted that impeachment and removal from office would come first but would not necessarily be the end of it. Consequently, to avoid a double jeopardy problem, the Constitution explicitly states that an impeachment conviction does not bar a subsequent criminal proceeding. The purposes and consequences of impeachment and criminal punishment are completely different. It is absurd to treat impeachment as a sort of dress rehearsal for the criminal prosecution, with all the same formalities and burdens of proof.

Impeachment is not a frivolous matter, but it will not lead to an execution or jail term, as it might have in fourteenth-century England. (Instead of Americans becoming more like the French, as Clinton's flacks constantly recommend, so we can start warmly embracing those who violate their oaths to God and man, how about being more like the English?) Impeachment is nothing more than a constitutional process for removing rogues from office. Criminal punishment, if the impeachable act also happens to be a criminal act, comes by a different route.

It is often said that the impeachment of a president poses a "constitutional crisis." One may call whatever one likes a "constitutional crisis," but it can at least be said that this particular crisis is not unconstitutional. The Constitution specifically provides for impeachment, mentioning it six times. When other constitutional procedures are employed—elections, no naturalized citizens running for president, presidential vetoes, Senate confirmations, revenue bills originating in the House—no one speaks of a "crisis." Impeachment is serious business, but so are elections. Both are part of constitutional government.

In fact, the framers assumed Congress would leap to the task of impeachment with a little more alacrity than has been the case over the past fifty years. From the founding to 1945, there were fifty-four "documented House impeachment investigations" of federal judges alone. Since 1945 there have been four. Two of the four were convicted felons.[33] There have been fourteen impeachment trials in the Senate in the history of the country. In the past fifty years there have been only three, and these were rather unavoidable. All three concerned federal judges who had been indicted and tried for criminal offenses. Two were sitting in jail—continuing to draw their federal salaries—before the House and Senate finally moseyed around to removing them from office.[34]

The framers may have hoped for virtuous men in public office, but they weren't necessarily counting on it. The Constitution is nothing if not contingency-oriented. There is a backup mechanism in the Constitution for every imaginable glitch (except a populace indifferent to self-government). Presidents and any other "civil officers" who were not fit for office could be—were expected to be—removed from office.

A president who is so lacking in virtue that a V-chip is required to discuss his conduct in office surely warrants the impeachment remedy—"removal from office, and disqualification to hold and enjoy any office of honor, trust or profit under the United States." A president who is merely incompetent or neglectful—as the president would have us believe from his own explanations for the endless series of corrupt acts, abuses, and obstructions that have occurred on his watch—deserves the same: removal from office.

And if the president also happens to have perjured himself or conspired to break the laws in order to cover up his personal vices, he is also "liable and subject to Indictment, Trial, Judgment and Punishment, according to Law."

HIGH CRIMES AND MISDEMEANORS THROUGHOUT HISTORY

Though an impeachable act need not be a criminal offense, it does need to be a particular kind of conduct, and not just an unpopular policy decision. As the Rodino Report notes, the phrase "high Crimes and Misdemeanors" was a "term of art" that must be construed "according to what the Framers meant when they adopted them"—an oddly originalist argument.[35] Perhaps more to the point, records from the Constitutional Convention make clear that the framers were familiar with the English practice of impeachment and the particular technical meaning of the phrase "high Crimes and Misdemeanors" in that context.

Congressman Gerald Ford's famous formulation—in this book, infamous—was that "an impeachable offense is whatever a majority of the House of Representatives considers it to be at a given moment in history; conviction results from whatever offense or offenses two-thirds of the other body considers to be sufficiently serious to require removal of the accused from office."[36]

It could also be said that a constitutional right is whatever a majority of the Supreme Court says it is. That doesn't mean the words in the Constitution have no meaning, or that justices of the Supreme Court aren't supposed to give effect to those meanings. All it means it that there is no appeal, even when the court or Congress is wrong—such as when the Senate concluded in 1787 that senators were exempt from impeachment.

The framers did not choose the phrase "high Crimes and Misdemeanors" because it was imprecise; it was not imprecise to them. There is a fixed meaning to the term "high Crimes and Misdemeanors," no more uncertain or malleable than the meaning of "cruel and unusual punishment," "free press," or "reasonable man." The last thing the framers intended was to leave the Senate free to declare any conduct it chose to be an impeachable offense. Madison, for example, opposed a proposed version of the impeachment clause with the *reductio ad absurdum* argument that it would "be equivalent to tenure during pleasure of the Senate."[37] (Whose tenure Madison was talking about did not have to be explained.)

When the framers chose the phrase "high Crimes and Misdemeanors," they were designating specific types of conduct that would constitute an impeachable offense.[38] Hamilton described impeachable conduct as "those offenses which proceed from the misconduct of public men, or, in other words, from the abuse or violation of some public trust."[39] (Consequently, one of the punishments for impeachment is disbarment from ever holding an office of "Trust" or "honor" with the United States.)

Citing Berger,[40] the Rodino Report recites the categories of impeachable conduct to "emerge from 400 years of English parliamentary experience with the phrase 'high Crimes and Misdemeanors'":

- corruption
- abuse of official power
- neglect of duty
- betrayal of trust
- encroachment on Parliament's prerogatives
- misapplication of funds

Both the drafters of the Rodino Report and impeachment scholar Raoul Berger provide examples from each category.

Corruption

Lord Treasurer Middlesex, was charged with "corruption, shadowed under pretext of a New Year's-Gift," and with "using the power of his place, and countenance of the king's service to wrest [from certain persons] a lease and estate of great value." There is also a charge of corruption in that Middlesex bought assets conveyed by the King for the benefit of creditors at much less than their value. (1624)[41]

Perhaps, as with the first lady's financial wizardry in cattle futures, the lord treasurer just read the *Wall Street Journal*, which allowed him to make shrewd business moves in the land-leasing and asset businesses.

Earl of Suffolk and Lord Treasurer Middlesex "were charged with obtaining property from the King for less than its value." (1388)

> *Buckingham Danby, the Earl of Arlington, Earl of Orford, Lord*
> *Somers, and Lord Halifax were charged with procuring large gifts*
> *from the King to themselves.*
>
> *Lord Chancellor Macclesfield was charged with the sale of public*
> *offices.*
>
> *Lord Halifax was accused of "opening a way to all manner of cor-*
> *rupt practices in the future management of the revenues" by appoint-*
> *ing his brother to an office which had been designed as a check on his*
> *own, the profits to be held in trust for Halifax.*[42]

Poor Lord Halifax engaged in a little cronyism in a single appointment of his brother to "an office which had been designed as a check on his own." Upon assuming the presidency, Clinton fired all the United States attorneys—more than ninety—to replace them with, as Hillary might say, "his people." No other president in memory has fired all top federal prosecutors like this.

Abuse of Official Power

At least one impeachment charge against the Earl of Oxford suggests, painfully, that we could have gotten rid of this guy after the 1993 tax bill.

> *Edward Earl of Oxford, was charged in 1701 with "violation of his*
> *duty and trust" in that, while a member of the King's privy council,*
> *he took advantage of the ready access he had to the King to secure*
> *various royal rents and revenues for his own use, thereby greatly*
> *diminishing the revenues of the crown and subjecting the people of*
> *England to "grievous taxes."*[43]

Many examples of "abuse of official power" involve bad appointments.

Oxford was also charged with procuring a naval commission for William Kidd "known to be a person of ill fame and reputation" and ordering him "to pursue the intended voyage, in which Kidd did commit diverse piracies… being thereto encouraged through hopes of being protected by the high station and interest of Oxford, in violation of the law of nations and the interruption and discouragement of the trade of England."[44]

Duke of Suffolk (1450), treason and high crimes and misdemeanors: procured offices for persons who were unfit and unworthy of them; delayed justice by stopping writs of appeal (private criminal Prosecutions) for the deaths of complainants' husbands.[45]

Duke of Buckingham (1626), misdemeanors, misprisions, offenses, and crimes: though young and inexperienced, procured offices for himself thereby blocking the deserving: …procured titles of honor to his mother, brothers, kindred.[46]

Oxford's offense was to use his office to get a government job for a crook. Though it is not clear how much Oxford knew of William Kidd's piracies, Oxford was charged with having allowed Kidd to believe Oxford would protect him by virtue of his "high station and interest."

The Duke of Suffolk "procured offices for persons who were unfit and unworthy of them," and was impeached for it. Maybe that's why we still don't know who procured Craig Livingstone's job for him.

A slew of other "abuse of power" cases concern highly placed government officials' interference with legal processes—which included discouraging plaintiff's counsel, reviling the grand jury, and invoking phony points of law.

Justice Berkley (1637), treason and other great misdemeanors: reviled and threatened the grand jury for presenting the removal of the communion table in All Saints Church; on the trial of an indict-ment, he "did much [to] discourage complainants' counsel" and "did overrule the cause for matter of law."[47]

Viscount Mordaunt (1660), high crimes and misdemeanors: pre-vented Tayleur from standing for election as a burgess to serve in Parliament; caused his illegal arrest and detention.[48]

Chief Justice Scroggs (1680), treason and high misdemeanors: discharged grand jury before they made their presentment, thereby obstructing the presentment of many Papists; arbitrarily granted general warrants in blank.[49]

Attorney General Yelverton (1621), high crimes and misde-meanors: committed persons for refusal to enter into bonds before he had authority so to require; commencing but not prosecuting suits.[50]

One wonders if Justice Berkley's attempts to "discourage com-plainants' counsel" included outing homosexuals on the counsel's staff. Berkley was also charged with improperly overruling a cause of action as a "matter of law." Clinton has repeatedly invoked invented principles of law for no other purpose than to delay legal pro-ceedings—as former presidential adviser Dick Morris has expressly admitted in the case of Clinton's "presidential immunity" claim.[51] The contrived nature of this claim was evidenced by the fact that it was rejected by all nine Supreme Court justices—including the two Clinton himself appointed. Later, Clinton would begin introducing privilege claims ranging from the absurd secret service officer "protec-tive services privilege" to the outrageous claim of "executive privilege" for communications about the president's interactions with a White House intern. This last claim was directly at odds with the president's media strategy: the president's defenders themselves all insisted his relationship with the intern was a purely personal affair, making it completely off-limits to executive privilege claims.

Neglect of Duty

*Duke of Buckingham (1626), misdemeanors, misprisions, offenses,
and crimes: ...neglected as great admiral to safeguard the seas....*[52]

*Peter Pett, Commissioner of the Navy (1688), high crimes and
misdemeanors: negligent preparation for the Dutch invasion; loss of
a ship through neglect to bring it to mooring.*[53]

Buckingham and Pett were charged with safeguarding the seas;
the president is charged with safeguarding the executive branch.
Yet the president has habitually deflected charges of corruption or
abuse of power by eagerly claiming the mantle of negligence and
incompetence. That was the White House's defense of, for example, Lippo operative John Huang's access to classified material at
Clinton's Commerce Department; the disappearance of subpoenaed documents, such as the first lady's billing records; the Travel
Office firings; the FBI investigation of Billy Dale; the nine hundred FBI files being illegally reviewed by Craig Livingstone; the
obstruction of the FBI's investigation of Vince Foster's office; the
felonious solicitation or receipt of campaign donations by Vice
President Al Gore[54] and the first lady's chief of staff, Maggie
Williams; the presidential audience accorded "hustler" Johnny
Chung. And so on, and on, and on.

The one common thread running through all these corrupt
practices and abuses has been that Clinton was president. But forget what that might mean. The very least President Clinton can be
accused of is neglect of duty—an impeachable offense. And this is
the very claim the president invariably raises as his *excuse.*

"Mistakes were made" didn't suffice to duck responsibility in
the seventeenth century.

Betrayal of Trust

*Buckingham put valuable ships within the grasp of the French, and
when Orford weakened the navy while invasion threatened. (1626)*[55]

After a one-year investigation into the transfer of technology to Red China by two American companies, the Pentagon concluded: "United States national security has been harmed." But as the Justice Department was impaneling a grand jury, President Clinton gave the companies "a get-out-of-jail-free card." They were big Clinton campaign contributors.

Why does Red China now operate the Long Beach Naval Facility?

Encroachment on or Contempt of Parliament's Prerogatives

Sir Richard Gurney, lord mayor of London (1642), high crimes and misdemeanors: thwarted Parliament's order to store arms and ammunition in storehouses.[56]

Chief Justice North (1680), high crimes and misdemeanors: assisted the Attorney General in drawing a proclamation to suppress petitions to the King to call a Parliament.[57]

Justice Berkley and other Justices were impeached for uttering opinions that Charles I could obtain "Ship Money Taxes" without resort to Parliament. (1637)[58]

One of the president's most risible acts of lawlessness occurred on September 18, 1996, when he declared 1.7 million acres of state and federal lands in southern Utah a "National Monument." Only Congress can create national wilderness areas or national parks. Congress was not about to declare this land a national wilderness: in addition to being remote, barren, and ugly, the area contained the Kaiparowits coal field, one of the largest untapped resources of high-Btu clean coal in North America.

But the president's maneuver cut Congress out of the process by declaring the land a national "monument" under the Antiquities Act of 1906, which allows the president to so designate "objects of historic and scientific interest." Some objects declared monuments under this act have been large—the Grand Tetons and the Grand Canyon, for example. But they have also been coherent natural objects... the Grand Tetons and the Grand Canyon, for example. Yet this was merely undistinguished land mass. It was an encroachment on Congress's prerogatives to designate wilderness areas.

Various Utah counties and administrative agencies promptly sued the president for this "mother of all land grabs," as Senator Orrin Hatch (R-UT) called it. According to some in the Utah delegation, Clinton's interest in blocking the use of clean coal mines in southern Utah may be explained by the alternative source for high-grade coal: Indonesian coal mines, owned by Clinton's friends, the Lippo Group.[59]

Misapplication of Funds

Chancellor Michael de la Pole, Earl of Suffolk (1386), high crimes and misdemeanors: applied appropriated funds to purposes other than those specified.[60]

Sir Edward Seymour (1680), high crimes and misdemeanors: applied appropriated funds to public purposes other than those specified.[61]

One of the least noticed facets of the cover-up of Vince Foster's office after his suicide is that he had been performing personal legal work for the Clintons. Government lawyers are not supposed to be running their private legal practices out of the Department of Justice or the White House. Forget whatever corrupt dealings Foster may have been working on in his White House office—Bernard Nussbaum squirreled those away, and, as one senator put it, "the American people will never know really what was in there." Foster was not given a White House office and a government salary so he could perform personal legal work for the Clintons.

President Clinton isn't even embarrassed about using government staff for his multifarious legal problems: his administration has boldly raised the attorney–client privilege to block testimony about any communications between the Clintons and their taxpayer-supported White House lawyers. The communications have absolutely nothing whatsoever to do with official White House business. In order to obstruct justice, Clinton casually cites his administration's misapplication of government funds.

AMERICAN RIPPLE: NO KING

Though the framers were adopting a "term of art" when they designated "high Crimes and Misdemeanors" as impeachable offenses, they were inserting it in a Constitution "established by the people and unalterable by the government."[62] Impeachable offenses would clearly have new color and tone under a constitutional republic.

For openers, there was no king; the Constitution was "paramount."[63] In the English system anyone could be impeached, save members of the royal family. By contrast, impeachment American-style was pointedly directed toward impeaching the very nonroyal president—though all other civil officers remain impeachable, as well. The president could be impeached, as Madison said, merely for "neglect[ing] to superintend" his subordinates, thus allowing them to perpetrate with impunity their own impeachable offenses.[64] And, of course, the Constitution's impeachment power was praised at the state ratifying conventions for applying to a president who himself "misbehaves"[65] or "behave[s] amiss."[66]

The other difference is that conviction for high crimes and misdemeanors in the English system might be consummated with a hanging or, at the very least, a prison sentence. This is striking since an impeachable offense was never thought to require criminal conduct, even in Great Britain. But it was used as a weapon against great abuses of power by the king's ministers—or the "tools of royal oppression." The idea was to impeach and hang the king's ministers before they hanged the impeaching officers.[67]

In American impeachments, the punishment can be only

removal from office and possibly a prohibition on holding any other office of public trust with the United States. Quite obviously, lesser punishments presuppose lesser abuses of power.

Moreover, such punishments also suggest a particular kind of offense: high crimes and misdemeanors in the American system were intended to address "the misconduct of public men." As Hamilton noted, impeachable offenses are those that violate "some public trust." It is simply "the first step in a remedial process."[68] In the words of the Rodino Report, "The purpose of impeachment is not personal punishment; its function is primarily to maintain constitutional government."[69]

Section 3 of the Rodino Report, titled "Grounds For Impeachment," cites numerous statements from the Constitutional Convention, the state ratifying conventions, and constitutional scholars describing impeachable offenses under the new Constitution:

> [T]hose who behave amiss, or betray their public trust.
> —Charles Cotesworth Pinckney of South Carolina[70]

> The President may be impeached if he "misbehaves."
> —Edmund Randolph of Virginia[71]

> The President using his pardoning power to "pardon crimes which were advised by himself."
> —George Mason of Virginia

> If the President were to "stop inquiry and prevent detection" before indictment or conviction.[72]

> [P]olitical offenses, growing out of personal misconduct...
> —Justice Joseph Story, Commentaries on the Constitution[73]

As the Rodino Report notes, "From the comments of the framers and their contemporaries, the remarks of delegates to the state ratifying conventions, and the removal power debate in the First Congress, it is apparent that the scope of impeachment was not viewed narrowly." Nor, in practice, have Americans ever viewed the impeachment remedy narrowly. The seven federal impeachment convictions in the nation's history were for:

- Drunkenness and Senility (Judge John Pickering, U.S. District Judge for the District of New Hampshire—1803–1804);
- Incitement to Revolt and Rebellion Against the Nation (Judge West W. Humphreys, U.S. District Court Judge for the District of Tennessee—1862);
- Bribery (Judge Robert W. Archibald, Circuit Judge, U.S. Court of Appeals for the Third Circuit—1912–1913);
- Kickbacks and Tax Evasion (Judge Halstead Ritter, U.S. District Court Judge for the Southern District of Florida—1936);
- Tax Evasion (Judge Harry E. Claiborne, U.S. District Judge for the District of Nevada—1986);
- Conspiracy to Solicit a Bribe (Judge Alcee Hastings, U.S. District Judge for the Southern District of Florida—1988–1989);
- False Statements to a Grand Jury (Judge Walter L. Nixon, Jr., U.S. District Judge for the Southern District of Mississippi—1988–1989).[74]

Impeachment "of dreary little judges for squalid misconduct,"[75] including purely personal misconduct, was consistent with the purpose of impeachment in a self-governing republic.

THE IMPEACHMENT OF PRESIDENT JOHNSON: NOT POLICY

The 1868 impeachment of President Andrew Johnson, and his hairs-breadth escape from removal by the Senate, illustrates the difficulty of meeting the requirement of a two-thirds Senate vote, even during an era when Congress would just as soon impeach the president as override his veto. Congress was whipped up over President Johnson's opposition to its Radical Reconstruction designs on the South after the Civil War.[76]

Without going into great detail about the policy and constitutional disputes between Congress and President Johnson, both had plausible arguments.[77] Immediately after the Civil War, Congress refused to recognize the congressional delegations sent by the eleven southern states. With the abolition of slavery, the size of congressional delegations was no longer limited by the three-fifths rule for slaves. Obviously, but ironically, this was a great boon to the southern delegations. The North did not relish the prospect of losing in the legislature what it had just won on the battlefield. Still, Johnson believed Congress was acting unconstitutionally, that states had the right to choose their own delegations to Congress. A war had just been fought to keep the southern states from seceding, and now Congress was essentially telling southerners they couldn't quit, they were being fired.

Johnson communicated his view by refusing to recognize the laws enacted by this Northern-only Congress. Johnson vetoed a series of Reconstruction bills and refused to enforce the military occupation of the Southern states. The final straw came when he fired Secretary of War Edwin Stanton, who was overseeing the military reconstruction in the South. Anticipating just this action, Congress had recently enacted the Tenure of Office Act of March 2, 1867. The Tenure Act required Senate approval for Stanton's removal. Impeachment proceedings were begun immediately for

Johnson's refusal to obey the Tenure Act, a law he correctly perceived to be unconstitutional.

Articles of Impeachment were enacted by the House on March 3, 1868; they were sent to the Senate on March 5; and the trial began March 30. A request by the defense for more time before beginning the trial was refused. And when the defense counsel took ill during the proceedings and requested an adjournment for a day or two, the prosecutor's response to the request, which typically would be "honored without demur,"[78] was Kennedyesque demagoguery, with shades of the "Robert Bork's America" speech.[79] Congressman Benjamin Butler said: "[W]hile we are waiting for the attorney general to get well… numbers of our fellow citizens are being murdered day by day. There is not a man here who does not know that the moment justice is done on this great criminal [President Johnson] these murders will cease."[80]

Feeling against Johnson was bitter. Indeed, Johnson had failed so stupendously to ingratiate himself with Congress[81] that one of the managers of the prosecution called for abolishing the presidency altogether if the president was so uppity that he refused to follow an unconstitutional law.[82] Another House manager proposed charging Johnson as an accessory to Lincoln's murder.[83]

More than a century later all indications are that the president has hit up a White House intern for oral sex, sexually assaulted a White House volunteer, obstructed justice, suborned perjury, and perjured himself, among many other infractions. The leader of the Senate—and the opposition party—quickly stepped to the plate… to criticize the prosecutor. They don't make opposition parties like they used to.

In the case of Johnson's impeachment, what the spunky 1868 Congress had in the way of enthusiasm, it lacked in constitutional authority. The mistake Congress made with respect to impeachment was to think mere policy disagreements sufficed for an impeachment. A policy disagreement is an example of what impeachment was *not* intended to address. In the words of constitutional scholar Raoul Berger, "A president... is not to be removed merely for differing with Congress."[84] Each branch of government has its arsenal of powers by which it may frustrate the will of another.

As Supreme Court Justice Louis Brandeis explained in his duly famous description of the Constitution's distribution of powers:

> *The doctrine of the separation of powers was adopted by the convention of 1787 not to promote efficiency but to preclude the exercise of arbitrary power. The purpose was not to avoid friction, but, by means of the inevitable friction incident to the distribution of the governmental powers among three departments, to save the people from autocracy.*[85]

Opposing Congress's will, within his constitutionally delegated powers, was Johnson's offense, and for that he was impeached. Mercifully, the two-thirds vote requirement was stiff enough to save Johnson—by a single vote—from conviction and removal by the Senate. Today, it seems, one would need a five-person vote requirement in the "Republican Senate," to say nothing of the constitution's two-thirds vote requirement, to remove any president for even enormous, impeachable crimes.

THE NEAR IMPEACHMENT
OF PRESIDENT NIXON

Whatever one thinks of the "evolving Constitution," the framers' abstract statements about what could get a president impeached are not as powerful as what almost got a president impeached, and did lead to a president's resignation, just a couple of decades ago. Watergate is recent precedent. The articles of impeachment against President Nixon constitute compelling evidence of the sort of conduct that constitutes a "high Crime and Misdemeanor."

Impeachment proceedings against President Nixon were set in

motion not by the underlying crime committed by persons known to the president but by Nixon's resistance to the investigation. Nixon refused to produce tapes of his conversations with top advisers, claiming executive privilege.[86] He offered a series of compromises including providing the grand jury with summaries of "private presidential papers and meetings," to be authenticated by a Democratic senator—albeit a "nearly deaf" Democratic senator.[87] Special Prosecutor Archibald Cox refused to entertain these offers, believing he was entitled to every man's evidence, including the president's.

The special prosecutor served at the pleasure of the president, so on Saturday, October 20, 1973, the president ordered him fired, and the investigation returned to the "career professionals" at the Department of Justice. But Attorney General Elliot Richardson immediately resigned rather than follow the president's order; Nixon then called on Deputy Attorney General William Ruckelshaus, who likewise refused to fire Cox and resigned instead.

That was it. The following Tuesday impeachment resolutions in the House were "raining down."[88] Though the polls showed substantial majorities of Americans opposed removing the president through impeachment,[89] *that* Congress was not cowed by the polls, and formal impeachment hearings were begun in the House. They don't even make opposition parties like they used to twenty-five years ago.

President Richard Nixon became the second president to face impeachment hearings in more than one hundred years. Almost a year later—after the Supreme Court had, on July 24, 1974, rejected Nixon's executive privilege claim for all presidential communications—he became the first president to resign.

Nixon had the legal right to fire Cox, who, unlike today's independent counsels, was an employee of the executive branch. This, incidentally, is what inspired the creation of the "independent counsel" law. It created a procedure outside normal constitutional chains of command to appoint a prosecutor to investigate potential crimes by the executive branch, but wholly independent of executive branch authority.[90] An independent counsel can be removed only by the personal action of the attorney general (except in the case of impeachment) for good cause, physical or mental disability (except as forbidden by the Americans with Disabilities Act and the Rehabilitation Act), or any other condition that substantially impairs the performance of the independent counsel's duties. The attorney general serves at the president's pleasure.[91]

Cox was being obstinately inflexible in refusing to entertain any compromise on the tapes when actual national security issues were at stake. It was not just the Vietnam War and violent anti-war protests at home. In the midst of Cox's demand for tapes of Nixon's conversations with his top advisers—privileged communications, as Nixon saw it—an all-new world crisis erupted. On October 6, 1973, Egypt and Syria bombed Israel in a sneak attack. Nixon ordered airlifts to Israel. The Soviet Union did the same for Egypt and Syria. The Yom Kippur War had morphed into a superpower crisis overnight. Nixon accelerated the airlifts to Israel,[92] dispatched Secretary of State Henry Kissinger to negotiate with Soviet leader Leonid Brezhnev—and then watched Cox on television refusing to accept the White House's proposed compromise on the tapes, taunting Nixon to fire him. Back then, getting back to the country's business meant "nuclear combat, toe to toe with the Russkies,"[93] not naming the First Dog.

Though the president was wholly within his rights firing Cox, and there were national security reasons for Nixon to resist Cox's request for tapes, it just didn't look good for the president to fire even an irritatingly inflexible special prosecutor during a superpower crisis.

Nixon's attorney general and deputy attorney general resigned rather than fire Cox themselves only because the Senate resolution calling for appointment of a prosecutor independent of the Justice Department had specified that the attorney general "will not countermand, nor interfere with the special prosecutor's decisions."[94] Accordingly, Elliot Richardson and William Ruckelshaus had pledged noninterference.[95] White House Press Secretary Ron Ziegler explained Cox's discharge that evening at 8:24 PM, saying that Cox had "pressed for a confrontation at a time of serious world crisis."[96]

Congress saw it differently. Firing Cox because he had refused to relent in his demand for tapes of Nixon's Oval Office meetings smacked of obstruction of justice. There was no evidence that Nixon had broken any law. Nixon may have had the Constitution—even national security—on his side, but firing his own investigator didn't have a good-government ring to it. When Nixon ordered the office of the special counsel guarded by an FBI agent to prevent files from being removed, the Nazi comparisons began to fly. Cox's press spokesman, James Doyle, announced to the press that he was "going home to read about the Reichstag fire." The *Times* of London reported a "whiff of the Gestapo" in America's capital city.

In the end, instead of being rid of an overzealous prosecutor, Nixon had forced his own defeat on the tapes issue.

The Cox firing came in the wake of Vice President Spiro Agnew's resignation, for reasons unrelated to Nixon or the Watergate break-in. Until Vice President–designate Gerald Ford was confirmed, the man next in line to be president was Speaker of the House Carl Albert, a Democrat. The Middle East crisis was still simmering, and there was no vice president.

There was no action on Ford's nomination, however, when the House reconvened on Tuesday after the so-called "Saturday Night Massacre." Instead, House business was focused on consideration of the numerous impeachment resolutions. House Republicans refused to oppose impeachment unless Nixon turned over the tapes. That day, Nixon agreed to turn the tapes over to the grand jury.

In dramatic contradistinction to Clinton, Nixon had raised a plausible and novel constitutional objection to releasing the tapes: that tape-recorded conversations between the chief executive and his high-level aides were privileged communications. There was no clear precedent—as there is now—regarding Nixon's claim of executive privilege. The Supreme Court would have to decide the issue. But the Supreme Court had not yet ruled on Nixon's executive privilege claim when the House and Senate impeachment committees got under way. The court would *not* rule on it for another nine months.

Nixon's legal argument was not frivolous. The court did, after all, accept in principle his argument that a privilege presumptively attaches to high-level presidential communications. The court rejected only the idea that the privilege was absolute and applied to *all* high-level presidential communications.

Clinton's assertion of executive privilege twenty-five years later to cover high-level communications about the president's relationship with a White House intern, coming *after* the Supreme Court's holding in *Nixon* v. *United States*, is completely frivolous and outrageous. No one has resigned from this administration. The Republican leader of the Senate tried to weasel out of impeachment hearings by proposing a completely meaningless "censure" of the president.[97] They really don't make opposition parties like they used to.

Two days after Nixon relented on the tapes issue—without waiting for the Supreme Court to rule—he took the Watergate investigation away from the Justice Department and returned it to a reconvened office of the special counsel, this time headed by Leon Jaworski.

Nixon's public resistance to turning over the tapes, even before the court had ruled on his privilege claim, had set the impeachment hearings in motion. The hearings would be conducted by Congressman Peter Rodino, chairman of the House Judiciary Committee, with the able assistance of Hillary Rodham and Bernie Nussbaum.

Invoking a single, somewhat legitimate privilege once, telling one lie to the public, allowing one part of an investigation to be delayed for two weeks—this was how Nixon engaged in "conduct that might adversely affect the system of government" and committed "offenses that subverted the system of government."

THE OKIE FROM MUSKOGEE
Pattern of Corruption

According to recent precedent, a president is impeachable for the misconduct of his subordinates. The House Judiciary Committee approved three articles of impeachment against President Nixon: obstruction of justice, abuse of presidential power, and unconstitutional defiance of House subpoenas. The articles of impeachment are accusations only, but even as accusations they repeatedly rely on allegations against Nixon's employees or "agents."

Article I, charging Nixon with obstruction of justice, claims he "engaged personally and through his close subordinates and agents in a course of conduct of plan designed to delay, impede, and obstruct the investigation [of a third-rate burglary committed by private citizens without Nixon's knowledge, much less approval]."

Article II, charging Nixon with abuse of presidential power, listed as one of Nixon's impeachable acts that he had "failed to take care that the laws were faithfully executed *by failing to act* when he knew or *had reason to know that his close subordinates* endeavoured to impede and frustrate lawful inquiries by duly constituted executive, judicial and legislative entities" (emphasis added).

Apart from Nixon's lie to the public, which was the very first impeachable offense listed in Article I, the only impeachable act committed directly by Nixon himself was invoking "executive privilege." (This was back when presidents admitted that they were president, and it was they who were invoking executive privilege.) While Nixon's privilege claim was being duly appealed through the courts, the House initiated impeachment proceedings against him because he had invoked a privilege rather than giving the materials directly to Congress.

All other charges and accusations against Nixon rely on the actions of Nixon's subordinates, which he allegedly "condoned," "acquiesc[ed] in," or "fail[ed] to act [to prevent]." Conveniently, the Rodino Report, written "to assist the Committee in working toward [a] resolution" of Nixon's impeachment, enthusiastically endorsed the notion that the president is to be made responsible for the actions of his subordinates, through impeachment. "[T]he impeachability of the President was considered to be an important element of his responsibility," so that, in Hamilton's words, "there should be a single object for the jealousy and watchfulness of the people."[98]

On calm reflection, Rodham and Nussbaum were probably overreaching when they uncritically quoted James Wilson's statement that a president could be impeached for "his negligence or inattention" to the actions of subordinates. When George Washington was president he had four cabinet members, and the executive branch, practically speaking, consisted of a few dozen men under his direction and control. Today, President Clinton has fourteen cabinet members, more than a thousand White House employees, and thousands of executive branch employees under his control.

But they were eager to "fix the blame," and the odds were, tying Nixon to the actions of his subordinates would be the only way to tie him to an impeachable offense. After all, even the most paranoid Nixon haters never seriously contemplated discovering evidence that Nixon had been involved in the Watergate break-in. As the abundant use of "expletive deleted" demonstrated, Nixon was not guarded in his Oval Office taped statements. He can be heard on the tapes saying that the main thing that embarrassed him about the break-in was that "it was so dumb—tying it to us is an insult to our intelligence." But even before the tapes came out, it didn't make any sense.[99]

The evident hope was that some of the president's "men" *had* been so dumb, and that Nixon would try to protect them. Consequently, the Rodino Report provides a bounty of historical support for the proposition that the president can be impeached for the misconduct of his subordinates.[100]

Stop the Madness—A Rational Standard for the President's Accountability

Still, it seems rather severe to suggest, as the Rodino Report does, that a bad act by a single one of these subordinates, if not remedied on account of mere "negligence" or "inattention," should merit impeachment of the president. With thousands of executive branch employees, the president cannot reasonably be held responsible for giving positions to a few persons who may later turn out to be "unfit and unworthy" of the job (as the Duke of Suffolk was in 1450).

On the other hand, the president should not be able to hire an endless stream of crooks and hoodlums to do his bidding, and then insist that all he knows about their misbehavior—after they get caught by some congressional or media watchdog—is what he reads in the papers. Surely the president is responsible for any bad acts that he has himself encouraged implicitly or explicitly.

As James Madison noted:

> If the President be connected, in any suspicious manner with any per-son, and there be grounds to believe he will shelter him, the House of Representatives can impeach him; they can remove him if found guilty.[101]

Nobody's Fault But the President's

There are several "grounds" on which to believe a president will "shelter" his misbehaving subordinates. Clinton illustrates at least four of them. First, the misconduct in Bill Clinton's administration almost always benefits Bill Clinton. Second, the president has never routed out or punished malfeasance in his administration on his own. Indeed, the president invariably acts like he is responsible—but not in the sense of being accountable, only in the sense of being guilty. Third, the president's accomplices generally end up with promotions, attractive job offers, or lucrative Lippo consulting fees. Moreover, the president's criminal accomplices are somehow left with the impression that President Clinton is dangling a presidential pardon before them.

Finally, though, the sheer number of mishaps the Clinton administration has stumbled into starts to make it look like it's not an accident. This is not a subjective point. A president's impeachability is not a function of the number of indignant Anthony Lewis columns prattling about an Imperial Presidency. But no one—maybe Anthony Lewis, not Clinton anyway—disputes the wrongdoing in the Clinton administration. The president, for example, does not dispute that Craig Livingstone's collection of private FBI files on Republicans was wrong. Nor does the president dispute that William Kennedy's demand for an FBI investigation of the Travel Office was an abuse of power. POTUS admits that he should not have met with "hustler" Johnny Chung and the DNC should not have been eagerly accepting illegal foreign contributions.

Whatever the scandal, Clinton's defense is the same: POTUS is not responsible. It was a bureaucratic snafu, and he knows only what he reads in the papers.[102] But he is responsible—it's *his* administration. And the fact that it is his administration is the one recurring factor in the never-ending series of bureaucratic snafus.

If any one of the slew of Clinton administration lies, abuses of power, corruption, and obstructions of justice were dropped into an otherwise totally clean and honest administration, the president might plausibly be given a pass. Once. It would at least be a nonfrivolous debate. Giving Clinton a pass on every scandal in his administration—from the government persecution of Billy Dale to the sale of technology to Red China—is frivolous. And this is to say nothing of the president's own perjuries and obstructions of justice exposed since 1997.

You Win Again

Noticeably, much of the misconduct in the Clinton administration keeps benefiting one person: Bill Clinton. And that is Bill Clinton, personally—or "the current occupant of that office," as the Supreme Court referred to him in *Clinton* v. *Jones.*

Clinton's first White House counsel, for example, resigned, if not in disgrace then at least under a cloud, for having obstructed the FBI's attempted investigation of Vince Foster's office. Why would the counsel, heretofore respected lawyer Bernard Nussbaum, have had any interest in obstructing an investigation of Foster's office? Foster, it seems, had been doing personal legal work for the Clintons. It was their tax records and their Whitewater documents that Nussbaum would not allow the FBI to see. Neither before nor after Nussbaum's tenure at the White House has he found himself accused of improper conduct. Clinton has.

Another victim of Clinton's reverse Pygmalion effect was Mr. Clean, Bruce Babbitt, whom Clinton made secretary of the Interior. Was President Clinton, once again, the innocent victim of a corrupt subordinate? The secretary of the Interior apparently sold government policy for large donations to the DNC. It is difficult to believe Secretary Babbitt was freelancing in his abuse of power and, completely unbeknownst to the president, selling government policy for his own ends. Especially since *his* ends weren't served. Babbitt wasn't running for any office. A more credible scenario is that the sale of casino rights was part of Clinton's acknowledged frenzy for campaign dollars. Padding DNC coffers advantaged Clinton, not Babbitt.

Whose enemies were being audited by the IRS? Against whom might an impoverished Webb Hubbell have testified? Whose campaign coffers swelled with the sale of the Lincoln Bedroom, plots at Arlington cemetery, and White House coffees? To whose campaign had Loral and Hughes contributed?

Earning Presidential Kneepads:
Promotions and Pardons

A president is responsible for the behavior of his subordinates if he allows them to believe he will protect them if they are caught engaging in improper conduct. The Earl of Oxford was held responsible for William Kidd's piracies, on the theory that Kidd had been emboldened "through hopes of being protected by the high station and interest of" Oxford, since Oxford had appointed him. The point was not that Oxford had actually solicited Kidd's piracies or had been videotaped offering Kidd a pardon if he were to go out and engage in piracies. Oxford had simply done nothing to dash Kidd's hopes that he would be protected by Oxford's good station.

This is similar to the accusation often leveled at President Nixon—that he had set a tone that encouraged others in his administration to engage in misconduct. And that was when misconduct consisted of White House staff keeping "enemies lists" that the president never ordered or saw, not White House staff using secret FBI files to compile dossiers on the president's perceived enemies.

If the worst that could be said of Clinton was that he had managed to set a *tone* that permitted others in his administration to engage in misconduct, he could start popping champagne corks. Clinton is constantly getting caught hinting at pardons and granting promotions to potential witnesses against him.

Kathleen Willey was provided a series of positions with the government for which she was not obviously qualified as long as she stayed quiet about the president's grope. Monica Lewinsky was given jobs both in and out of the government for her silence. Webb Hubbell made more money than he ever had earned or stolen in a comparable period in his life for keeping his mouth shut about the president. The United States attorney for the District of Columbia, who did not indict the vice president after Gore admitted on national television to committing all elements of a federal felony, was soon promoted. The government flunky at the Defense Department who illegally released information from Linda Tripp's personnel file was given a promotion weeks later. (This despite Clinton's promise during the 1992 campaign that "[i]f I catch anybody [going through State Department personnel files] I will fire them the next day. You won't have to have an inquiry or rigmarole or anything else.")[103]

Six months after U.N. Ambassador Bill Richardson's role as faithful mule to the president was exposed in the Monica Lewinsky scandal, Clinton chose Richardson to serve as secretary of Energy (a field of endeavor about which he probably knows even less than he did about diplomacy). To go from the cesspool of the U.N. to the Energy Department was considered a step up, if only because Richardson was then in a position to shake down some really big fat cats. In all of the press reports of Richardson's promotion there was barely a mention of Richardson's involvement in the Lewinsky affair. No one paused to consider: *Hmmm, six months ago Richardson was offering Monica a taxpayer-funded job in the Clinton administration, now he's being promoted to a much more important cabinet job. I wonder if.... But no.*

What kind of tone might this set?

Webb Hubbell's attorney was taped on the prison phone telling Hubbell, "[T]here is some chance that the day after Election Day they will make a move that moots everything. And I don't want to discourage it." The attorney, John W. Nields, later insisted the "move" to which he had referred had "absolutely nothing to do with a pardon." Instead, he sportingly averred he was raising the possibility of "immunity granted by the independent counsel, which I was hopeful we would get right after the election, and we did."[104] This is a laughable claim since (1) whether Hubbell would be given immunity was entirely in his own hands, and (2) the grant of immunity Hubbell did get could hardly be described as "moot[ing] everything"—it sent Hubbell to prison for eighteen months.

James McDougal said it was the expectation of a presidential pardon that persuaded his wife, Susan McDougal, to refuse to answer the grand jury's question, "Did Bill Clinton lie at your trial?" Mr. McDougal explained: "The turning point is that I feel that he led Susan to believe she would be pardoned." Because she believed that, he pointed out, "She is now in jail. She is in jail because she wouldn't answer a question before the grand jury, not for anything we were convicted of."[105]

Perhaps some will say James McDougal isn't credible on this point. And Hubbell's lawyer may have been dreaming. But the standard the framers gave was precisely whether crooks had reason to believe that the president would protect them, not whether the president actually intended to protect them. Madison said a president could be impeached if there were "grounds to believe he will shelter" any person. Somehow Clinton's criminal associates have fallen under the impression that he will pardon them, and President Clinton has done nothing to dispel that impression.

During the first presidential debate in the 1996 campaign, Senator Bob Dole asked President Clinton to rule out granting pardons to his felonious friends in a second term. Clinton refused to do so, saying only that he would "adhere to the law." The "law" is, of course, that, except in the case of an impeachment, the president has absolute authority to pardon anyone but himself.[106]

Protecting the Guilty

It has to be said, though, that the *Saturday Night Live* skit of the Clinton character introducing his secretary of state as "former Arkansas State Trooper Warren Christopher" was somewhat unfair to Clinton. Some scandals would become just too public and notorious to leave the president much room to give the miscreant a promotion. But there is little reason to suppose Craig Livingstone would not now be Clinton's White House chief of staff if not for the publicity accorded his romp through the FBI files.

Whether or not the president's disreputable subordinates can be confident of receiving a promotion under Clinton, they definitely can be confident that neither President Clinton nor any member of his administration will ever uncover the wrongdoing or mete out any punishment. Clinton emboldens the knaves in his administration by consistently allowing misconduct to go undetected, unaccounted for, and unpunished. Indeed, there is no evidence that the Clinton administration has taken appropriate steps to prevent or to discover malfeasance in its ranks. Rather, the bad acts of Clinton's employees have almost invariably been brought to light by congressional investigators, the independent prosecutor, or the media.

This includes—and this is just a brief sampling—the president's White House counsel obstructing the FBI's attempted search of Vince Foster's office; his top staffers arranging for the payment of more than half a million dollars in "consulting fees" to Webb Hubbell, a potential witness against the president; his employees illegally collecting and perusing nine hundred sensitive FBI files; his vice president making felonious fund-raising calls from the White House; his IRS director auditing the president's two leading private citizen "enemies"; and the talking points intended to tamper with a witness in a case against the president personally, passed to the witness by a former employee of the president (a.k.a. "that woman").

Moreover, once a White House scandal is exposed, the Clinton administration has never quickly and thoroughly investigated the wrongdoing, produced the purported miscreant, and taken adequate remedial measures. The Clinton administration moves with lightning speed only when producing things like the affectionate letters to the president from the groped Kathleen Willey.

Instead, when caught red-handed, the White House has consistently reacted by lying, withholding documents, and denouncing the whistleblowers. For the obstruction of justice charges surrounding the Lewinsky matter, the White House has truly gone to the mattresses. One wonders if the Clintons may have actually been innocent in some of the scandals, but just assumed the worst of themselves and acted guilty.

Consider the files scandal. If those files were *not* being gathered with the consent of the president, he hasn't done much to erase that impression. Two employees of the Clinton White House were engaging in egregious violations of the privacy rights of American citizens by husbanding and reviewing extremely sensitive FBI background files. It cannot be disputed that these two—Craig Livingstone and Anthony Marceca—were "unfit and unworthy" of the job. Placing these goons in those positions shows a fundamental lack of seriousness about the background process, which is supposed to be a key component in determining qualifications of employees.

Yet no one has taken responsibility for even giving these two their jobs—apart from the question-begging admission that Livingstone hired Marceca. The White House acts as if no one higher than the former bar bouncer can be held accountable. This cannot help but suggest that Livingstone's benefactor was the president (or the first lady). At the very least, whoever did hire Livingstone is being "protected by the high station and interest of" the president.

Moreover, consider what the White House did not do. There was no horrified reaction to the news that nine hundred FBI files had been improperly obtained. The Clinton administration never really ginned up any interest in figuring out how this outrageous abuse could have occurred. This brings the irresponsibility directly back to the president. (Recall that when President Bush discovered that someone had been looking through Clinton's passport file, the guilty party was immediately fired without further ado.)

The Clinton administration's handling of the FBI files scandal is surely a paradigm of when a president could be impeached for a single instance of misconduct by his subordinates. Madison remarked during the First Session of the First Congress that since the president would have absolute authority to fire any employee of the executive branch, his subordinates' misconduct would "subject him to impeachment himself, if he suffers them to perpetrate with impunity high crimes or misdemeanors against the United States, or neglects to superintend their conduct, so as to check their excesses."[107]

President Clinton's culpability for the unfit and unworthy Livingstone and Marceca results from the unavoidable facts that (1) the president did not put in place adequate systems to detect or correct their wrongdoing, and (2) he is still, now—as you read this—protecting the person who was responsible for hiring and supervising Livingstone and Marceca.

If nothing else, the threat of impeachment ought to be able, at least, to prod the president into telling the public who was responsible for hiring Livingstone and for supervising his activities. The threat of impeachment ought to be able to force the president—the executive in charge of the executive branch—to produce the culprits responsible for all corrupt practices and abuses of power. Whose idea was it to fire the Travel Office employees and then use the FBI to charge Billy Dale, the head of that office, with criminal wrongdoing? How did Dale come to be audited by the IRS after his notorious termination? How about Paula Jones? How did so many well-known Clinton critics come to be audited by the IRS?

Someone at the White House was responsible for these acts. But President Clinton just announces that all he knows about it is what he reads in the paper and he has to get back to the important business of naming his dog. *Washington Post* reporter Sue Schmidt ought to be president. She has more authority to decide when the country goes to war, since, as Clinton constantly acknowledges, she knows more about what goes on in the White House under his watch than he does.

The Music Never Stops

If one eliminates a handful of players from the Watergate scandal, it is easy to imagine President Nixon serving out his second term uneventfully. In fact, remove just G. Gordon Liddy from the picture, and there might well have been no Watergate break-in, and consequently no cover-up and no presidential lie. How many characters would have to be removed from Clinton's administration to create an ethical administration? Not "the most ethical administration in the history of the Republic," just moderately ethical. You'd be left with Donna Shalala running the government. The president has filled his administration with crooks and rogues—and if they weren't that way before, they have become so under his tutelage.

This much corruption can't be a staffing problem. It has been true since long before Clinton came to Washington. (Try to imagine, for example, Bernie Nussbaum finding himself in a partnership with the likes of James McDougal.)

Clinton might have been able to duck responsibility for his Health Care Task Force's "reprehensible lies" to a court; his associate attorney general's thievery from the Rose Law Firm; his Housing and Urban Development secretary's lies to the FBI about payoffs to a mistress; and his secretary of Agriculture's acceptance of gifts from those he was supposed to be regulating. A lie about a mistress or individual bribe-taking have no apparent value to the president. But it didn't end with that.

There was White House Associate Counsel William Kennedy, who ordered the FBI to investigate Billy Dale in "fifteen minutes" or he would call in the IRS (which he did anyway). There were Craig Livingstone and Anthony Marceca rifling though private FBI files— including Dale's file, requested by some unknown Clinton employee about the time Kennedy was demanding an investigation. There was Clinton friend, supporter, and IRS Commissioner Margaret Milner Richardson, who according to White House memos was "on top of" the Dale matter. As luck would have it, Dale was later audited by the IRS. There were the various top Clinton administration officials calling around to scare up massive "consulting fees" for Webb Hubbell, including Clinton's then and future White House Chiefs of Staff Mack McLarty and Erskine Bowles; Clinton's trade representative, Mickey Kantor; and informal Clinton adviser Vernon Jordan. And, of course, there was Webb Hubbell himself.

It didn't end when Kennedy got the boot. It didn't end once the administration finally made sacrificial lambs out of Livingstone and Marceca. It didn't end when Nussbaum headed back to New York. It never ends. And it won't end until Clinton is gone. There is no more room for giving the president the benefit of the doubt. Even if it were possible to believe Clinton were an innocent dupe of this endless stream of nefarious staffers, his incompetence in hiring them is enough to impeach him. This isn't a simple matter of saying the fish rots from the head. It is saying the whole administration, the whole country, is gagging on Clinton's rotting fish. That was true even before January 21, 1998.

IMPEACHMENT OF A PRESIDENT FOR OBSTRUCTION OF JUSTICE
The Nixon Precedent

President Clinton has almost certainly perjured himself about Monica Lewinsky, as well as her many "Jane Doe" competitors. He has just as surely obstructed justice in an attempt to cover his own perjury as well as his own underlying misconduct.

Nixon's obstruction of justice consisted of: invoking executive privilege to avoid turning over the tapes of his Oval Office conversations to the Congress; allowing his aides to ask the CIA to stall an FBI investigation into one aspect of the Watergate investigation, though the delay lasted only two weeks; and telling a single lie to the American people. Nixon didn't believe it was a lie, and under the nation's newly minted Clinton standards, it wasn't.

Just that much interference with an investigation—invoking executive privilege just one time, delaying an FBI investigation for a couple of weeks, and not owning up to the Watergate burglars' day job as "Plumbers"—was Nixon's version of "shredding the Constitution." Apparently, investigations into possible misconduct within the executive branch are treated very seriously. Minor interference with legal processes concerning even low-level crimes, like spying on the DNC by individuals with only tenuous connections to the president, were deemed grave threats to the constitutional order.

Admittedly much of this was overblown, irrational anti-Nixon hysteria. The "shredding the Constitution" rhetoric was really imbecilic. But that's the precedent: minor stonewalling of an investigation by the president was deemed a threat to constitutional government, even if it was not as colossal a threat as the *Washington Post* let on.

There actually are some real reasons the president shouldn't be breaking the law. The president has vast powers as chief executive, including control over the use of force. It is his constitutional duty to take care that the laws be faithfully executed. And indeed, the Constitution spells out the president's oath—and only his— in similar words. If the president himself engages in obstruction of justice, that undermines confidence in the legal system.

It is one thing for the president to have an understanding of the law that is different from that of the federal courts or of Congress. But people must have confidence that he is acting on some plausible view of the law and not simply twisting it to his own convenience—or worse, flouting or obstructing the law to his own advantage. If the president does this in one area, the public cannot have confidence that he is not doing it in all sorts of other areas—to benefit loyal supporters, core constituencies, campaign contributors, China, and so on.

There is no need to hyperventilate about anyone "shredding the Constitution"; it is enough to say that it is very bad for the president to break the law, even those unimportant felonies members of the Clinton administration admit to breaking.[108]

Clinton's Perjury

President Nixon never gave a single statement under oath throughout the Watergate investigation. So however he obstructed justice, it could not have been by perjuring himself. He was said to have "subverted constitutional government," because his *aides* gave false statements under oath about their own "personal conduct." It wasn't even personal to Nixon. No one thinks Nixon had the bright idea of wiretapping the DNC. That "dumb" foray, as Nixon called it,[109] was committed by people who were neither president nor even drawing government salaries.

Twenty-five years later, there is more reason to believe in visitors from another planet than to believe the president has not perjured himself. Even if Clinton ever does, as his former chief of staff, Leon Panetta, has urged, "[a]t some point… tell the American people the truth of what was behind this relationship," he has already given his statements under oath. And not just about Monica Lewinsky. He has also given sworn statements, with a federal judge presiding, about Paula Jones, Gennifer Flowers ("once"), Kathleen Willey— even statements about loyal Betty Currie's role in all this.

As journalist Stuart Taylor has pointed out, believing Clinton strains mathematical probabilities. Noting that at least ten major players (so far) have given statements under oath directly contradicting Clinton's own statements under oath, Taylor calculated, "If we posit at 50-50 the probability that any one of the top ten witnesses against Clinton is lying, then the mathematical probability that all ten are lying—and thus that Clinton has told the whole truth in his own sworn testimony—comes to one chance in 1,024."[110]

Whether or not it is unconstitutional to indict a sitting president (it isn't), alleged Clinton mouthpiece Monica Lewinsky certainly can be indicted. If Lewinsky were to plead guilty to, or be convicted of, perjury or an obstruction crime, even the yellow-bellied Republican Congress would come close to having their criminal standard of proof that the president committed a felony. Lewinsky and Clinton's alleged perjuries are the same—that they did not have "a certain kind of sex," as Paula Jones termed it. If Lewinsky perjured herself, so did Clinton. And if Lewinsky committed an obstruction crime to prevent the court or grand jury from discovering evidence of her relationship with Clinton, there is one person with whom she would have had to conspire: the other party to that relationship. Unless she was sure Clinton was going to perjure himself, too, she would have been walking right into open and obvious obstruction offenses. And she would have been begging for a perjury conviction with her affidavit denying the affair.

Lying is an impeachable offense. Perjury, suborning perjury, concealing evidence, and obstruction of justice are not only impeachable offenses, they are also crimes. These are real crimes, far surpassing the quantum of misconduct necessary for an impeachment. About this there is absolutely no question. Even Clinton aide Paul Begala would not have the cheek to claim otherwise. That the president has committed them may be properly deemed an attempt "to subvert the Constitution."[111]

Invoking Executive Privilege
As Obstruction of Justice

If the legal talents of Hillary Rodham and Bernie Nussbaum are to be credited, impeachment for invoking executive privilege to thwart congressional subpoenas is an impeachable offense. The entire third article of impeachment against Nixon was based solely on the fact that he had "failed without lawful cause or excuse to produce papers and things as directed by duly authorized subpoenas issued by the Committee on the Judiciary of the House of Representatives...."

This was for a somewhat legitimate invocation of executive privilege, being appealed through the courts. Ultimately, of course, the Supreme Court did recognize the existence of executive privilege, and created a new privilege. But the new privilege did not cover all presidential communications, as Nixon had argued. So the court ordered Nixon to hand over the tapes. Nixon, by the way, at least admitted he was the one invoking executive privilege.

Flash forward twenty-five years: the nation's chief executive, Bill Clinton, was asked about the invocation of executive privilege to shield high-level conversations about Monica, such as those his wife had with communications adviser Sidney Blumenthal. Executive privilege, of course, is the privilege of the executive; he's the executive, and only he can assert or waive the privilege. The response from the president of the United States was this: "That's a question that's being asked and answered back home by the people who are responsible to do that.... All I know is, I saw an article about it in the papers today."[112]

In trying to pawn off the executive privilege gambit on his subordinates, Clinton was reversing the whole idea of a single executive held accountable for his subordinates through impeachment. The Constitution makes the president responsible for the actions of his subordinates precisely in order to prevent him from saying, "Well, I just appointed them but now it's on their heads." Here, Clinton was saying, "I like that dodge so much I'll double it." He made his subordinates take the rap for invoking executive privilege, even though they legally, constitutionally, *cannot* invoke executive privilege. By no stretch of the law can this be anyone's decision but the president's. Nixon did it once and had an article of impeachment voted against him for it.

The framers explicitly posited obstruction of justice as an impeachable offense. Interestingly, though, the framers did not contemplate that the obstruction would be actually be committed by the president himself, but assumed it would be committed by persons with whom the president was connected. "Those who adopted the Constitution," as the Rodino Report calls the framers, expressly stated that the president could be impeached if "there be grounds to believe he will shelter" any person who has broken the law.[113]

One chance in 1,024, that the president himself has not committed perjury.

IMPEACHMENT OF A PRESIDENT FOR LYING
The Issue

Lying to the American people may not be a criminal offense, but it is a breach of trust by the president. It is a "high crime or misdemeanor." It is unquestionably an impeachable offense. As Hamilton suggested, the president could be impeached for acts that make him "unworthy of being any longer trusted," even if immune from "legal punishment."

The idea that the nation has a right to expect the truth from the president has become a quaint anachronism. Since he is just a politician, no one believes him anyway. His words are treated as mere pleasantries. But there is a chance that the president will have to, for example, send men into battle. He has to be able to tell the country that we really need to do this and not have people assume it's just some political stunt.

It is roundly assumed that Clinton is lying. His partisans are only waiting to see if there is criminal proof that he lied under oath about something they deem important.

The Precedent

It wasn't always this way. One president was almost impeached for lying—lying on one single narrow point that had nothing to do with his own misconduct. The first article of impeachment voted against President Nixon included—as a separate and independent ground—that he had lied to the American people. He was accused of "making or causing to be made false or misleading public statements for the purpose of deceiving the people of the United States...."[114] It wasn't under oath, and it was enough.

As Nixon's first special prosecutor, Archibald Cox, explained:

> *The President is not merely the only active government official elected in America by all the people; he is the nation's image of itself, the symbol of the nation... Woe betide him who sullies the nation's image of itself. In my view, Watergate proved the conscience of the nation as well as the ability of a self-governing people to vindicate, by the processes of open government, their own moral sense....* [115]

The president as "symbol of the nation," "sully[ing] the nation's image of itself," the people vindicating "their own moral sense"— and Nixon wasn't even getting oral sex from an intern. He wasn't even the one wearing latex gloves in the Watergate Hotel.

Nixon's second special prosecutor, Leon Jaworski, summarized the "infamy and disgrace" of President Nixon: "What sank him was his lying.... People can tolerate a great deal in their public officials. If a person is big enough to say 'I did it,' he'll be forgiven."[116]

In a prediction that later events would sadly disprove, Jaworski exulted that the Watergate scandal had made "tremendous" strides for "better government":

Those who seek office know there's a very high standard expected of them.... There aren't many who now think they can depart from the straight line. There'll be less use of influence. The attention given to this case will give its results a more lasting effect. It has made its impressions deep-rooted. The good that comes out of it won't be a passing fancy.[117]

Elliot Richardson, the attorney general who resigned during Nixon's "Saturday Night Massacre," similarly described Watergate as a shot over the bow for politicians ambivalent about the truth: "[T]hey can't risk cutting corners or hoarding dirty little secrets, if only because they've learned that honesty is the best politics—whether or not there is a real regeneration of morality."[118] (Sam Ervin, chairman of the Senate Watergate Committee, was more subdued in his estimate of the salubrious effect of Watergate on other politicians, saying that it would be "up to the media to keep reminding people.")[119]

Some "better government" we got. President Clinton has announced to the American people: "[L]isten to me. I'm going to say this again. I did not have sexual relations with that woman—Miss Lewinsky."[120] More than twenty hours of taped conversations of an unsuspecting witness, thirty-seven Lewinsky visits to the White House, Betty Currie's testimony, a dress, a brooch, a hat pin, and much additional evidence say otherwise.

A few days after the Lewinsky story broke on January 21, 1998, Ben Bradlee, who had been editor of the *Washington Post* during Watergate, ticked off some of the "eerie" comparisons with Nixon during Watergate: "You have a president lying. You have a president wounded and hurt by trying to cover it up. What will the consequences be? Well, it's going to be very difficult for Clinton to get out of this."[121]

Clinton's Friends Say He Is Lying

Clinton's flacks defend their man with these points: (1) even if Clinton is lying, it has to do with sex; (2) even if Clinton is lying, the vast right-wing conspiracy is out to get him; (3) even if Clinton is lying, Starr is a really, deeply evil man; (4) even if Clinton is lying, his poll numbers are high; and so on. But no one denies that he is lying (except Eleanor Clift and the first lady, going beyond the call of duty to earn their presidential kneepads).

Oddly, even his paid White House defenders openly acknowledge that the president is lying. One "adviser" gave the *Washington Post* this spin to Kathleen Willey's groping allegation: "Clinton's not a coercive guy; he's very subtle.... Were they together? Yes. Did something happen? Possibly.... I think she is lying about how she felt about it." But his boss says unequivocally that he didn't grope her—not that he did it but she liked it.[122]

Leon Panetta, Clinton's former chief of staff, said of Clinton: "At some point he's going to have to tell the American people what the truth of that relationship was."[123]

And, of course, George Stephanopoulos, former senior Clinton aide, said of the Lewinsky affair: "These are probably the most serious allegations yet leveled against the president. There's no question that... if they're true, they're not only politically damaging but it could lead to impeachment proceedings." He elaborated later, saying Clinton had violated a "loyalty contract" with the American people by asking people to lie:

> I don't think a president is loyal to his people if he either know-ingly asks them to lie or asks them to say things which he realizes are not very credible, asks them to take him on his word without giving them reasons to take him at his word. And I think that is the trap that the president has set right now.[124]

Press Secretary Mike McCurry: "If it turns out what the president has said has not been fair and square with the American people, that has enormous implications."[125]

Albert Eisele, who served as press secretary to Vice President Walter Mondale, pointed out another trap Clinton has set for himself, and this one is unavoidable. In an editorial for *The Hill*, Eisele wrote that Clinton "has disgraced and degraded the presidency and betrayed his family and friends, his party and his country." (Meanwhile, Republican Senators Trent Lott and Arlen Specter were calling on Ken Starr to wrap up his investigation.) Eisele continued, "Americans are willing to forgive their elected officials almost anything as long as they tell the truth." But, he continued, "We do not believe that Clinton has done that in the present case, and we don't know if he will, *or is even able to, without exposing himself to charges of perjury*" (emphasis added). For the president to come clean now, he would have to admit that he has already committed a felony.

At least one recent Democratic presidential candidate considered the trustworthiness of the president a matter of public concern:

> *Every time [the president] talks about trust it makes chills run up and down my spine. The very idea that the word "trust" could ever come out of [his] mouth after what he has done to this country and the way he is trampled on the truth is a travesty of the American political system.*[126]
>
> *   *   *
>
> *There's just no such thing as truth when it comes to him.... He just says whatever sounds good and worries about it after the election.*[127]

That was what candidate Bill Clinton had to say about President Bush during the 1992 campaign.

Lying "About Sex"

Ironically, the argument that Clinton's relationship with Lewinsky is a "personal" matter—only "about sex"—has effectively deprived Clinton of any possible defense if he is lying. Probably the only defense the president of the United States could pony up to a charge of lying to the American people would be that the lie was required by his duty as the chief executive—something like a secret military maneuver, troop movements in a war zone, or an impending sting operation against domestic terrorists. Obviously, even a presidential lie told to save lives is problematic in a democracy. Lying about oral sex with a White House intern cannot possibly have anything to do with saving American lives or any other official presidential duties.[128]

As Ben Bradlee said, "[I]t's going to be very difficult for Clinton to get out of this."

IMPEACHMENT OF A PRESIDENT FOR PERSONAL MISCONDUCT

Any impeachment hearings against Clinton could stray beyond his wily subordinates invoking executive privilege without telling him. Unlike Nixon, who was largely being held responsible for the misconduct of his subordinates, the weight of the evidence against President Clinton concerns the misconduct of the president himself.

Former Clinton Chief of Staff Leon Panetta discussed the White House staff's efforts to restrain the president's "dark side":

> *We were sensitive to those issues.... [Let's say] a woman wanted to ride with him in the limo, we took steps to make sure that didn't happen. In the evenings, we always made sure he had company when he was with friends.... [Clinton] was cooperative. I never saw him in a situation that you would call reckless. You never control all of the private moments.... If it turned out that somehow his dark side prevailed in these moments of temptation, it would be a disappointment.*[129]

But can the president be impeached for having a "dark side" that had to be suppressed by a corps of his top advisers?

Yes, absolutely.

Hamilton wrote that presidents would derive their confidence and firmness—critical qualities in a president—directly from "the proofs he had given of his wisdom and integrity" and "to the title he had acquired to the respect and attachment of his fellow citizens."[130] Recall that James Madison said the primary object of the Constitution was to secure leaders with the "most virtue" and to "take the most effectual precautions for keeping them virtuous whilst they continue to hold their public trust."[131] For that purpose, Madison said, the impeachment power was "indispensable." Impeachment would counter "the perfidy of the chief magistrate."[132] The impeachment of statesmen would be tried "upon the enlarged and solid principles of morality."[133]

In 1701 a member of the king's council was impeached for procuring an office for someone "known to be a person of ill fame and reputation." Now it is assumed that the president can actually *be* the "person of ill fame and reputation" without risking anything more than a censure.

One of the longest quotes on impeachable conduct given in the Rodino Report is this:

> *Not but that crimes of a strictly legal character fall within the scope of the power… but that it has a more enlarged operation, and reaches, what are aptly termed political offenses, growing out of personal misconduct or gross neglect, or usurpation, or habitual disregard of the public interests, in the discharge of the duties of political office. These are so various in their character, and so indefinable in their actual involutions, that it is almost impossible to provide systematically for them by positive law. They must be examined upon very broad and comprehensive principles of public policy and duty. They must be judged… by a great variety of circumstances, as well those which aggravate as those which extenuate or justify the offensive acts which do not properly belong to the judicial character in the ordinary administration of justice, and are far removed from the reach of municipal jurisprudence.*[134]

There are undoubtedly grey areas in determinations of when personal misconduct constitutes grounds for impeaching a president. The president's obtaining oral sex from a White House intern does not fall in the grey area. If a congressman's married chief of staff was caught being sexually serviced by a Capitol Hill intern thirty years his junior, it would rank as a major scandal and would be a major political embarrassment for the congressman. This isn't a congressman, and it certainly isn't a congressman's chief of staff. It is the president of the United States himself.

The argument against impeachment for "mere personal misconduct" misconceives the nature of an impeachable offense. When Alexander Hamilton described impeachment proceedings as related "chiefly to injuries done immediately to the society itself," he meant a betrayal of a public trust, not partisan gamesmanship. Such "political" offenses range from abuse of power to personal misbehavior. But they exclude policy differences, since an erroneous policy decision might result from "a wilful mistake of the heart, or an involuntary fault of the head,"[135] as Edmund Randolph said. Since policy matters are necessarily off the table, in a sense, that leaves only "personal misconduct."

Even in Great Britain, where impeachment was "initiated to topple giants," high crimes and misdemeanors encompassed personal misconduct. American impeachments were, from their inception, concerned with more modest abuses. The Constitution had clearly eliminated the need for impeachment to be used in a power struggle with any king. Consequently, impeachments under the American Constitution have always had more to do with "squalid misconduct" of office holders than the sort of grand offense that might warrant a hanging.

The Senate has convicted officers after impeachments for such disreputable acts as drunkenness, tax evasion, and false statements to a grand jury.[136] Be it drunkenness, conspiracy to solicit a bribe, tax evasion, covering up a third-rate burglary attempt, or groping female staffers—all these involve "personal misconduct."

Clinton has literally disgraced the office in the sense that people's expectations for what goes on in the Oval Office are remarkably, historically low. One of the most devastating blows to President Nixon when the tapes came out was the introduction of the phrase "expletive deleted" into the vernacular. Nixon was a Quaker; he wasn't even using the really good curse words. But the idea that cursing was going on in the White House offended people's sense that the Oval Office was sacrosanct.

One of the most peculiar defenses raised by Clinton's claque is its very active aggressive campaign to persuade people that Starr is just going after sex. As if it's outrageous to suggest that the president should have a minimally decent personal life.

A president whose own behavior in the Oval Office introduces the term "presidential kneepads" into the nation's vocabulary, and who conspires to break laws to hide that behavior—conducted on the presidential seal, no less—surely warrants, as the Constitution provides, "removal from Office, and disqualification to hold and enjoy any Office of honor, Trust or Profit under the United States."

EYES OF THE WORLD

Now it is problematic even to discuss what the president has been doing in his office. The whole country is tongue-tied with a series of convoluted euphemisms for the president's sexual perversions and inadequacies laid bare in the Oval Office.

The Rodino Report cited Benjamin Franklin's odd argument that including an impeachment power in the Constitution was "favorable to the executive"[137]:

> *What was the practice before this in cases where the chief Magistrate rendered himself obnoxious? Why recourse was had to*

assassination in [which] he was not only deprived of his life but of the
opportunity of vindicating his character.[138]

It's funny—the one defense you never hear Clinton partisans make
is that he deserves the opportunity to "vindicate his character."

Now it is a laugh to read Alexander Hamilton's calm assurance in
Federalist No. 68 that the president would always be a virtuous man.
But recall that he was confident that the office of the presidency would
be filled only by "characters pre-eminent for ability and virtue":

> *This process of election affords a moral certainty that the office of*
> *President will seldom fall to the lot of any man who is not in an emi-*
> *nent degree endowed with the requisite qualifications. Talents for low*
> *intrigue, and the little arts of popularity, may alone suffice to elevate*
> *a man to the first honors in a single State; but it will require other*
> *talents, and a different kind of merit, to establish him in the esteem*
> *and confidence of the whole Union.... It will not be too strong to say*
> *that there will be a constant probability of seeing the station filled by*
> *characters pre-eminent for ability and virtue.*[139]

This is what was expected of the rulers in the new country
forged from "a revolution which has no parallel in the annals of
human society." They had "reared the fabrics of governments,"
Madison wrote, to create a Constitution that had "no model on
the face of the globe." And they had done so, "happily we trust for
the whole human race."[140]

At the end of the Constitutional Convention, Franklin was
asked what they had wrought. "A Republic," he said, "if you can
keep it."

Notes

CHAPTER 1

1   For the record, conservative commentators seem to have openly abandoned consistency on only one point—the question of whether the Kathleen Willey letters released by the White House immediately after her *60 Minutes* appearance belied a sexual harassment claim. Many conservatives promptly adopted the impotent victim excuse. This was silly. If Willey had been suing for sexual harassment, those fawning letters would have damaged her credibility. But she wasn't. She was an extremely unwilling witness called by the Jones lawyers. The letters didn't damage her credibility for that purpose. For the purposes of Jones's lawsuit, the only thing that mattered with Willey was that Clinton did it, not Willey's reaction. *See* Chapter 7.

2   George Orwell, *1984*, 69 (1949).

3   *See, e.g.,* CNN's *CNN Late Edition with Wolf Blitzer*, March 22, 1998 (Congressman Tom Delay (R-TX): "[W]e're waiting for the facts to come out."); *The NewsHour with Jim Lehrer*, March 16, 1998 (Former Clinton Special Counsel Lanny Davis: "I think people are withholding judgment. I think they're waiting to see if the facts come out."); CNBC's *Rivera Live*, February 11, 1998 (Lanny Davis: "[President Clinton] is to be believed when he says that he did not have this relationship. And until evidence comes in, until facts come in to prove otherwise..."); Liz Stevens, "Hill-billy Relations," *Fort Worth Star-Telegram*, January 31, 1998 ("Whatever you think of the president's guilt or innocence, there's *no way to judge* him or his wife—or, for that matter, Monica Lewinsky—*until all the facts are in*. And maybe not even then.").

4   Sonya Ross, "First Lady Says President Will Weather Latest Scandal," Associated Press, January 22, 1998.

5   Peter Goldman, "Was Justice Finally Done?" *Newsweek*, January 13, 1975.

6 Staff Report, House Committee on the Judiciary, 93rd Congress, "Constitutional Grounds for Presidential Impeachment" (released February 22, 1974) [hereafter "Rodino Report"] at 4.

7 Raoul Berger, *Impeachment: The Constitutional Problems*, 211 and 201 (1973) (quoting 8 Howell 197, 200, Art. 8.).

8 Rodino Report at 6.

9 Berger at 200.

10 Berger at 58.

11 Rodino Report at 17 (quoting 1 J. Story, *Commentaries on the Constitution of the United States* sec. 764 at 559 [5th ed. 1905]).

12 Rodino Report at 17 (quoting 1 J. Story, *Commentaries on the Constitution of the United States* sec. 764 at 559 [5th ed. 1905]).

13 R.M. Jackson, *The Machinery of Justice in England* 289 n.1 (London 5th ed. 1967) (quoted in Berger at 211, n. 96) (emphasis added).

14 Federalist No. 65, at 396 (Alexander Hamilton) (Clinton Rossiter ed., 1961).

15 Paul Langford and P.J. Marshall, ed., *The Writings and Speeches of Edmund Burke*, 333 (1991).

16 7 Edmund Burke, *Works* 11,14 (1839) (quoted in Laurence H. Tribe, *American Constitutional Law*, 294 [2d ed. 1988]). A number of variants of the morality quote have been given, including, most popularly, Burke's explanation that impeachment requires statesmen to try statesmen upon principles of "state morality." Even in these versions it is clear that Burke is referring to the honor of statesmen, and not their technical competence. There have been various renditions of Burke's speeches during the Hastings impeachment from the very beginning. There was no official reporter for either house of Parliament (and indeed it may have been a technical breach of privilege even to report debates at all). So compilations of Burke's speeches have been pieced together from (possibly clandestine) note-takers whose versions conflict with one another—as well as with the versions Burke produced later.

17 Langford and Marshall at 333.

18 Laurence H. Tribe inserted "[criminal]" in his work *American Constitutional Law*.

19 Federalist No. 57, (James Madison).

20 Berger at 14.

21 Federalist No. 70, at 427 (Alexander Hamilton). *See also* Rodino Report at 9 (The president is "personally responsible for any abuse of the great trust reposed in him." [quoting framer and Supreme Court Justice James Iredell]).

22 116 Cong. Rec. H 3113–3114 (Statement of Representative Gerald Ford) (daily ed. April 15, 1970).

23 Rodino Report at 16 (quoting 1 J. Story, *Commentaries on the Constitution of the United States* sec. 764 at 559 (5th ed. 1905).

24 Berger at 44–45.

25   Berger at 43.

26   Report of the National Commission on Judicial Discipline and Removal, at 30 (August 1993).

27   Berger at 3.

28   Berger at 71–72.

29   Berger at 71.

30   Berger at 74.

31   Rodino Report at 14 (quoting Edmund Randolph).

32   Federalist No. 65, (Alexander Hamilton).

33   Report of the National Commission on Judicial Discipline and Removal at 27 (August 1993) (quoting 2 *The Records of the Constitutional Convention* 65 [M. Farrand ed. 1911]).

34   Rodino Report at 13 (quoting Charles Cotesworth Pinckney of South Carolina and Edmund Randolph of Virginia, respectively).

35   Rodino Report at 10.

36   *See, e.g.*, Charles McCarry, "Bill Clinton's John Dean?" *New York Times*, July 12, 1998. The assistant special prosecutor offered this conclusion in a letter to Special Prosecutor Leon Jaworski.

37   Anthony Lewis, "Abroad at Home: Again, the Imperium," *New York Times*, November 17, 1986 ("The example of such unlimited executive power that must have most impressed the forefathers was the prerogative exercised by George III, and the description of its evils in the Declaration of Independence leads me to doubt that they were creating their new Executive in his image.") (quoting opinion of Justice Robert H. Jackson in the Steel Seizure case).

38   Rodino Report at 15.

39   Peter Goldman, "Was Justice Finally Done?" *Newsweek*, January 13, 1975.

40   *See* Information Bank Abstracts, Anthony Lewis, *New York Times*, January 21, 1974: ABSTRACT:
A Lewis holds lawsuit against Pres Nixon has not inhibited Nixon from exercising Pres powers despite Nixon's protestations that it would do so when he recd grand jury subpoena for Watergate tapes and documents last summer. *Holds Nixon's problem is loss of public belief in his word.* Notes Nixon's latest assertion of his right to ignore subpoena from Sen Watergate com. Holds legal test of Sen subpoena is highly significant as *control of information has played crucial part in rise of imperial Presidency* (emphasis added).

41   Peter Goldman, "Was Justice Finally Done?" *Newsweek*, January 13, 1975.

42   Bob Woodward and Carl Bernstein, "The Final Days: Part Two," *Newsweek*, April 12, 1976.

43   Martha Sherrill, "Interview: Grave Doubts. Senator Bob Kerrey," *Esquire*, January 1996.

44 "Excerpts From Clinton's News Conference on Investigations and Middle East," *New York Times*, May 1, 1998.

45 Despite the talk of "absolute Despotism," taxes were actually relatively moderate under King George III. Fair and just, in fact, compared to Clinton's 1993 "tax stimulus bill" that swept in a Republican Congress for the first time in forty years.

46 Chuck Raasch, "Bennett Asks: Where's Religious Right in Clinton Fight?" *Gannett News Service*, February 27, 1998:

Though the Christian Coalition has preached family values for almost a decade, the organization has not officially come to conclusions about the Clinton-Lewinsky controversy, spokesman Arne Owens said....

"They truly believe you are innocent until proven guilty. They want to see the facts... Everyone we talk to, certainly within our grass roots, is very, very concerned about this."

[Former Christian Coalition Spokesman Ralph] Reed maintained that when he headed the coalition, he turned down an invitation from conservative supporters of Paula Corbin Jones to appear at her first press conference—before she filed suit alleging Clinton sexually harassed her.

47 Federalist No. 65, at 396 (Alexander Hamilton).

48 Federalist No. 51, at 322 (James Madison).

49 Rodino Report at 13.

50 Peter Goldman, "Was Justice Finally Done?" *Newsweek*, January 13, 1975.

CHAPTER 2

1 *Agence France Presse*, January 24, 1998.

2 Eric Pooley, with reporting by Michael Duffy and Charlotte Faltermayer, "Monica's World," *Time*, March 2, 1998.

3 ABC's *Good Morning America*, January 21, 1998.

4 NBC's *Today*, January 22, 1998.

5 Editorial, "The Allegations," *Washington Post*, January 22, 1998.

6 Susan Schmidt, Peter Baker, and Toni Locy, "Starr Investigates Whether Clinton Told Intern to Deny Affair," *Washington Post*, January 21, 1998.

7 In *Black* v. *Zaring Homes*, Clinton's EEOC issued a "right to sue" letter and filed repeated amicus briefs in support of a woman whose claim of discrimination consisted of five in-between-color remarks made by male colleagues. These included such whoppers as a coworker saying, "Nothing I like more in the morning than sticky buns," while reaching for a pastry and—as the complainant put it—"wriggl[ing]" his eyebrows. Once, she also overheard her supervisor refer to a woman as a "broad." The jury awarded the plaintiff $250,000 for such indignities. Clinton's EEOC fought to vindicate the plaintiff's rights in *Zaring Homes* until January 1997, when the Sixth Circuit Court of Appeals, mercifully, reversed the jury's verdict.

8   President Clinton's press conference, Friday, February 6, 1998.

9   Complaint, *Jones* v. *Clinton*, No. 94-290, at para. 6–11 (May 6, 1994).

10   Complaint, *Jones* v. *Clinton*, No. 94-290, at para. 20–21 (May 6, 1994).

11   42 U.S.C. sec. 1983. This statute codifies constitutional rights, including the Four-teenth Amendment right to be free from discrimination by the government on the basis of sex.

12   *United States Postal Service Board of Governors* v. *Aikens*, 460 U.S. 711, 716 (1983).

13   Dick Morris said of Clinton's presidential immunity claim in the *Jones* case: It "was basically a trumped-up argument that [Clinton lawyer Bob] Bennett threw together at the last minute to get this thing put off until after the election. And of course by 9-0, it had no legal merit. I never thought it had any legal merit. But the point was, we weren't going to let this thing be adjudicated in August, October, November, near the election." Quoted in Ross Mackenzie, "Between The Grand Inquisitor & The Church Lady, Assessing The Clintons," *Richmond Times Dispatch*, June 22, 1997.

14   *See, e.g., Quick* v. *Donaldson Co.*, 90 F.3d 1372, 1379 (8th Cir. 1983); *Heyne* v. *Caruso*, 69 F.3d 1475 (9th Cir. 1995) (holding that exclusion of evidence of different type of sexual harassment than that alleged by plaintiff constitutes reversible error).

15   *Clinton* v. *Jones*, Oral Argument before Supreme Court (January 12, 1997).

16   An anonymous caller to the Rutherford Institute was described as a "nervous young woman" by the man who took her calls. Tim Weiner and Neil A. Lewis, "Testing of a President: The Unraveling," *New York Times*, February 9, 1998.

17   Michael Isikoff and Evan Thomas, "The Secret War," *Newsweek*, February 9, 1998.

18   As we will see, Hubbell had worked on a fraudulent land deal at the prestigious Rose Law Firm—as had Hillary Clinton. The prosecution's theory was that the White House arranged for Hubbell to be paid hush money to keep him from testifying against Mrs. Clinton. In the months following his indictment, Hubbell managed to pull down more than $500,000 in "consulting fees" with "little work, if any" expected in return. Jordan had been of great "help" to Hubbell. *See, e.g.*, Susan Schmidt, "Hubbell Meetings with Riady Draw Probers' Scrutiny," *Washington Post*, March 23, 1997.

19   Susan Schmidt, Peter Baker, and Toni Locy, "Starr Investigates Whether Clinton Told Intern to Deny Affair," *Washington Post*, January 21, 1998.

20   "The invocation of executive and other privileges in this context also presents a ques-tion of overriding concern to the full and impartial administration of justice: the cir-cumstances under which the Executive Branch may withhold information from a fed-eral grand jury investigating allegations of misconduct against the president, other Executive Branch officials, and various private individuals."
     Petition For a Writ of Certiorari Before Judgment, *United States* v. *Clinton*, May 28, 1998.

CHAPTER 3

1   This is not as extraordinary as it may sound. Three sitting presidents have been sued for acts they committed before taking office. These suits, against Theodore Roosevelt, Harry Truman, and John F. Kennedy, were dismissed or settled out of court. At least six other sitting presidents have responded to written interrogatories, given depositions, and provided videotaped trial testimony "with sufficient frequency that such interactions between the Judicial and Executive Branches can scarcely be thought a novelty." *Clinton* v. *Jones*, 117 S.Ct. 1636 (1997). President Clinton had already given videotaped testimony twice in criminal proceedings: *United States* v. *McDougal*, 934 F.Supp. 296 (E.D.Ark.1996); *United States* v. *Branscum*, No., LRP-CR-96-49 (E.D. Ark., June 7, 1996). President Carter also voluntarily gave videotaped testimony for use at a criminal trial. President Nixon, of course, produced tapes in response to a subpoena. *United States* v. *Nixon*, 418 U.S. 683 (1974). President Ford gave a deposition in a criminal trial, *United States* v. *Fromme*, 405 F.Supp. 578 (E.D.Cal.1975). Presidents Monroe and Grant answered an interrogatory and gave a deposition, respectively, in criminal cases. *See generally* Rotunda, *Presidents and Ex-Presidents as Witnesses: A Brief Historical Footnote* (1975) L.F. 1.

No sitting president has, however, "ever testified, or been ordered to testify, in open court." *Clinton* v. *Jones* at n.14. So far.

2   Pursuant to a subpoena, the tapes themselves had been turned over to Starr Friday morning, the day before.

3   Judge Wright explained that she assumed Fisher could provide a good faith basis for asking the questions about Lewinsky, noting that he would be sanctioned later if it turned out that he could not. The judge also offered to review the good faith basis for the questions in private, at which point Bennett relented.

4   Deposition of William Jefferson Clinton, *Jones* v. *Clinton*, at 65–66 (January 17, 1998).(emphasis added).

5   "Throughout last year's [1997's] controversy over Democratic campaign fund-raising, the White House strategically released entry logs, telephone records, notes and other internal documents that may not have provided a flattering portrait of its activities but at least preempted congressional critics from putting the information out first.... But information about White House visits and presidential phone calls that was made public last year is now being guarded with fierce protectiveness."

Peter Baker, "White House, Changing Tactics, Guards Records; During Fund-Raising Flap, Documents Were Strategically Released to Limit Bad Spin," *Washington Post*, February 3, 1998.

6   *See, e.g.*, Matthew Campbell, "Hillary in Retreat," *Sunday Times* (London), March 8, 1998.

7   Deposition of William Jefferson Clinton, *Jones* v. *Clinton*, at 73–76 (January 17, 1998).(emphasis added).

8   Deposition of William Jefferson Clinton, *Jones* v. *Clinton*, at 76–77 (January 17, 1998).

9 *See, e.g.*, David Brock, "His Cheatin' Heart," *The American Spectator*, January 1994.

> *On yet another occasion that Patterson described, the governor and his security detail arrived at the Little Rock airport and Clinton told his bodyguards that he was going to be driven back to the residence by the Arkansas lawyer, who had met the plane, so that she could show him her new Jaguar. "On the ride back he drove and she was nowhere to be seen in the car," Patterson said. "Later he told me that he had researched the subject in the Bible and oral sex isn't considered adultery."*

To himself if to no one else, Brock may be a totally discredited journalist, but the point is that the president's oral-sex-is-not-adultery position had been reported, not that it was necessarily true.

10 Deposition of William Jefferson Clinton, *Jones* v. *Clinton*, (January 17, 1998) Exhibit 1 (emphasis added).

11 CBS's *60 Minutes*, January 26, 1992.

12 Susan Yoachum, "New Flareup Over Singer's Claim of Affair with Clinton," *San Francisco Chronicle*, January 24, 1992.

13 Interviewer Steve Kroft: "I'm assuming from your answer that you're categorically denying that you ever had an affair with Gennifer Flowers?"

Clinton: "I said that before.... And so has she."

Kroft: "You feel like you've leveled with the American people?"

Clinton: "I have absolutely leveled with the American people."

CBS's *60 Minutes*, January 26, 1992.

CHAPTER 4

1 John M. Broder, "Testing of a President: The Investigation," *New York Times*, March 7, 1998; Michael Isikoff and Evan Thomas, "The Secret War," *Newsweek*, February 9, 1998; John Harris, "Starr-Lewinsky Talks About Immunity Slow," *Washington Post*, February 1, 1998.

2 Peter Baker, "White House, Changing Tactics, Guards Records; During Fund-Raising Flap, Documents Were Strategically Released to Limit Bad Spin," *Washington Post*, February 3, 1998.

3 Peter Baker and Susan Schmidt, "Clinton Discussed Lewinsky Testimony with His Secretary," *Washington Post*, February 6, 1998.

4 Affidavit of Monica S. Lewinsky, dated January 7, 1998.

5 Deposition of William Jefferson Clinton, *Jones* v. *Clinton*, at 68 (January 17, 1998).

6   White House records indicate she had been cleared to enter the White House on Sunday, December 28.

7   John M. Broder, "Testing of a President: The Investigation," *New York Times*, March 7, 1998.

8   John M. Broder, "Testing of a President: The Investigation," *New York Times*, March 7, 1998.

9   John M. Broder, "Testing of a President: The Investigation," *New York Times*, March 7, 1998.

10 "Text of Vernon Jordan's Statement," Associated Press, March 5, 1998.

11 NBC's *Today*, January 27, 1998.

12 Tripp told Newsweek that the talking points sounded like Bruce Lindsey's words, especially the suggestion that Tripp say she believed Willey had misinterpreted the president's attempt to console a grieving widow. That talking point stated that the alleged Oval Office groping had taken place "at around the time of her husband's death. (The president has claimed that it was after her husband died. Do you really want to contradict him?)" Tripp identified the parenthetical as probably coming from Lindsey. Evan Thomas, Martha Brant, and Pat Wingert with Michael Isikoff, "What Made Linda Do It?" *Newsweek*, March 23, 1998.

13 Michael Isikoff, "Diary of a Scandal," *Newsweek,* January 21, 1998.

CHAPTER 5

1   Michael Isikoff, "A Twist in *Jones* v. *Clinton*," *Newsweek,* August 11, 1997.

2   *See, e.g.*, Michael Isikoff, "A Twist in *Jones* v. *Clinton*," *Newsweek,* August 11, 1997.

3   After the article appeared, Tripp sent a letter to Isikoff clarifying her position, but retracting nothing: "Whatever happened that day in the Oval Office, if anything, is known to only two people." Seven months and one enormous presidential scandal later, Tripp told *Newsweek* that the reason she sent the follow-up letter was because, in *Newsweek*'s words, she "felt pushed" by Lewinsky, "who advised her that it would be a wise career move." Evan Thomas, Martha Brant, and Pat Wingert with Michael Isikoff, "What Made Linda Do It?" *Newsweek*, March 23, 1998.

4   Willey had been volunteering in the White House Social Office, but had requested a meeting with President Clinton to ask for a full-time, paying job in the White House. She and her husband had just signed a note for $274,495 to repay a court judgment against Mr. Willey, who had been found guilty of embezzling that amount from two of his former clients, Josephine Abbott and Anthony Lanasa. According to Isikoff, Willey told others she saw Treasury Secretary Lloyd Bentsen waiting when she came out of the president's office. Bentsen's records, Isikoff added, show he had a meeting with Clinton on November 29, 1993, at 3 PM.

5   Jonathan Peterson and Alan C. Miller, "New Questions Raised Over Willey's Account," *Los Angeles Times*, March 19, 1998.

6   Michael Isikoff, "A Twist in *Jones* v. *Clinton*," *Newsweek,* August 11, 1997.

7   She was apparently taking the FOB lawyers' line on "relevance" in a sexual harassment

case—and meant only that she was not present when Jones met Clinton in the Excelsior Hotel on May 8, 1991. Noticeably, she did not deny having information relevant to President Clinton's practice of sexually harassing female underlings.

8   Michael Isikoff, "A Twist in *Jones* v. *Clinton*," *Newsweek*, August 11, 1997.

9   *See, e.g.,* Tucker Carlson, "The Scandal That Wasn't," *The Weekly Standard,* August 18, 1997 ("Willey could wind up in the headlines again if Paula Jones's attorneys succeed in forcing her to sit for a deposition, but it seems likely a judge will quash the subpoena before events get that far."). The *Human Events* legal reporter was consistently correct in predicting legal rulings in the *Jones* case.

10 Amy Goldstein, "Willey's Career Path Had a Sharp Upturn," *Washington Post,* March 15, 1998.

CHAPTER 6

1   Jones's papers were likely to contain copies of Willey's deposition transcript, which until then had not been made public on account of Judge Wright's gag order.

2   Nor, in fact, would it be the first time the Clinton administration had turned against one of their own to protect the "reputation" of the president. When David Watkins, assistant to the president for management and administration, released a document detailing the first lady's role in the White House Travel Office firings, the White House reportedly prepared to leak information to the press about Watkins's own sexual harassment problems.

3   "Ex-Miss America Apologizes to First Lady Over Alleged One-Night Stand with Clinton," Associated Press, April 25, 1998.

4   ABC's *Good Morning America*, March 16, 1998.

CHAPTER 7

1   James Bennet and Adam Nagourney, "The President Under Fire: The Strategy," *New York Times*, January 30, 1998.

2   ABC's *This Week with Sam and Cokie*, February 8, 1998.

3   ABC's *This Week with Sam and Cokie*, February 8, 1998.

4   Lois Romano, "The Monday Interview; On the Warpath for Clinton," *Washington Post*, September 21, 1992.

5   David Brock, "Living with the Clintons," *The American Spectator*, January 1994.

6   CNN's *Larry King Live*, January 27, 1992.

7   Thomas M. DeFrank and Thomas Galvin, "Inside the Clinton Attack Machine," *The Weekly Standard*, August 4, 1997.

8   William P. Cheshire, "The Story the Media Won't Touch," *Arizona Republic*, February 13, 1994.

9   A dead dog at that: "I had a dog like that who just wanted to catch cars, and he suc-

cessfully caught one one day, and I have a new dog. So if they're insisting on proceeding, we'll proceed." NBC's *Meet the Press*, June 1, 1997.

10 Bennett's bald-faced threat was so openly contrary to a feminist article of faith that he managed to finally flush them out of the bushes on this one. Within a few days, Bennett had retracted his threat to go into Jones's sexual history, saying "I'm not a fool."

11 Defendant Danny Ferguson could have dug up dirt on Paula in order to reduce her damages in the event that she won her defamation claim against Ferguson. The theory is that if she had had a lousy reputation anyway, she didn't lose much when Ferguson defamed her. Ferguson is the trooper who escorted her to the hotel room and then told *The American Spectator* that she willingly engaged in a sexual act with Clinton.

   It would be nice to know who is paying Ferguson's legal bills.

12 CBS's *60 Minutes*, March 14, 1998.

13 Michael Isikoff, "Willey and the Mogul," *Newsweek*, March 23, 1998.

14 Michael Isikoff, "A Twist in *Jones* v. *Clinton*," *Newsweek*, August 11, 1997.

15 "Excerpts of Kathleen Willey Letters," Associated Press (AP Online), March 17, 1998 (May 3, 1993, letter).

16 Jill Abramson and Don Van Natta, Jr., "Testing of a President: The Volunteer," *New York Times*, March 20, 1998.

17 *See, e.g.*, Alan C. Miller, "Willey's Credibility Takes Hits," *Los Angeles Times*, March 22, 1998.

18 "Excerpts of Kathleen Willey Letters," Associated Press (AP Online) March 17, 1998 (February 14, 1995, letter).

19 "Excerpts of Kathleen Willey Letters," Associated Press (AP Online) March 17, 1998 (February 14, 1995, letter).

20 Michael Isikoff, "A Twist in *Jones* v. *Clinton*," *Newsweek*, August 11, 1997 ("The cost of her trips to the taxpayers was about $7,000. Frank Provyn, the director of the State Department Office of International Programs, said he was 'kind of surprised' to see her on the trip to Indonesia. But, he added, 'a good way to get yourself into a jam is to ask too many questions when someone comes from the White House.'").

21 "Excerpts of Kathleen Willey Letters," Associated Press (AP Online) March 17, 1998 (December 5, 1995, letter).

22 Steele is not Willey's only corroborating witness. In addition to Linda Tripp, *USA Today* quoted another Willey friend as confirming that Willey had told a similar story to the unnamed friend shortly after the presidential grope. Willey, the friend reported, "said [Clinton] had given her a big old kiss… and then said something to the effect of 'I've been wanting to do that for a long time.'" Peter Eisler, "Willey's Life Dramatically Altered One Cold Day in Fall," *USA Today*, March 11, 1998.

23 Michael Isikoff, "Newsweek Had Story, But Held It," *Arkansas Democrat-Gazette*, January 23, 1998.

24 CNN's *CNN Late Edition with Wolf Blitzer*, March 15, 1998.

25 Tony Snow, "Will Leak Trip Up Clinton White House?" *Detroit News*, June 15, 1998.

26 Donna Abu-nasr, "Pentagon to Investigate Linda Tripp," Associated Press (AP Online), March 14, 1998.

27 Elaine Sciolino, "Testing of a President: The Pentagon; Linda Tripp's Security Form Draws Inquiry," *New York Times*, March 14, 1998; CNN's *Larry King Live*, May 26, 1998.

28 Editorial, "Lot of Lying Going on, But Question Is: By Whom?" *USA Today*, March 16, 1998.

29 Tim Weiner with Neil A. Lewis, "Testing of a President: The Unraveling," *New York Times*, February 9, 1998.

30 Jay Nordlinger, "Bacon Tripps Up," *The Weekly Standard*, May 18, 1998.

CHAPTER 8

1 NBC's *Today*, March 23, 1998.

2 Peter Baker, Susan Schmidt, "Starr Subpoenas Lewinsky to Testify," *Washington Post*, February 10, 1998.

3 William Ginsburg with Nathaniel Speights, "Behind the Scenes with Monica," *Time*, February 16, 1998.

4 Doug Ireland, "Of Closets and Clinton," *The Nation*, March 30, 1998.

5 Michael Kelly, "Clinton's Whisperers," *Washington Post*, March 5, 1998.

6 Lou Chibbaro, Jr., and Lisa Keen, "Clinton Adviser Denies Outing Starr Staffers," *Washington Blade*, March 20, 1998.

CHAPTER 9

1 CNN's *Larry King Live*, June 11, 1998.

2 Ann Gerhart and Annie Groer, "The Reliable Source," *Washington Post*, April 30, 1998.

3 Peter Baker, "Shrinking Public Role For Lewinsky Attorney; Family May Add Another Lawyer to Team," *Washington Post*, May 24, 1998.

CHAPTER 10

1 Federalist No. 75, at 453 (Alexander Hamilton). This was not the framers' expectation for all public servants. Quite different characteristics would define congressmen, for example. The "people's House," as the House of Representatives was called, was expected to be a raucous, spirited place. With its many members and short terms of office, the House was designed to have a "fluctuating" and "multitudinous composition," as Alexander Hamilton put it in Federalist No. 75.

2 Federalist No. 76, at 455–456 (Alexander Hamilton).

3   Federalist No. 46, at 296 (James Madison).

4   Matthew Andrew Rich and Kara Hopkins, "Feminists Still Hypocrites on Clinton's Character," *Human Events*, February 13, 1998.

5   Gloria Steinem, "Feminists and the Clinton Question," *New York Times*, March 22, 1998.

6   Gloria Steinem, "Feminists and the Clinton Question," *New York Times*, March 22, 1998.

7   CNBC's *Equal Time*, February 18, 1998:

Buchanan: Oh, no, that adds up perfectly.

Prof. Estrich: What they do add up is 65 percent right now are saying—70 percent are saying we believe he lied about having a sexual relationship. We think he's dumb on the matter of sex. But we don't think a mother should be investigated over it. We don't think we should have a—a sexual witch-hunt in Salem, Washington, and we'd like to get on with the business of figuring out whether we're going to war.

Buchanan: Call it perjury, my friend.

*   *   *

Prof. Estrich: I call it lying about sex.

8   Peter Brimelow, "An Interview with Nobel Laureate Milton Friedman," *Forbes*, December 12, 1988.

9   *See, e.g.*, CNBC's *Equal Time*, June 10, 1998 (Susan Estrich: "Most Americans believe, for themselves, that some hanky-panky went on here....").

CHAPTER 11

1   Federalist No. 76, at 456 (Alexander Hamilton).

2   Susan Schmidt, "Papers Detail Clinton Friend's Contract Push; House Panel Reviews '93 Travel Office Firings," *Washington Post*, October 25, 1995.

3   Matthew Cooper, "The Arkansas Impresarios," *The New Republic*, September 9, 1996.

4   House Report 104-849: "Investigation of the White House Travel Office Firings and Related Matters," Report by the Committee on Government Reform and Oversight, September 26, 1996.

5   World Wide Travel was owned by the Worthen Bank, which in turn was controlled by the Stephens family. The Riady family held an interest in the bank, where James Riady was once president, and Worthen's legal work was performed by the prestigious Rose Law Firm.

6   Steven Heilbronner, "Memo at Variance with White House Explanation on Travel Office," UPI, May 21, 1993.

7   House Report 104-849: "Investigation of the White House Travel Office Firings and Related Matters," Report by the Committee on Government Reform and Oversight, September 26, 1996.

8   Steven Heilbronner, "Memo at Variance with White House Explanation on Travel Office," UPI, May 21, 1993.

9   The White House's own report on the Travel Office firings admitted that Cornelius was copying and smuggling documents out of the office on Watkins's instructions, to help build a case against the Travel Office employees. Thomas L. Friedman, "White House Rebukes 4 in Travel Office Shake-up," *New York Times*, July 3, 1993.
Soon after Cornelius began work in the Travel Office, a photocopier repairman had found a copy of a $288,000 check stuck in the machine, suggesting that someone was copying the office's files. "Later it would be revealed that [Cornelius] was gathering information about charges for charter travel and other matters that she thought might implicate the travel-office staff in wrongdoing." Kim I. Eisler, "Fall Guy; Everyone Liked Billy Dale, But Clinton Pals Wanted His Job. In the End, Vince Foster Was Dead and Billy Dale Was Ruined. Here's the Story Behind the Headlines," *Washingtonian*, February 1996. Even the General Accounting Office's whitewash report of the Travel Office firings conceded that Cornelius took papers from the office and brought them home with her.

10   Kim I. Eisler, "Fall Guy; Everyone Liked Billy Dale, But Clinton Pals Wanted His Job. In the End, Vince Foster Was Dead and Billy Dale Was Ruined. Here's the Story Behind the Headlines," *Washingtonian*, February 1996.

11   Toni Locy, "Fired Travel Office Director Acquitted of Embezzlement; Dale Charged After Ouster From White House," *Washington Post*, November 17, 1995.

12   David Brock, *The Seduction of Hillary Rodham*, 374 (1996).

13   Susan Schmidt, "McLarty Recalls 'Pressure to Act' on Travel Office from First Lady," *Washington Post*, August 6, 1996.

14   Susan Schmidt, "Papers Detail Clinton Friend's Contract Push; House Panel Reviews '93 Travel Office Firings," *Washington Post*, October 25, 1995. *See generally* Richard L. Berke, "Travel Outfit Tied to Clinton Halts Work for White House," *New York Times*, May 22, 1993 ("During today's briefing [May 21, 1993], Mr. Stephanopoulos said Mr. Thomason had raised his concerns about the travel staff directly to the President.").

15   Susan Schmidt, "Papers Detail Clinton Friend's Contract Push; House Panel Reviews '93 Travel Office Firings," *Washington Post*, October 25, 1995.

16   House Report 104-849: "Investigation of the White House Travel Office Firings and Related Matters," Report by the Committee on Government Reform and Oversight, September 26, 1996.

17   House Report 104-849: "Investigation of the White House Travel Office Firings and Related Matters," Report by the Committee on Government Reform and Oversight, September 26, 1996.

18   Terence Hunt, "White House Trying to Find Where It Went Wrong," Associated Press, May 26, 1993.

19   Kim I. Eisler, "Fall Guy; Everyone Liked Billy Dale, But Clinton Pals Wanted His Job.

In the End, Vince Foster Was Dead and Billy Dale Was Ruined. Here's the Story Behind the Headlines," *Washingtonian*, February 1996.

20 House Report 104-849: "Investigation of the White House Travel Office Firings and Related Matters," Report by the Committee on Government Reform and Oversight, September 26, 1996.

21 Susan Schmidt and Toni Locy, "Papers Detail Clinton Friend's Contract Push; House Panel Reviews '93 Travel Office Firings," *Washington Post*, October 25, 1995.

22 House Report 104-849: "Investigation of the White House Travel Office Firings and Related Matters," Report by the Committee on Government Reform and Oversight, September 26, 1996.

23 ABC's *Good Morning America*, May 26, 1993.

24 Ann Devroy, Al Kamen, "Longtime Travel Office Staff Given Walking Papers," *Washington Post*, May 20, 1993.

25 Editorial, "Blame the Dead Guy," *Investor's Business Daily*, June 27, 1996.

26 Richard L. Berke, "Travel Outfit Tied to Clinton Halts Work for White House," *New York Times*, May 22, 1993.

27 ABC's *20/20*, January 12, 1996.

28 Thomas L. Friedman, "White House Rebukes 4 in Travel Office Shake-up," *New York Times*, July 3, 1993.

29 George Lardner, Jr., "White House Contradicted on FBI Files," *Washington Post*, October 5, 1996.

30 Mary Jacoby, "More FBI Files Traced to White House," *Chicago Tribune*, June 26, 1996.

31 Kim I. Eisler, "Fall Guy; Everyone Liked Billy Dale, But Clinton Pals Wanted His Job. In the End, Vince Foster Was Dead and Billy Dale Was Ruined. Here's the Story Behind the Headlines," *Washingtonian*, February 1996.

32 Michael Isikoff, Ann Devroy, "FBI Says White House Invoked IRS," *Washington Post*, June 11, 1993. Thomason had been encouraging the Cornelius-instigated rumors that UltrAir was paying kickbacks. Kim I. Eisler, "Fall Guy; Everyone Liked Billy Dale, But Clinton Pals Wanted His Job. In the End, Vince Foster Was Dead and Billy Dale Was Ruined. Here's the Story Behind the Headlines," *Washingtonian*, February 1996.

33 An FBI memo summarizing this point in the conversation stated that Kennedy "commented that the matter had to be handled immediately or the matter will be referred to another agency, the IRS." *See, e.g.*, Michael Isikoff, Ann Devroy, "FBI Says White House Invoked IRS," *Washington Post*, June 11, 1993. The White House's own internal report on the matter states, "Kennedy said that he needed to hear from Bourke within the next fifteen minutes and that if the FBI were unable to provide guidance, Kennedy might have to seek guidance from another agency, such as the IRS," citing the notes of Jim Bourke, the FBI Unit chief to whom Kennedy spoke. Thomas L. Friedman, "White House Rebukes 4 in Travel Office Shake-up," *New York Times*, July 3, 1993.

34 This was acknowledged in the White House's internal report on the firings. Thomas L. Friedman, "White House Rebukes 4 in Travel Office Shake-up," *New York Times*, July 3, 1993.

35 Michael Isikoff, Ann Devroy, "FBI Says White House Invoked IRS," *Washington Post*, June 11, 1993. ("An article this week in Tax Notes, a tax industry newsletter, raised questions about the propriety of the UltrAir audit, saying it appears to deviate in major ways from IRS rules. Such IRS audits, according to the article, generally are done after a tax return has been filed. In this case, UltrAir—formed in 1992—was audited before it had ever filed a tax return.")

36 Jeff A. Taylor, "Will Travelgate Affair Ever Die?" *Investor's Business Daily*, May 29, 1996.

37 House Report 104-849: "Investigation of the White House Travel Office Firings and Related Matters," Report by the Committee on Government Reform and Oversight, September 26, 1996.

The notes from a June 28, 1993, White House Management Review interview of Beth Nolan and Cliff Sloan of the White House Counsel's Office revealed that Kennedy has said this. The notes read:

"BK [Associate White House Counsel Bill Kennedy] said PR [IRS Commissioner Peggy Richardson] on top of it. She said at a party IRS on top of it and some reference to IRS agents aware or something like that."

38 Michael Isikoff, Ann Devroy, "FBI Says White House Invoked IRS," *Washington Post*, June 11, 1993.

39 Mitch Clarke, "Where Is Deep Throat Now? Watergate Reporter Wants 'Credible' Clinton Witness," *Macon Telegraph*, May 13, 1998.

40 They were: David Watkins, assistant to the president for management and administration; William Kennedy, an associate White House counsel; Jeff Eller, director of media affairs; and Catherine Cornelius, the current head of the Travel Office. Thomas L. Friedman, "White House Rebukes 4 in Travel Office Shake-up," *New York Times*, July 3, 1993.

CHAPTER 12

1 Sandy Grady, "Clinton's Klutzes Aren't Crooked," *Denver Post*, June 12, 1996.

2 CNN's *Inside Politics Weekend*, June 9, 1996.

3 Sandy Grady, "Clinton's Klutzes Aren't Crooked," *Denver Post*, June 12, 1996.

4 John F. Harris, "White House Admits Having Background Files; Administration 'Blunder' Sets Off Rhetorical Firefight with Hill Republicans," *Washington Post*, June 8, 1996.

5 David A. Price, "More from the 'Filegate' Front; Livingstone Was Hired over More Qualified Woman," *Investor's Business Daily*, October 23, 1997.

6 Investigators for the Senate Judiciary Committee, which held hearings on "Filegate" in 1996, discovered this.

7 Editorial, "Phantom Appointment," *Washington Post*, June 28, 1996.

8   Former U.S. Attorney Joseph diGenova discussed the nature of FBI background files with the Scripps-Howard News Service. "Expert Says Filegate 'Stinks to High Heaven,'" *Patriot Ledger* (Quincy, MA), June 19, 1996.

9   George Lardner, Jr., "GOP Not Ready to Presume Innocence in FBI Files Fiasco," *Washington Post*, September 9, 1996.

10   David A. Price, "More from the 'Filegate' Front; Livingstone Was Hired over More Qualified Woman," *Investor's Business Daily*, October 23, 1997.

11   William Safire, "Their Just Powers," *New York Times*, July 4, 1996.

12   In the letter, dated August 11, 1994, DeConcini referred to "operational inefficiencies" in White House security that had created the backlog in issuing permanent White House passes.

13   David A. Price, "More from the 'Filegate' Front; Livingstone Was Hired over More Qualified Woman," *Investor's Business Daily*, October 23, 1997.

14   Jane Crawford, "From Beaver County to White House: He Keeps Official Activities on Even Keel," *Pittsburgh Post-Gazette*, May 22, 1994.

15   Al Kamen, "The Livingstone Flip-Flop," *Washington Post*, June 21, 1996.

16   Rodino Report at 9.

17   Sculimbrene's notes were introduced as an exhibit at William Clinger's House Government Reform and Oversight Committee hearings on August 1, 1996.

18   Stuart Taylor, Jr., "Starr's Newest Maneuver Works Against Him; Starr Subpoena Starts First Amendment Frenzy," *Texas Lawyer*, March 9, 1998.

19   David Brock, "Living with the Clintons," *The American Spectator*, January 1994.

20   Karen Gallo, "Candidate: Marceca Offered 'Dirt' on Arlen Specter," Associated Press, July 10, 1996.

21   George Lardner, Jr., "GOP Not Ready to Presume Innocence in FBI Files Fiasco," *Washington Post*, September 9, 1996.

22   Editorial, "The White House and the FBI," *New York Times*, June 17, 1996.

23   Juliet Eilperin, "Nearly Dozen Hill Staff Also Make FBI List," *Roll Call*, June 13, 1996.

24   Paul Johnson, *Modern Times*, 651 (1991).

25   Carl Bernstein and Bob Woodward, *All the President's Men*, 313 (1974).

26   Bernstein and Woodward at 314.

27   Rodino Report at 9.

CHAPTER 13

1   Rodino Report at 9 (quoting James Iredell).

2   Thomas L. Friedman, "White House Rebukes 4 in Travel Office Shake-up," *New York Times*, July 3, 1993; *See also* Michael Isikoff, Ann Devroy, "FBI Says White House Invoked IRS," *Washington Post*, June 11, 1993.

3   House Report 104-849: "Investigation of the White House Travel Office Firings and

Related Matters," Report by the Committee on Government Reform and Oversight, September 26, 1996.

4 Maureen Dowd, "Liberties: Something Sacred, After All," *New York Times*, November 22, 1997.

5 Federalist No. 70, at 428 (Alexander Hamilton).

6 Rodino Report at 9.

7 *See e.g.*, Editorial, "White House Ethics Meltdown," *New York Times*, March 4, 1994 ("It is, of course, long past time for Mr. Nussbaum to be dismissed.").

CHAPTER 14

1 Walter Goodman, Television Review: "Tangled Tale of Friends, Partners, and Politicians," *New York Times*, October 7, 1997.

2 Michael Wines, "Whitewater Investigation's Focus: Another Tangled Arkansas Deal," *New York Times*, July 11, 1996.

3 During an interview with Matt Lauer of NBC's *Today* show on Tuesday, January 27, 1998, for example, Mrs. Clinton said:

This is what concerns me: This started out as an investigation of a failed land deal. I told everybody in 1992, we lost money. People said, it's not true. You know, they made money. They have money in a Swiss bank account.

As a certified member of the "politically motivated... right-wing opponents of [Mrs. Clinton's] husband," I have never heard anyone claim that the Clintons had ferreted away money in a Swiss bank account. In any event, Mrs. Clinton went on to answer her own straw man question:

Well, it was true. It's taken years, but it was true. We get a politically motivated prosecutor who is allied with the right-wing opponents of my husband, who has literally spent four years looking at every telephone....

4 Editorial, "Whitewater Disinformation," *New York Times*, July 26, 1994. ("It is possible that if Mr. McDougal engaged in such shenanigans, he did so without telling his partners. But at least one Resolution Trust Corporation investigator has said publicly that she finds it hard to believe that the Clintons never even tried to find out who was paying off their debts. [Clinton lawyer] Mr. Cutler seems also to have forgotten that Mrs. Clinton once represented Madison.")

5 The bill Mr. Clinton vetoed would have given small water companies—like the one at Castle Grande—the ability to raise their rates. *See* Special Committee, Investigation of Whitewater Development Corporation and Related Matters, S. REP. NO. 280, 104th Cong., 2d Sess., at 338 (1996).

6   Special Committee, Investigation of Whitewater Development Corporation and Related Matters, S. REP. NO. 280, 104th Cong., 2d Sess., at 333–334, 338 (1996). A "couple years" earlier, on April 4, 1985, James McDougal held a fund-raiser for Governor Clinton to retire approximately $50,000 in personal debt Clinton had acquired in his 1984 gubernatorial race. More than $30,000 was raised, including three consecutively numbered Madison Guaranty cashier's checks, each for $3,000. This and other evidence—individuals named on these checks denied having written them—suggested to investigators that Madison deposits had been laundered through phony contributors at the fund-raiser. Tucker, the future convicted governor of Arkansas, and his partner Randolph attended the fund-raising event.

7   Michael Wines, "Whitewater Investigation's Focus: Another Tangled Arkansas Deal," *New York Times*, July 11, 1996.

8   "Some buyers received loans that far exceeded the purchase price, but risked losing only the land if they defaulted. Some reaped sales commissions as rewards for playing the role of straw man in a deal. One loan was linked to other transactions that richly benefited the borrowers and others. Federal prosecutors say Mr. McDougal gave at least one buyer private assurances that he would not be liable for his debt. The biggest loan went to a corporation, putting the actual borrowers beyond the reach of any effort to collect on it." Michael Wines, "Whitewater Investigation's Focus: Another Tangled Arkansas Deal," *New York Times*, July 11, 1996.

9   Michael Wines, "Whitewater Investigation's Focus: Another Tangled Arkansas Deal," *New York Times*, July 11, 1996.

10 Special Committee, Investigation of Whitewater Development Corporation and Related Matters, S. REP. NO. 280, 104th Cong., 2d Sess., at 357 and 355 (1996).

11 Special Committee, Investigation of Whitewater Development Corporation and Related Matters, S. REP. NO. 280, 104th Cong., 2d Sess., at 356 (1996).

12 Special Committee, Investigation of Whitewater Development Corporation and Related Matters, S. REP. NO. 280, 104th Cong., 2d Sess., at 357 (1996).

13 David Maraniss and Susan Schmidt, "Hillary Clinton and the Whitewater Controversy: A Close-Up; Her Public Record Suggests Conflicts with Self-Portrait of Naivete," *Washington Post*, June 2, 1996. ("And most of her work came in a concentrated period of those 15 months. What may be most significant about the billing records in any case was not the amount of time Hillary Clinton put into her Madison representation, but the nature of the work itself and when it took place. What was she actually doing during most of the hours she billed to the Madison account? According to the billing records, most of Hillary Clinton's hours on the Madison account involved not the securities issue but a development in the swampland south of Little Rock [Castle Grande].")

14 Special Committee, Investigation of Whitewater Development Corporation and Related Matters, S. REP. NO. 280, 104th Cong., 2d Sess., at 356 (1996).

15 Although the testimony of another Madison official initially supported Mrs. Clinton's

position by saying that "in his mind" Castle Grande referred solely to the trailer park, he admitted that he did not know whether that particular distinction existed in anyone else's mind at Madison. His testimony was further undermined by a check made out to him that referred to the entire development as "Castle Grande." David Maraniss and Susan Schmidt, "Hillary Clinton and the Whitewater Controversy: A Close-Up; Her Public Record Suggests Conflicts with Self-Portrait of Naivete," *Washington Post*, June 2, 1996.

16 The Madison loan officer was H. Don Denton, quoted in David Maraniss and Susan Schmidt, "Hillary Clinton and the Whitewater Controversy: A Close-Up; Her Public Record Suggests Conflicts with Self-Portrait of Naivete," *Washington Post*, June 2, 1996.

17 David Maraniss and Susan Schmidt, "Hillary Clinton and the Whitewater Controversy: A Close-Up; Her Public Record Suggests Conflicts with Self-Portrait of Naivete," *Washington Post*, June 2, 1996.

18 David Maraniss and Susan Schmidt, "Hillary Clinton and the Whitewater Controversy: A Close-Up; Her Public Record Suggests Conflicts with Self-Portrait of Naivete," *Washington Post*, June 2, 1996 ("Articles in the Arkansas newspapers about that trial consistently referred to the entire property as Castle Grande.").

19 Special Committee, Investigation of Whitewater Development Corporation and Related Matters, S. REP. NO. 280, 104th Cong., 2d Sess., at 355–356 and n. 822 (1996).

20 Special Committee, Investigation of Whitewater Development Corporation and Related Matters, S. REP. NO. 280, 104th Cong., 2d Sess., at 356 (1996).

21 Michael Wines, "Whitewater Investigation's Focus: Another Tangled Arkansas Deal," *New York Times*, July 11, 1996.

22 Bob Franken, "Hale Gives Loan Specifics in Arkansas Whitewater Trial," CNN, April 2, 1996.

23 Susan Schmidt, "Clinton Discussed Loan, Hale Testifies; Jury Is Told of Meeting in Trailer with Then-Governor and McDougal," *Washington Post*, April 3, 1996.

24 Michael Wines, "Whitewater Investigation's Focus: Another Tangled Arkansas Deal," *New York Times*, July 11, 1996.

CHAPTER 15

1   John Hanchette, "Questions on Land Deal, S&L Still Dog Clintons," *USA Today*, January 1994.

2   Senate Hearing 104-869: Hearings Before the Special Committee to Investigate Whitewater Development Corporation and Related Matters, Administered by the Committee on Banking, Housing, and Urban Affairs, Vol. I, 313.

3   Senate Hearing 104-869: Hearings Before the Special Committee to Investigate Whitewater Development Corporation and Related Matters, Administered by the

Committee on Banking, Housing, and Urban Affairs, Vol. I, 320.

4   Senate Hearing 104-869: Hearings Before the Special Committee to Investigate Whitewater Development Corporation and Related Matters, Administered by the Committee on Banking, Housing, and Urban Affairs, Vol. I, 334.

5   Senate Hearing 104-869: Hearings Before the Special Committee to Investigate Whitewater Development Corporation and Related Matters, Administered by the Committee on Banking, Housing, and Urban Affairs, Vol. I, 417.

6   "Senate, House Committees Conclude Whitewater Hearings," *Facts on File World News Digest*, August 17, 1995. Also on July 21, Bruce Abbott, a Secret Service agent, said he saw Livingstone and an unidentified man step off an elevator in the West Wing just below the White House Counsel's Office, carrying a box and a briefcase. Susan Schmidt, "Probe Into Handling of Foster Files May Highlight Some Discrepancies; Papers Are Intact and 'Innocuous,'" *Washington Post*, July 10, 1995. It is unknown whether this was a coincidence or if investigators have connected the box of papers and briefcase to papers being removed from Foster's office.

7   Special Committee to Investigate Whitewater Development Corporation and Related Matters, August 9, 1995 (Statement of Bernard W. Nussbaum) ("But I did not speak to the President or the First Lady about this matter. Nor did Susan Thomases, or anyone else, convey a message to me, from either of them. Susan Thomases did not discuss the First Lady's views with me."). Phone records clearly indicate that Thomases called Nussbaum moments after getting off the phone with the first lady.

8   Bill Turque and Michael Isikoff, "Lost in Whitewater," *Newsweek*, December 18, 1995.

9   Bill Turque and Michael Isikoff, "Lost in Whitewater," *Newsweek*, December 18, 1995.

10 Senate Hearing 104-869: Hearings Before the Special Committee to Investigate Whitewater Development Corporation and Related Matters, Administered by the Committee on Banking, Housing, and Urban Affairs, Vol. I, 762.

11 "Senate Whitewater Hearings—Day 10—Part 7," CNN, Transcript #1083-6, August 9, 1995.

12 Senate Hearing 104-869: Hearings Before the Special Committee to Investigate Whitewater Development Corporation and Related Matters, Administered by the Committee on Banking, Housing, and Urban Affairs, Vol. I, 417.

13 Kim Isaac Eisler, "All the President's Lawyers," *Washingtonian*, August 1996.

14 Sara Fritz, "First Lady's Top Aide Said to Remove Foster Office Files," *Los Angeles Times*, July 27, 1995.

15 Sara Fritz, "First Lady's Top Aide Said to Remove Foster Office Files," *Los Angeles Times*, July 27, 1995.

16 The two aides were Thomas Castleton, a Counsel's Office clerk, and Carolyn Huber, a longtime aide to the Clintons.

17 Bill Turque and Michael Isikoff, "Lost in Whitewater," *Newsweek*, December 18, 1995.

18 Editorial, "White House Ethics Meltdown," *New York Times*, March 4, 1994.

CHAPTER 16

1   CNN's *Larry King Live*, April 21, 1997.

2   Starr, a former judge and solicitor general, was appointed independent counsel on August 5, 1994.

3   ABC's *Nightline*, April 30, 1998.

4   NBC's *Meet the Press*, May 3, 1998.

5   Michael Isikoff with Daniel Klaidman, "Oh, What a Tangled Webb...," *Newsweek*, April 14, 1997.

6   Susan Schmidt, "Clinton Aides Sought Help for Hubbell," *Washington Post*, April 2, 1997.

7   Susan Schmidt, "Lippo Paid Hubbell after Call from Friend; Former Clinton Partner Contacted Company to Aid Ex-Justice Official," *Washington Post*, December 10, 1997.

8   Susan Schmidt, "Hubbell Meetings with Riady Draw Probers' Scrutiny," *Washington Post*, March 23, 1997 ("Little work, if any, was expected from Hubbell in return for the money, according to a source familiar with some of Lippo's activities.").

9   Brian McGrory, "'Mistakes Were Made,' President Says of Funds," *Boston Globe*, January 29, 1997.

10 Susan Schmidt, "Lippo Paid Hubbell after Call from Friend; Former Clinton Partner Contacted Company to Aid Ex-Justice Official," *Washington Post*, December 10, 1997.

11 Susan Schmidt, "Lippo Paid Hubbell after Call from Friend; Former Clinton Partner Contacted Company to Aid Ex-Justice Official," *Washington Post*, December 10, 1997.

12 Susan Schmidt, "Clinton Aides Sought Help for Hubbell," *Washington Post*, April 2, 1997.

13 Susan Schmidt, "Hubbell Meetings with Riady Draw Probers' Scrutiny," *Washington Post*, March 23, 1997 (correction appended).

14 Jeff Gerth, "Money from Private Sources Helps Clinton and Associates with Bad Times and Good," *New York Times*, December 19, 1996.

15 William C. Rempel and David Willman, "Starr Looks for a Pattern in Job Offers by Clinton Camp," *Los Angeles Times*, February 9, 1998.

16 Susan Schmidt, "Hubbell Meetings with Riady Draw Probers' Scrutiny," *Washington Post*, March 23, 1997.

17 Susan Schmidt, "Lippo Paid Hubbell after Call from Friend; Former Clinton Partner," *Washington Post*, December 10, 1997; Susan Schmidt, "Hubbell Meetings with Riady Draw Probers' Scrutiny," *Washington Post*, March 23, 1997.

18 Jeff Gerth, "White House Says Clintons Didn't Know Scope of Hubbell Matter," *New York Times*, May 6, 1997.

19 William C. Rempel and David Willman, "Starr Looks for a Pattern in Job Offers by Clinton Camp," *Los Angeles Times*, February 9, 1998.

20 William C. Rempel and David Willman, "Starr Looks for a Pattern in Job Offers by Clinton Camp," *Los Angeles Times*, February 9, 1998.

21 William C. Rempel and David Willman, "Starr Looks for a Pattern in Job Offers by Clinton Camp," *Los Angeles Times*, February 9, 1998.

22 Bob Herbert, "The Clinton M.O.," *New York Times*, February 5, 1998.

23 William C. Rempel and David Willman, "Starr Looks for a Pattern in Job Offers by Clinton Camp," *Los Angeles Times*, February 9, 1998.

24 William C. Rempel and David Willman, "Starr Looks for a Pattern in Job Offers by Clinton Camp," *Los Angeles Times*, February 9, 1998.

25 William C. Rempel and David Willman, "Starr Looks for a Pattern in Job Offers by Clinton Camp," *Los Angeles Times*, February 9, 1998.

26 CBS's *60 Minutes*, January 26, 1992.

27 The fact that Nixon and his lawyer called it living expenses and Dean called it "hush money" has added to the speculation that it was Dean who had something to hide in the Watergate burglary. *See* Len Colodny and Robert Getlin, *Silent Coup* (1991).

28 CNN's *Larry King Live* "Larry King Talks to Whitewater Figure James McDougal," (Guest: James McDougal) April 21, 1997.

29 House Judiciary Committee, Article of Impeachments, Article I, July 27, 1974.

30 Susan Schmidt, "Hubbell Meetings with Riady Draw Probers' Scrutiny," *Washington Post*, March 23, 1997.

CHAPTER 17

1   Howard Fineman and Michael Isikoff with Karen Breslau, Daniel Klaidman, and Lucy Shackelford, "Strange Bedfellows," *Newsweek*, March 10, 1997.

2   Howard Fineman and Michael Isikoff with Karen Breslau, Daniel Klaidman, and Lucy Shackelford, "Strange Bedfellows," *Newsweek*, March 10, 1997.

3   James A. Barnes, "A Question of Context," *National Journal*, March 8, 1997.

4   James A. Barnes, "A Question of Context," *National Journal*, March 8, 1997.

5   Don Van Natta, Jr., "Campaign Finance: Raising the Money; Party Officials Orchestrated White House Sleepovers," *New York Times*, October 4, 1997.

6   Don Van Natta, Jr., "Campaign Finance: Raising the Money; Party Officials Orchestrated White House Sleepovers," *New York Times*, October 4, 1997.

7   Alan C. Miller and Mark Gladstone, "White House Events Raised Cash For Health Care Fight," *Los Angeles Times*, April 4, 1997.

8   Alan C. Miller and Mark Gladstone, "White House Events Raised Cash For Health Care Fight," *Los Angeles Times*, April 4, 1997.

9   Don Van Natta, Jr., "Campaign Finance: Raising the Money; Party Officials Orchestrated White House Sleep overs," *New York Times*, October 4, 1997.

10 Transcript of President Clinton's Press Conference (Part 3 of 5), U.S. Newswire, March 7, 1997.

11 Alison Mitchell, "White House Kept Close Tabs on Cash Raised at Coffees," *New York Times*, March 23, 1997.

12 Don Van Natta, Jr., "Democratic Math at a Coffee: 10 Texans and $500,000 Goal," *New York Times*, February 28, 1997.

13 Glenn F. Bunting and Ralph Frammolino, "Cash-for-Coffee Events at White House Detailed," *Los Angeles Times*, February 24, 1997.

14 Don Van Natta, Jr., "Courting Donors: Party Workers," *New York Times*, February 26, 1997.

15 Don Van Natta, Jr., "Courting Donors: Party Workers," *New York Times*, February 26, 1997.

16 It is not altogether clear on what issues the bankers might have wished to lobby Ludwig about. His spokeswoman, Lee Cross, said he might have wished to brief them on changes in banking regulations that had taken place over the previous six months. That sort of reverse lobbying—where the government official is presenting his views to the interested private citizen, not vice versa—is unobjectionable. But there were other issues on which the bankers might have wanted to lobby the administration. The Reuters Financial Service noted in its February 7, 1997, report on the Ludwig coffee that at the time it took place, House Banking Committee Chairman Jim Leach was supporting a bill to make the Federal Reserve the primary regulator for financial services companies. Ludwig was opposed. Did the bankers have a view that they might have wanted to put to him?

17 Glenn F. Bunting and Ralph Frammolino, "Cash-for-Coffee Events at White House Detailed," *Los Angeles Times*, February 24, 1997.

18 Glenn F. Bunting and Ralph Frammolino, "Cash-for-Coffee Events at White House Detailed," *Los Angeles Times*, February 24, 1997.

19 Howard Fineman and Michael Isikoff with Karen Breslau, Daniel Klaidman, and Lucy Shackelford, "Strange Bedfellows," *Newsweek*, March 10, 1997.

20 *Evans* v. *United States*, 504 U.S. 255,258 (1992).

21 Campaign Finance Investigation Senate Governmental Affairs Committee, Chairman Senator Fred Thompson, Federal News Service, September 19, 1997 (testimony of R. Warren Meddoff).

22 William Raspberry, "Too Crass for Comfort," *Washington Post*, February 27, 1997.

CHAPTER 18

1 Thomas Corcoran at O'Connor's firm has said under oath that on the next day, April 25, O'Connor told him about his successful buttonholing of the president and conversation with Lindsey.

2 George Lardner, Jr., "Wisconsin Tribes Press for Withheld White House Papers," *Washington Post*, November 30, 1997.

3 Hearing of the House Government Reform and Oversight Committee, Interior Department Indian Casino Decision Chaired by Representative Daniel Burton, Federal News Service, January 28, 1998.

4   House Hearings Before the Committee on Government Reform and Oversight, on the Department of the Interior's Denial of the Wisconsin Chippewa's Casino Applications, Vol. I, 914.

5   George Lardner, Jr., "Lobbyist Contradicted Babbitt Aide on Casino," *Washington Post*, March 11, 1998.

6   This is the meeting Patrick O'Connor mentioned in his May 8 letter to Harold Ickes.

7   This was according to documents produced in the civil litigation arising out of the casino dispute.

8   Hearing of the Senate Governmental Affairs Committee, Chaired by Senator Fred Thompson, Federal News Service, September 9, 1997.

9   Don Van Natta, Jr., "Babbitt Attended Political Session Days Before the Initial Decision on a Casino," *New York Times*, February 21, 1998. This part of Babbitt's schedule was not disclosed until February 1998.

10 Don Van Natta, Jr., "Babbitt Attended Political Session Days Before the Initial Decision on a Casino," *New York Times*, February 21, 1998.

11 James Rowley, "Lawyer Quotes Babbitt Saying White House Ordered Casino Decision " Associated Press, October 30, 1997.

12 James Rowley, "Lawyer Quotes Babbitt Saying White House Ordered Casino Decision " Associated Press, October 30, 1997.

13 Don Van Natta, Jr., and Jill Abramson, "Web of Influence," *New York Times*, January 11, 1998.

14 "Statement by Interior Secretary Bruce Babbitt," Federal Document Clearing House, Inc., February 11, 1998.

15 Hearing of the Senate Governmental Affairs Committee, Chaired by Senator Fred Thompson, October 8, 1997.

16 George Landow, Jr., "Lobbyist Contradicted Babbitt Aide on Casino," *Washington Post*, March 11, 1998.

17 House Hearings before the Committee on Government Reform and Oversight, Exhibits 356-1–356-59.

CHAPTER 19

1   Maureen Dowd, "Liberties: Something Sacred, After All," *New York Times*, November 22, 1997.

2   Maureen Dowd, "Liberties: Something Sacred, After All," *New York Times*, November 22, 1997.

3   Bob Woodward, "Findings Link Clinton Allies to Chinese Intelligence," *Washington Post*, February 10, 1998.

4   Bob Woodward, "Findings Link Clinton Allies To Chinese Intelligence," *Washington Post*, February 10, 1998.

5   Bob Woodward, "Findings Link Clinton Allies To Chinese Intelligence," *Washington Post*, February 10, 1998.

6   Ivan Tong, "China Resources to Acquire 50pc Stake in Bank," *South China Morning Post*, July 17, 1993.

7   Jeff Gerth and Stephen Labaton, "Wealthy Indonesian Businessman Has Strong Ties to Clinton," *New York Times*, October 11, 1996.

8   The three-page letter, marked "personal and confidential," was released by the White House on December 3, 1996.

9   Jim Mann and Glenn F. Bunting, "Clinton Aided Indonesia Regime," *Los Angeles Times*, October 16, 1996.

10 Jim Mann and Glenn F. Bunting, "Clinton Aided Indonesia Regime," *Los Angeles Times*, October 16, 1996.

11 Jim Mann and Glenn F. Bunting, "Clinton Aided Indonesia Regime," *Los Angeles Times*, October 16, 1996.

12 "Excerpts From Interview with Clinton: 'Global Economy' and the U.S.," *New York Times,* November 16, 1996.

13 Jim Mann and Glenn F. Bunting, "Clinton Aided Indonesia Regime," *Los Angeles Times*, October 16, 1996.

14 James Rowley, "Reno Doesn't Budge on Campaign Probe," Associated Press, April 30, 1997.

15 This information was not admitted to congressional investigators until January 1997, in response to repeated letters from House Rules Committee Chairman Gerald Solomon (R-NY). At one point, Solomon even wrote directly to President Clinton, deploring this pattern of stalling, stonewalling, and obstructing justice. Eventually then–Commerce Secretary Mickey Kantor released a large batch of documents relating to Huang's activities at Commerce, and described the weekly intelligence briefings in a cover letter to Solomon.

16 Letter from Commerce Department Chief Financial Officer Raymond G. Kammer, Jr., to House Rules Committee Chairman Gerald Solomon, dated January 28, 1997.

17 Hearing of the Senate Governmental Affairs Committee, Chaired by Senator Fred Thompson, Federal News Service, July 16, 1997.

18 James Risen and Alan C. Miller, "Huang's Security Status Raises New Questions," *Los Angeles Times*, June 17, 1997. On December 12, 1995, the Pentagon's Defense Industrial Security Clearance Office granted Huang a "consultant top-secret" clearance without running a new background check.

19 Kenneth R. Timmerman, "All Roads Lead to China," *The American Spectator*, March 1997.

20 According to Commerce Department spokesmen, Huang's application for government employment as well as his applications for security clearances listed his birthdate as April 14, 1945. Yet, on two consecutive days, May 15 and May 16, 1995, Huang signed

visa applications for South Korea and China (the country of his birth) legally certifying that his birthdate was in fact April 14, 1941.

21 On October 9, 1996, Assistant White House Counsel Mark Fabiani described the meeting as "an informal chat." On October 14, 1996, the *Los Angeles Times* reported that Fabiani referred to both the April 1993 meeting among the president, Riady, and Huang and the September 13, 1995, meeting as "meet and greet" social visits. On October 16, 1996, the *Times* reported that "one of Clinton's senior advisers, Bruce Lindsey, said he had been present for two meetings between Riady and Clinton in the past two years, including one in the last few months. 'It was basically a social visit,' Lindsey said."

22 James Risen and Alan C. Miller, "Huang's Security Status Raises New Questions," *Los Angeles Times*, June 17, 1997. On December 12, 1995, the Pentagon's Defense Industrial Security Clearance Office granted Huang a "consultant top-secret" clearance without running a new background check.

23 William C. Rempel and Alan C. Miller, "First Lady's Aide Solicited Check to DNC, Donor Says," *Los Angeles Times*, July 27, 1997.

24 James Sterngold, "White House Aide Pushes Plan Benefiting Chinese Shipping Concern," *New York Times*, May 9, 1997.

25 This was apparently in response to a request from Chairman Solomon of the House Rules Committee.

26 David Johnston, "FBI Denied Data the White House Sought on China," *New York Times*, March 25, 1997.

27 At a press conference on Friday February 6, 1998, CNN's Wolf Blitzer asked President Clinton, "Monica Lewinsky's life has been changed forever—her family's life has been changed forever. I wonder how you feel about that and what, if anything, you'd like to say to Monica Lewinsky at this minute?" "That's good," the president said. "That's good, but at this minute, I'm going to stick with my position in not commenting."

28 Clinton said of Riady, "[I]f I said to him, I want a good, strong, positive relationship with China, and my objective is to engage China, not to isolate it… it wouldn't surprise me if he said that to somebody the next time he was in China because I expect that to be done by—I mean, a lot of times I do it deliberately knowing that it would be communicated." "Excerpts from Interview with Clinton: 'Global Economy' and the U.S.," *New York Times*, November 16, 1996.

29 U.S. Senate Committee on Governmental Affairs, Hearing on Investigations into Fund-raising Activities During the 1996 Elections, Tuesday, July 8, 1997, FDCH Political Transcripts (1997).

30 Sandy Grady, "The Chinese Commies Are Coming!" *Miami Herald*, July 13, 1997.

31 U.S. Senate Committee on Governmental Affairs, Hearing on Investigations into Fund-raising Activities During the 1996 Elections, Tuesday, July 8, 1997, FDCH Political Transcripts (1997).

32 U.S. Senate Committee on Commerce, Science, and Transportation, Hearing on NASA's

FY 1998 Budget Request, Thursday April 24, 1997, FDCH Political Transcripts (1997) (Testimony of Marcia S. Smith, Specialist in Aerospace and Telecommunications Policy).

33 Earl Lane, "John Glenn Rides Again/Spot Saved for Him on Oct. Shuttle," *Newsday*, January 16, 1998.

34 Jeff Gerth, "Democrat Fund-Raiser Said to Detail China Tie," *New York Times*, May 15, 1998.

35 Editorial, "China Deal for Campaign Cash?" *Investor's Business Daily*, May 6, 1998.

36 Jeff Gerth, "Companies Are Investigated for Aid to China on Rockets," *New York Times*, April 4, 1998.

37 A few months later, this exchange occurred at a press briefing:

SARAH MCCLENDON: Mr. President, it looks as if you're getting ready to sign an agreement with China which would give them help and some of our secrets and not just be a friendly thing. Would you sign this without the American people having had wide discussion over this and debate on—don't you need approval of Congress? Would you just go ahead and sign this, because, after all, that's one of our greatest contemporary enemies, is China?

CLINTON: Well, Sarah, I'm not sure I know the specific issue you're referring to, but I—I would not make any agreements with China in secret and they would be subject to the knowledge of the Congress and the debate of the American people.

White House Press Conference April 30, 1998.

38 Editorial, "China Deal For Campaign Cash?" *Investor's Business Daily*, May 6, 1998.

39 Editorial, "China Deal For Campaign Cash?" *Investor's Business Daily*, May 6, 1998.

40 Editorial, "The Sanctity of Missile Secrets," *New York Times*, April 15, 1998.

41 CNN's *Larry King Live*, February 15, 1996.

42 Maureen Dowd, "Liberties: Something Sacred, After All," *New York Times*, November 22, 1997.

43 Federalist No. 64, at 396 (John Jay).

CHAPTER 20

1 Federalist No. 57, (James Madison).

2 Federalist No. 64, at 391 (John Jay). Jay was referring to the electoral college.

3 The process of selection Hamilton praises is the electoral college—not the popular election the electoral college has become. "It was equally desirable that the immediate election should be made by men most capable of analyzing the qualities adapted to the station and acting under circumstances favorable to deliberation.... A small number of persons, selected by their fellow-citizens from the general mass, will be most

likely to possess the information and discernment requisite to so complicated an investigation." Federalist No. 68, at 412. Still the desideratum of a man of virtue for the office of the president can hardly be disputed.

4   Federalist No. 68, at 414 (Alexander Hamilton).

5   Federalist No. 68, at 413 (Alexander Hamilton).

6   Rodino Report at 22.

7   Berger at 62.

8   Rodino Report at 23.

9   Michael de la Pole had "purchas[ed] property of great value from the King while using his position as Chancellor to have the lands appraised at less than they were worth all in violation or his oath, in deceit of the King and in neglect of the need of the realm." Rodino Report at n. 8.

10   Michael de la Pole had "brok[en] a promise he made to the full Parliament to execute in connection with a parliamentary ordinance the advice of a committee of nine lords regarding the improvement of the estate of the King and the realm: 'this was not done, and it was the fault of himself as he was then chief officer.'" Rodino Report at 5. After describing thirteen English impeachments for noncriminal conduct, Berger observes that "[t]he foregoing examples by no means exhaust the list which could be adduced to illustrate that English impeachments did proceed for misconduct that was not 'criminal' in the sense of the general criminal law." Berger at 69.

11   After describing thirteen English impeachments for noncriminal conduct, Berger observes that "[t]he foregoing examples by no means exhaust the list which could be adduced to illustrate that English impeachments did proceed for misconduct that was not 'criminal' in the sense of the general criminal law." Berger at 69.

12   U.S. Constitution, Article II, section 2.

13   U.S. Constitution, Article III, section 2.
     This was not true in the English practice: even though impeachable offenses did not have to be "indictable crimes," impeachment could be punished by death or imprisonment (Berger at 67). By contrast, the Constitution specifically provides that the sole punishments for impeachment and conviction are "removal from office, and disqualification to hold and enjoy" any other office of profit or trust with the United States. Article II, section 3.

14   *See* Berger at 81–82.

15   Tribe at 293–294.

16   Report of the National Commission on Judicial Discipline and Removal at 25 (August 1993).

17   Rodino Report at 23.

18   Rodino Report at 23.

19   Rodino Report at 22.

20   Federalist No. 66, at 402 (James Madison).

21   Berger at 80 (quoting James Wilson, from his *Philadelphia Lectures*, I Wilson at 324).

22 Rodino Report at 9 (emphasis in original).

23 Federalist No. 67, at 408–409 (Alexander Hamilton).

24 Federalist No. 69, (Alexander Hamilton).

25 James Wilson quoted in Rodino Report at 9.

26 Federalist No. 70, at 428 (Alexander Hamilton).

27 Federalist No. 70, at 429 (Alexander Hamilton).

28 Rodino Report at 9.

29 U.S. Constitution, Article II, section 4.

30 Though "impeachment" is assumed in common parlance to effect removal of the accused official from office, it does no such thing. Impeachment by the House of Representatives is the equivalent of indictment by a grand jury in a criminal proceeding. The trial is then held by the Senate, and only if two-thirds of the members present vote to "convict" is the officer removed from office. The term "impeachment" is often used to refer to the whole megillah—impeachment and removal from office—presumably to distinguish convictions of impeachment from criminal convictions.

31 U.S. Constitution, Article I, sections 2–3.

32 Federalist No. 70, at 427 (Alexander Hamilton). *See also* Rodino Report at 9. The president is "personally responsible for any abuse of the great trust reposed in him" (quoting James Iredell).

33 Report of the National Commission on Judicial Discipline and Removal at 29 and 31 (August 1993).

34 Report of the National Commission on Judicial Discipline and Removal at 37 (August 1993).

35 Rodino Report at 12.

36 116 Congressional Record H 3113–3114 (daily ed. April 15, 1970). To this extent Ford was right: the impeachment and removal of government officials is left entirely to the legislative branch, and in the case of a criminal conviction, some legislative body must first have written a law making the specific act criminal. In addition, some executive branch official must have decided to prosecute. Hamilton explained that the Constitution had limited the legislature's power of removing executive branch officials by granting the House the power of impeachment, and the Senate the power of conviction: "The division of them between the two branches of the legislature, assigning to one the right of accusing, to the other the right of judging, avoids the inconvenience of making the same persons both accusers and judges; and guards against the danger of persecution from the prevalency of a factious spirit in either of those branches" (Federalist No. 66, at 420). In the case of actual criminal acts by an impeachable official, the accusing or prosecuting function, falls to the attorney general, or through the attorney general and a three-judge panel to an independent counsel.

37 Berger at 74.

38   As Berger has written, the phrase "'high Crimes and Misdemeanors' was adopted [by the framers] with knowledge that it had a 'limited' and 'technical meaning,' a meaning to be sought by recurrence to English practice." Though it was "not as sharply defined as 'treason' or 'bribery,'... it does have an ascertainable content in English practice" (Berger at 107 and 106).

39   Federalist No. 65, at 396 (Alexander Hamilton).

40   Berger at 70.

41   Berger at 70 and n. 83.

42   Berger at 70.

43   Rodino Report at 6.

44   Rodino Report at 6.

45   Berger at 67. The Rodino Report described the Duke of Suffolk's "high Crimes and Misdemeanors" as "such various offenses as 'advising the King to grant liberties and privileges to certain persons to the hindrance of the due execution of the laws,' 'procuring offices for persons who were unfit and unworthy of them' and 'squandering away the public treasure.'" Rodino Report at 6.

46   Berger at 68.

47   Berger at 68.

48   Berger at 68.

49   Berger at 68.

50   Berger at 67.

51   See, e.g., Ross Mackenzie, "Between The Grand Inquisitor & The Church Lady, Assessing the Clintons," Richmond Times Dispatch, June 22, 1997.

52   Berger at 68.

53   Berger at 68.

54   This is a felony under Section 607 of the U.S. criminal code.

55   Berger at 71.

56   Berger at 68.

57   Berger at 68.

58   Berger at 70, n. 82.

59   Brent Israelsen, "A Year Later, Grand Staircase-Escalante Issues Simmer; Grand Staircase Issues Simmer a Year Later," Salt Lake Tribune, September 14, 1997.

60   Berger at 67.

61   Berger at 69.

62   Federalist No. 53, at 332 (James Madison).

63   Federalist No. 53, at 331 (James Madison).

64   Rodino Report at 15.

65   Rodino Report at 13 (Edmund Randolph of Virginia).

66   Rodino Report at 13 (Charles Cotesworth Pinckney of South Carolina).

67   Berger at 433–435.

68   Rodino Report at 13.

69   Rodino Report at 13.

70   Rodino Report at 13.

71   Rodino Report at 13.

72   James Madison was responding to these hypotheticals posited by George Mason of Virginia with the impeachment remedy. Rodino Report at 13–14.

73   Rodino Report at 17 [quoting 1 J. Story *Commentaries on the Constitution of the United States* sec. 764 at 559 (5th ed. 1905)].

74   Report of the National Commission on Judicial Discipline and Removal, at 30 (August 1993).

75   Berger at 3.

76   Eric L. McKitrick, *Andrew Johnson and Reconstruction*, 328 (1988) (cited in Berger at 261).

77   Johnson's preferred course of action was to implement a "reconstruction of the Southern minds" before undertaking a "restoration of the Southern States." *See* Berger at 261. Most historians now believe Johnson's policy "contained the greatest long-range wisdom," but the post–Civil War Congress was in no mood for gradualism. Berger at 261.

78   Berger at 268.

79   In 1987 Senator Edward Kennedy (D-MA) denounced the respected federal judge by stating: "Robert Bork's America is a land in which women would be forced into back-alley abortions, blacks would sit at segregated lunch counters, rogue police could break down citizens' doors in midnight raids, schoolchildren could not be taught about evolution, writers and artists would be censored at the whim of government, and the doors of the federal courts would be shut on the fingers of millions of citizens for whom the judiciary is often the only protector of the individual rights that are the heart of our democracy." 133 Congressional Record S9188–S9189 (daily ed. July 1, 1987).

80   Berger at 268.

81   The Senate erupted in hoots of laughter when number 10 of the articles of impeachment against Johnson was read aloud: It charged the president with being "unmindful... of the harmony and courtesies which ought to exist and be maintained between the executive and legislative branches." Berger at 273.

82   Berger at 270–271 [Benjamin Butler].

83   Berger at 270–271 [George S. Boutwell]. Another referred to the Constitution as that "worthless bit of old parchment" [Stevens].

84   Berger at 262.

85   *Myers* v. *United States*, 272 U.S. 52, 293 (1926) (Brandeis, J. dissenting).

86   Everett Carll Ladd, "Nixon, Clinton, and the Polls," *Wall Street Journal*, April 1, 1998. ("In an April 1974 Harris survey, only 30 percent said Nixon was right to assert executive privilege in refusing to turn over tapes; 56 percent thought 'he is using it as an excuse to keep important information from Congress which might convict him.'")

87   Fred Emery, *Watergate*, 391, 393 and 395–396 (1994). Senator John Stennis was to

authenticate the summaries. Though Senator Sam Ervin later claimed that he understood the agreed-upon compromise to consist of Nixon providing "whole verbatim transcripts" of the tapes to the committee, no one else at the meeting understood it this way. Senator Stennis understood that he alone would view or listen to the conversations unedited. The White House had flown Ervin in from North Carolina by a special Air Force plane to meet with the president in order to discuss the compromise. It is not clear what Ervin might have thought Nixon was getting out of a "compromise" to provide "whole verbatim transcripts," other than keeping his personal secretary, Rose Mary Woods, very, very busy for a very long time. *See* Emery at 395–396.

88   Emery at 404.

89   Everett Carll Ladd, "Nixon, Clinton, and the Polls," *Wall Street Journal*, April 1, 1998. ("In response to questions on whether Nixon should resign or should be forced out through impeachment, substantial majorities said throughout 1973 that he should not. Support for Nixon's removal from office grew as the hearings proceeded in 1974—but even then tentatively. In early May 1974, three months before his resignation, 49% of respondents told Gallup interviewers that the president's actions were not serious enough 'to warrant his being impeached and removed from the presidency.'")

90   John M. Broder, "Hillary Clinton Declines to Answer Some of Starr's Questions," *New York Times*, April 29, 1998. President Clinton corrected House Speaker Newt Gingrich on this point, saying that Gingrich was mistaken in stating that the president could simply dismiss the independent counsel. As Clinton noted correctly, "[T]hat's not what the statute says."

91   28 U.S.C. 596(a)(1).

92   According to Henry Kissinger's memoirs, the Air Force was lackluster in its airlift efforts, until he complained to Nixon, who personally lit a fire under the appropriate general, leading to an enormous airlift, and, in Moshe Dayan's words, the saving of the "Third Temple."

93   *Dr. Strangelove*, Columbia Pictures, 1964.

94   Emery at 396. The Senate had passed the resolution unanimously on May 1, 1973. Emery at 355.

95   Emery at 396 and 398.

96   Emery at 400. Nixon's private response to the news that Richardson would not fire Cox was: "I'm not surprised that that pious bastard cares more for his ass than his country." Emery at 397.

97   Senator Lott, Republican leader of the Senate: "Well, just, you know, the House could say, well, it's not serious enough for impeachment, but this is clearly conduct that is on the margin, and we don't approve of, and the House Judiciary Committee would report out a censure resolution, and the House would vote on it." CNN's *Evans & Novak*, March 7, 1998.

98 Rodino Report at 9.

99 Nixon can be heard on the tapes saying, "What in the Christ did they think they were going to accomplish by bugging the National Committee of the Democratic Party?" Stuart Levitan, "Kutler's Stunning Book Proves Depth of Nixon Evil," *Capital Times* (Madison, WI) November 21, 1997.

100 Even Nixon believed he should be impeached if he had known about the Plumbers' planned break-in of office of Ellsberg's psychiatrist, Dr. Lewis Fielding, and did nothing to stop them. That act was at least in furtherance of a general request by Nixon for information on Ellsberg. "You see," he told Haldeman, "because if I was informed, then, frankly, I am derelict... [and] they've got to blame me for not firing Hunt and that bunch right then." Nixon remained tormented with the idea that he may have been informed of the Fielding break-in years after he left office, finally writing in his memoirs, "I do not believe I was told about the break-in." (To this day, despite committed efforts, there is no evidence that he was.)

101 The Rodino Report also cites remarks on impeachment made in the House of Representatives during the First Session of the First Congress: "Madison argued during the debate that the President would be subject to impeachment for 'the wanton removal of meritorious officers.'" Rodino Report at 15.

102 The familiar litany: Clinton on the White House's improper possession of hundreds of FBI raw files: "It appears to have been a completely honest bureaucratic snafu..." ("White House Apologizes for Seeking FBI Records," Reuters North American Wire, June 9, 1996). Clinton on the Travel Office firings: "I didn't personally know anything about it till I read about it in the press" (Associated Press, January 29, 1997). Clinton on invoking executive privilege for *Mrs.* Clinton's conversations: "All I know is, I saw an article about it in the paper today" (John F. Harris, "Clinton Finds There's No Escape," *Washington Post*, March 25, 1998).

103 Scrapbook, "Clinton's Pentagon Papers," *The Weekly Standard*, June 15, 1998.

104 George Lardner, Jr., "Democrats Hit Burton Over Tapes of Hubbell; House Chairman Accused of Doctoring Phone Transcripts," *Washington Post*, May 4, 1998.

105 CNN's *Larry King Live*, April 21, 1997. On June 25, 1998, Susan McDougal was released from prison for medical reasons (McDougal has a serious spinal condition).

106 Harvey Berkman, "Will the President Pardon His Friends?" *The National Law Journal*, November 4, 1996.

107 Rodino Report at 15. Citing 1 Annals of Congress at 872–878.

108 *See, e.g.*, 18 U.S.C. sec. 607.

109 Stuart Levitan, "Kutler's Stunning Book Proves Depth of Nixon Evil," *Capital Times* (Madison, WI) November 21, 1997.

110 Stuart Taylor, Jr., "Why Clinton Will Miss Paula Jones," *National Journal*, April 3, 1998. Taylor's list of contradicting witnesses included: Paula Jones, Monica Lewinsky, Gennifer Flowers, Dolly Kyle Browning, Betty Currie, the four former Clinton body-

guards "and self-described procurers of women," James McDougal, David Hale, and Webster Hubbell. Taylor writes that two of the troopers have also said under oath that "a Clinton political appointee warned them to keep quiet or risk unspecified consequences to themselves and their families."

111 *See* Rodino Report at 11.

112 "President Clinton's" Remarks," Federal News Service, March 24, 1998.

113 Rodino Report at 13–14.

114 Lying to the American people was shoe-horned into an obstruction of justice charge. The lie was that the White House had conducted its own thorough investigation and concluded that there was no involvement of White House personnel or campaign committee personnel in the Watergate break-in. This was a lie because the Watergate burglars had also performed national security plumbing work for the White House and one of the burglars worked at the campaign committee. It is less clear how lying to the American people—as distinct from lying to investigators or congressional committees, for example—could constitute obstruction of justice. Nonetheless, "making or causing to be made false or misleading public statements for the purpose of deceiving the people of the United States" was listed in the articles of impeachment against Nixon as an impeachable offense.

115 Peter Goldman, "Was Justice Finally Done?" *Newsweek*, January 13, 1975.

116 And, as Bob Woodward and Carl Bernstein portrayed Pat Buchanan's reasoning for Nixon's resignation, "The problem is… that he hasn't been telling the truth to the American people…. [T]he President can't lead a country he has deliberately misled for a year and a half." Bob Woodward and Carl Bernstein, "The Final Days: Part Two" *Newsweek*, April 12, 1976.

117 Peter Goldman, "Was Justice Finally Done?" *Newsweek*, January 13, 1975.

118 Peter Goldman, "Was Justice Finally Done?" *Newsweek*, January 13, 1975.

119 Peter Goldman, "Was Justice Finally Done?" *Newsweek*, January 13, 1975.

120 January 26, 1998, statement to the press from the Roosevelt Room of the White House.

121 James Langton, "Focus Clinton on the Rack: Bradlee: The End Could Come Within Weeks," *Sunday Telegraph*, January 25, 1998.

122 John F. Harris, "In Quick Shift, White House Brandishes Facts; A Sudden Blitz of Facts About Willey," *Washington Post*, March 18, 1998.

123 CBS's *Face the Nation*, February 8, 1998.

124 Jack Nelson, "Impeachment Cloud Darkens," *Los Angeles Times*, March 30, 1998.

125 Howard Kurtz, "McCurry Comments Provoke Speculation on White House Strategy," *Washington Post*, February 18, 1998.

126 Michael Kelly, "The 1992 Campaign: The Democrats," *New York Times*, October 29, 1992.

127 CNN's *Campaign USA '92—Voters and Media Picked and Panned*, November 1, 1992.

128 Arguably, a president's lies about official policy are worse than lies about his personal misconduct because they can have greater consequences for the nation. But distinguishing "lies" from, for example, "protecting vital national security information" would most likely boil down to partisan disputes about the underlying policy. For example, Arthur Schlesinger writes that Fidel Castro's request for nuclear missiles from Soviet leader Nikita Khrushchev was a direct response to President Kennedy's CIA maneuvers against Cuba. Noting this fact, Garry Wills has written, "Kennedy, calling that move unprovoked, was lying to the American people: He had provoked it." Garry Wills, "Son of Nixon. Oliver Stone's film on Richard Nixon," *Esquire*, January 1996. Should Kennedy have been expected to state that Castro's build-up was, perhaps, a "little provoked" by the CIA's covert operation against Cuba? There may be some lies that are so bald-faced and so distant from any serious national security interest that the policy/nonpolicy distinction is inapposite. It is enough to say that oral sex from the White House interns is not even vaguely, possibly related to Clinton's function as the chief executive.

129 James A. Barnes, "Flirting with Loyalties," *National Journal*, March 28, 1998.

130 Federalist No. 71, at 434 (Alexander Hamilton). Such vigor in the president, Hamilton said, was "essential to the protection of the community against foreign attacks; it is not less essential to the steady administration of the laws; to the protection of property against those irregular and high-handed combinations which sometimes interrupt the ordinary course of justice; the security of liberty against the enterprises and assaults of ambition, of faction and of anarchy." Federalist No. 70, at 423 (Alexander Hamilton).

131 Federalist No. 57, (James Madison).

132 Report of the National Commission on Judicial Discipline and Removal, at 27 (August 1993) (quoting 2 *The Records of the Constitutional Convention* 65 [M. Farrand ed. 1911]).

133 7 Edmund Burke, *Works* 11,14 (1839).

134 Rodino Report at 17 [quoting 1 J. Story, *Commentaries on the Constitution of the United States* sec. 764 at 559 (5th ed. 1905)].

135 Rodino Report at 14.

136 Report of the National Commission on Judicial Discipline and Removal, at 30 (August 1993).

137 Rodino Report at 10–11.

138 2 *The Records of the Federal Convention of 1787*, at 65 (M. Farrand ed. 1911) (from James Madison's notes from the Constitutional Convention debates, July 20, 1787).

139 Federalist No. 68, at 414 (Alexander Hamilton).

140 Federalist No. 14, at 104–105 (James Madison).

Index